THE *LANE VICTORY*

THE LAST VICTORY SHIP IN WAR AND IN PEACE

CAPT. WALTER W. JAFFEE

Dedication

To the United States Merchant Marine Veterans of
World War II

and to Joe Vernick and John Smith,
who made it all happen.

By the same author:

The Last Mission Tanker
The Last Liberty, the biography of the
        SS Jeremiah O'Brien
Appointment in Normandy
The Track of the Golden Bear, the California Maritime
        Academy Schoolships

These splendid ships, each with her grace, her glory,
Her memory of old song or comrade's story;
Still in my mind the image of life's need,
Beauty in the hardest action, beauty indeed.

They built great ships and sailed them, sounds most brave
Whatever arts we have or fail to have;
I touch my country's mind, I come to grips
With half her purpose, thinking of these ships.

— John Masefield

ACKNOWLEDGEMENTS

The story of the *Lane Victory* would not have been possible without the help of so many who contributed their time, effort and assistance. Special thanks to: Charles M. Baca, Capt. Robert Bryan, Alex S. Chambers, I. Roy Coats, Frank Filas, Isaac Givens, John A. Jansson, Phil Laudenschlager, Jenny Luckenbill, Don MacLean, Gil MacMillan, Sheila McIntyre, Manuel Medina, John Mena, Larry Miller, Capt. Ralph Moon, John (Jack) Morrison, Thomas Nation, Capt. James Nolan, Capt. Mark Owens, RADM Tom Patterson, Lucille Raymond, Vernon Richardson, John Smith, Capt. Morgan Vail II, Joe Vernick, Jane Weidringer, Jerry Werner.

Heartfelt thanks to my publisher, Shelby Rose, for her time, patience and judicious editorial eye.

The Forward is adapted from an article which appeared in the monthly publication of the U.S. Merchant Marine Veterans of World War II, the *Anchor Light*, Vol. 7, No. 9 & 10.

Most of the chapter on Isaac Lane comes from *Lane College: It's Heritage and Outreach 1881-1982*, by Anna L. Cooke. I am grateful to Ms. Cooke and Lane College for allowing me to use it.

Parts of the article "For All Those Born Before 1945" which appeared in the *Anchor Light*, Vol. 7, No. 9 & 10, were used in Chapter 3.

The beginning of Chapter 12 was adapted from the article "No Strain on the Lane" by Admiral Thomas J. Patterson, in Vol. 7, No. 6 of the *Anchor Light*.

CONTENTS

Preface to the Second Edition

Revising the story of the *Lane Victory* is like visiting a well-liked friend you haven't seen for years. You catch up on what's happened since your last meeting and share some of the old stories again. And, for the author, it provides the opportunity to correct some of the mistakes made the first time around.

Five years have passed since the first edition. Chapter 19 is entirely new and covers events of those years: the day cruises to Catalina Island, the move to the new berth, the valiant attempt to join "The Last Convoy" to Normandy, the *Lane*'s career in the film industry. We find Joe Vernick has stepped aside as president to allow a younger man, Bob Lace, to take the reins. But, as president emeritus, Joe is still very much part and parcel of what the *Lane Victory* is all about.

In the interim the ship has changed, the organization grown. In 1991 she hadn't seen a drydocking for more than two-dozen years, the ship's store was in a cramped cabin on the main deck, the museum in no. 4 was in its infancy and there was no shoreside office. Today, everything about the ship is well-laid out, carefully designed and "ship-shape in Bristol fashion." The entire operation has gone from an enthusiastic dream to a professionally-managed reality.

Less obvious changes in this edition include re-editing the existing chapters. Going through the book, I several times found myself saying, "Good God, did I say that? What the hell was I thinking?" Many of those parts were cut; the entire text was edited and tightened up.

The title was changed from *The Last Victory* to *The Lane Victory*. My thinking on the earlier title was it would make people curious enough to pick up the book and find out what "victory" the title referred to. Upon learning it was not a victory in battle but a Victory ship, they would be so intrigued by the play on words they would buy the book to read the story. I can still hear Joe Vernick saying, "Walter, nobody knows what the book is about. They see that title and think, 'Victory? I don't want to read another war story.'" Joe was right. The new title, *The* Lane Victory*, The Last Victory Ship in War and in Peace* tells the reader exactly what the book is about.

Some of the old photographs were retained but many new ones were added. The book now contains 120 photos and illustrations.

I hope you enjoy revisiting the story of the *Lane Victory* as much as I have. Some friends we never want to lose touch with; the *Lane* is one of them.

Capt. Walter W. Jaffee
Menlo Park, California

FOREWORD

The first American-built merchant ship was the thirty-ton *Virginia* laid down at the mouth of the Kennebec River [Maine] in 1607. Measuring fifty to sixty feet in length and carrying two masts she was active for several years in trans-Atlantic trade. From that time merchant seamen have played a vital role in our nation's commerce and prosperity, operating its ships in times of peace and, when we went to war, helping defend us by manning the vessels which provisioned and supplied our troops and allies.

The contribution and sacrifices of merchant seamen now span more than two centuries of the nation's existence. When, in 1775, the American colonies went to war with England without a single fighting ship in their service, the fledgling merchant marine leapt into the fray.

Their captains appeared before the Continental Congress and obtained "letters of marque" authorizing them to harass the enemy. By 1778, the privateers had captured 733 ships. Their total "catch" was 3,000 ships, but the price was high. In 1778 alone, 900 ships and thousands of seamen were lost to enemy action.

More casualties were suffered during the War of 1812. That war established the principle of freedom of the seas. Then came the age of clipper ships, the glorious Age of Sail, when American merchant mariners girdled the globe; the Civil War and more casualties; the transition to steam.

The merchant marine faded in importance at the turn of the century and by 1914 ships of other nations were carrying ninety percent of America's goods. In that year World War I broke out.

As always, war called for merchant ships and the United States started a rush program to build them. President Woodrow Wilson said, "Without a merchant marine our independence is provincial and it is independence only on land and within our borders."

The war ended just as the ship-building program reached its peak, and hundreds of vessels were laid up, rusting, in U.S. backwaters as the industry began another decline. It took the threat of another war to restore the merchant marine to a place of prominence, and again emergency measures were needed. In 1936 President Roosevelt signed The Merchant Marine Act, once again buttressing the oft-forgotten role of the merchant marine.

The merchant seamen of World War II did a magnificent job. They sailed their ships through hell and high water. Wolf packs of enemy submarines lay in wait off Cape Hatteras. Enemy submarines covered the convoy routes — on the Murmansk Run, in the Pacific, in the Indian Ocean, everywhere our ships carried men and supplies. Hundreds of ships were torpedoed and more were bombed by planes and still new men signed up for duty. Many thousands of seamen lost their lives in performance of their duty. In dying for their country they honored its ideals and greatness.

Their valor continued through wars in Korea, Vietnam and Iraq. Despite mines, rockets, snipers and missiles, they relentlessly delivered the necessary supplies to our fighting forces.

Never let it be said they did it for money. They were volunteers. They knew that without volunteers our ships could not supply our troops and our troops could not reach the enemy. Six thousand five hundred mariners were lost while engaged in vital and patriotic service in World War II, but the supply lines never failed.

What kind of men were those who signed on merchant vessels in wartime to run the risk again and again of meeting the enemy without the means or opportunity of fighting back?

How did they manage when enemy subs were below, enemy ships were on the surface and enemy planes were in the sky? How could they sail, unarmed, into such dangerous seas?

They had some protection from the U.S. Navy. A fortunate few had radar. The remainder relied on speed, maneuverability and, when possible, convoy. But, most of all, they relied on guts. It took courage, a spirit of adventure, a strong and hardy body and a great love of country to serve in the merchant marine in wartime.

"Give us the goods and we'll deliver," says the song of the merchant marine. The men honored by the *Lane Victory* helped deliver the goods and many made the ultimate sacrifice. In their quiet, unheroic ways, characteristic of merchant seamen, they wrote many glowing pages in the history of our nation. We should be proud of them.

INTRODUCTION

This story of the *Lane Victory* begins when the ship was more than forty years old. In 1989 she lay silent and idle. Her great days were long gone and she was consigned to "the mothball fleet," a warehouse of old, dying ships. And then things started to happen. For the *Lane Victory*, as for some fortunate people, "life begins (again) at forty."

It started with Joe Vernick and John Smith and a group known as the U.S. Merchant Marine Veterans of World War II. Made up of merchant seamen who served during that war, the Merchant Marine Veterans dedicated themselves to making the country aware of the sacrifices of their fellow mariners. It started with faith in their cause. It started with hope that they could find a ship to serve as a symbol of that cause. It started in the backwaters of Suisun Bay, California at the National Defense Reserve Fleet.

As superintendent of the Suisun Bay Reserve Fleet I frequently met people with ideas as to what to do with "all those ships just sitting there." Some wanted to make homes for the poor out of them. Others suggested using them to house criminals. Still others wanted them cut up to provide jobs for the poor. Few understood the purpose of the Fleet — "to provide a sizeable group of merchant ships at the outbreak of any national emergency."

"But they're so old," was the usual response. I countered that they were all we had. They would have to do if we ever needed them. So there they sat. We did our best to preserve them, but the mournful truth was that most of them were destined for the ship breakers.

Enter Joe Vernick and John Smith. They came looking for a ship to turn into a museum to honor merchant marine veterans. They had little money and no idea what it took to "get a ship." But they did have two unbeatable assets. First, their enthusiasm was unbridled; you could light a million-watt beacon with their energy and zeal. And, second, they didn't know that it was practically impossible. Ships, even old ones, are not just handed over for the asking.

So they came to look for a ship. Originally hoping to find a Liberty ship, Joe and John soon realized there were none left. Their second choice was a Victory ship, the next class produced after the Libertys in World War II. We had about forty of these ships at Suisun Bay at the time. One of them was the *Lane Victory.*

We considered the *Lane Victory* our "show ship." Most of the other ships in the fleet were simply sealed and put under dehumidification and cathodic protection. The *Lane Victory* was special. Years before my tenure, the interior was painted, the beds were made, lighting circuits were connected. You could enter the ship, throw a switch and, almost magically, be transported back to an active ship. It was as if the crew, after making their beds, had just gone out on deck to secure the cargo gear for sea. The quarters, galley, wheelhouse and engine room were clean and well-lighted. It was a pleasure to look at her.

Any time someone wanted to see a Victory ship we showed them the *Lane Victory.* This worked well with politicians, dignitaries from Washington, D.C., congressmen and others. Many a senator left the fleet with the remark, "Damn, those ships are in fine shape." With Joe Vernick it worked too well. Not only did he think the *Lane Victory* was in fine shape, he thought it was beautiful and wanted to take it home with him!

It's always a sad occasion when a proud ship leaves the Reserve Fleet, knowing that the wealth of stories, history, nostalgia and romance it carries will end up on some foreign shore where it will be cut into pieces. In that final moment it loses its soul and becomes merely a pile of steel plates, a bucket of bolts, a confusion of wires, to be sold to scrappers. What was once a noble work of art, with personality, character and life, is no more. Many of us will go to great lengths to prevent such an ignoble ending.

There were a few precedents. The *Jeremiah O'Brien*, a Liberty ship, was taken from the Suisun Bay Reserve Fleet in 1979 and, with hundreds of thousands of hours of sweat and toil from hundreds of volunteers, made into a museum ship in San Francisco. The *John W. Brown*, another Liberty, was taken from our sister fleet in Virginia and made into a museum ship in Baltimore. Some ships were taken from the Reserve Fleet and converted into training vessels for state maritime academies.

If Joe Vernick wanted to adopt the *Lane Victory* and give it a home, then, by God, I would do everything I could to help. What more fitting ending for an historic vessel than to be preserved as a museum. It would show generations to come some of our history. It would show people what America could do, and do well, when she had to. And it would remind everyone of the great contributions and sacrifices of the merchant mariners during World War II.

This, then, is the story of one ship. But, more than that, it is a story of faith in a good cause. It is a tale of hope in going against the odds to fulfill a dream. It is the story of the *Lane Victory*.

Capt. Walter W. Jaffee
Menlo Park
1991

PART ONE

1

THE PRE-WAR CHALLENGE

The story actually begins in 1936. National policy in Germany and Japan pointed toward war. The United States knew it must be prepared. We were especially concerned about our merchant fleet, a critical ingredient in the coming conflict. The American merchant fleet and the shipbuilding industry were in a slump. Fed by a huge construction program that began during World War I and continued until 1920, the ports, harbors and rivers of the country were plugged with idle ships. It was a case of too much too late. Too many ships were built as the war ended, and continued to be built for several years afterward. American ships flooded the industry, even as there was less and less for them to carry. By 1936 some 91% of the American merchant fleet was at or near the twenty-year mark. Most of these were capable of doing 10-11 knots at best. A few combination passenger-cargo carriers were built under the subsidy provisions of the Merchant Marine Act of 1928. But there was a crying need for dry cargo ships and tankers, fast ships that in an emergency could be used as naval auxiliaries. To address this need the Merchant Marine Act of 1936 was passed. Creating the United States Maritime Commission, the main thrust of the Act was to develop overseas trade and serve it with ships of a new, modern, efficient merchant marine.

The newly-formed Commission started building cargo ships in 1937. The long-range plan was for 500 ships with a total tonnage of four million, to be built over a ten-year period. The new ships were to be fast tankers and three standard designs of high-speed cargo ships. The cargo ships would be known as the "C" types. These were the C-1, C-2 and C-3 designs. The letter "C" represents "cargo" while the number refers to the length of the hull. At the time the design speed of 15 knots was noteworthy. (Today's standard is 20-25 knots.) The *Challenge*, one of the first C-2s reached a speed of 17 knots on her trials. Her design speed was 15.5. Most remarkable was the fact that the new "C" type ships had the same fuel consumption as the 10-knot ships they replaced.

By 1939 it was clear that construction of fifty ships a year was not fast enough to replace the old fleet. It was also not fast enough to maintain worldwide trade routes, even without a war. The Maritime Commission doubled the building schedule to 100 ships a year.

The growing threat of war could not be ignored. Germany quickly and ruthlessly overran most of Western Europe and gained control of the North Atlantic. Would she next turn her rapacious ambitions to the United States? Or to American trade routes? America could not afford to chance a "wait-and-see" attitude. In August of 1940 the shipbuilding schedule was doubled again, this time to 200 ships a year. There were nineteen shipyards building new ships.

Meanwhile, in a new phase of the war at sea, German U-boats began harassing Atlantic shipping from their stronghold in the Bay of Biscay. America wasn't ready for it, despite her best efforts. In just one four-week period in 1940, Britain lost over

300,000 tons of shipping. Although still officially "neutral," much of this tonnage was supplied by America through Lend-Lease. By the spring of 1941 Allied losses during a two-month period reached a staggering 815,000 tons and by the end of the year 750 ships totalling almost three million tons were lost.

Now fully realizing the crisis, the United States changed her shipbuilding policy. The concept in building the "C" ship was quality: produce a well-made, fast ship. The new policy was quantity: produce lots of ships. In February of 1941, President Roosevelt announced the new shipbuilding program in a nation-wide radio broadcast. Describing the new ships as "dreadful looking objects," he ruefully referred to them as "Ugly Duck-lings." These were the Liberty ships.

The *Patrick Henry*, the first of the Libertys, was launched in September of 1941, going on her trials a few days after Pearl Harbor. Eventually more than 2700 Liberty ships were built, becoming the bedrock of the "bridge of ships" that helped win the war.

German U-boats, meanwhile, began preying on American shipping. The Atlantic Coast and the Caribbean became virtual shooting galleries for Nazi submarines. The effects on Allied shipping were devastating.

"Quantity" shipbuilding became a desperate necessity. In the first half of 1942 more than six million tons of Allied shipping was lost. Some 1,200 ships went to the bottom. The old, estab-lished shipyards, as well as the new, emergency facilities soon reached a hectic shipbuilding pace. Steel was turned into ships so quickly that shipyards often outran their sources of supply.

The year 1943 was the turning point. Ship construction finally turned the corner from "they're getting sunk faster than they're built" to "build them faster than they can be sunk." Ship-yards turned out nineteen million tons of ships. With the produc-tion corner turned, policy once again changed. There was still a need for a fast cargo ship, both as part of the war effort and as a key to the merchant fleet after the war. This need would be filled by the Victory Ship.

2

LIBERTY
OR VICTORY?

To build ships in quantity meant the hull designs had to be standardized. Standardized hulls allowed for a heavy construction schedule. With standard designs came mass production and expansion of the shipyards. The delivery schedule for 1943 included 230 "C" type cargo ships, 209 tankers, 16 ore carriers, 69 frigates, 50 escort carriers, 54 LSTs, Army and Navy transports and more than 1,200 Liberty ships.

As the year drew to a close, the Liberty ship building program was considered an accomplished fact. Looking into the future, there was concern about a possible shortage of steel. If the available amount of this raw material was limited, then a decision must be made as to how best to use it. Should the Liberty ship program continue apace or might the steel be better used to build other types of ships that would operate faster and more efficiently?

Two groups pushed for newer ships. Commercial ship operators wanted a fast, efficient ship so they could compete in world markets when the war was over. The military services wanted fast, commercial-type ships to use as auxiliaries. An added factor was that faster ships could elude submarines. Convoys would not be necessary. This would mean that fewer ships were vulnerable to attack, so fewer ships were needed.

Because standardization worked so well with the Libertys and the yards were already "geared up" to that type of production, emphasis continued on quantity emergency ship construction rather than the quality "C" type building. It was clear from the start that the boxy hull and square lines of the Liberty wouldn't do for the new speedster. In early 1942 an entirely new design, known as the AP1, was created. Calling for a length of 445 feet and a beam of sixty-three feet, the guidelines for the new ship required that it have about the same deadweight capacity as the Liberty and that the minimum speed be fifteen knots. In the early stages of the Victory ship concept, the Maritime Commission planned on building 1,600 ships. Bethlehem Steel of Quincy, Massachusetts was assigned the task of creating working drawings. The Maritime Commission concentrated on stability calculations and other characteristics.

Production on the new ships should have started sooner. But there were too many bureaucracies involved. The Maritime Commission wanted to proceed with the new Victory-type ship. The War Production Board, an agency set up to regulate and consolidate American shipbuilding, was against it. The battle went on for months.

The first difficulty was that many shipyards could not build a ship with a sixty-three foot beam. Their ways were too narrow. But a sixty-two foot beam would just make it, so the design was changed to that figure. Of course, with a change in beam came a change in stability. The ends of the waterline were "filled" to correct this condition. There was an advantage. A fuller forebody created a drier ship in the right weather conditions.

Additional improvements to the plans included searchlights, gyro-compasses, larger cargo booms and more efficient winches (electric versus steam) and davits. The latter were needed to handle landing craft for the military. The additions were allowed with the proviso that they would not delay production.

Bethlehem was too busy doing other work to finish the drawings by the deadline. The task was then given to a design agent. One of the agent's challenges was to limit the size of the prefabricated sections to the lowest capacity of shipyard cranes. This let many shipyards work on the sections which could then be assembled in other yards with higher capacity cranes.

By March 1943 the drawings were complete. The Maritime Commission was ready to go public with the new design. Given the designator EC2-S-AP1, (Libertys were also designated EC2), the new ship design was ready to build. The design designator indicates "E" for emergency, "C" for cargo and "2" for length (between 450 and 500 feet). The letter "S" indicates a steam engine and the fact that there are no numbers with it means the ship is single screw. The third group "AP1" refers to the design and modification numbers.

The Maritime Commission thought the ship was ready to build. In a speech a few weeks later, the chairman of the Commission first referred to the new ship as a Victory.

"We have developed a new emergency ship — the Victory ship — to replace the Libertys. The new ship is designed to permit use of the Lentz engine, turbines or diesels. Its expected speed is fifteen to seventeen knots as against the Libertys' eleven knots, and it will be a good competition ship in post-war — which we cannot claim for the Liberty ship." (Ironically, the Liberty would become the postwar mainstay of most of the world's merchant fleets for years to come.)

A major problem with the Liberty ships was hull fractures. In fact, a good amount of shipyard time in 1944 was spent reinforcing them against structural failure. Modifications were made in the Victory so the same problem wouldn't occur. Internal frames were spaced at thirty-six inches, rather than thirty inches as in the Libertys. This made the ship more flexible, allowing it to "give" in heavy seas. The No. 1 hold deep tank was eliminated. Its capacity was included in two deep tanks at No. 4 hatch. These had the added versatility of being usable for fuel, water ballast or dry cargo. In addition there were deep tanks in No. 5 hold which were used for fuel or water only. The design enabled the ship to remain stable even after damage or partial flooding. Unlike the Liberty, the three forward holds of the Victory were fitted with 'tween decks. This feature gave the ship more versatility in cargo stowage. Much of the auxiliary equipment such as pumps, steering gear and the anchor windlass were electric instead of steam, as found on the Liberty.

Armament consisted of a 3-inch gun forward, a 5-inch aft, four 20mm mounts amidships, two 20mms on the forecastle and two 20mms on the poop deck house.

There was still one major problem. No one had an engine capable of producing fifteen knots in that type of hull. Steam turbines were the obvious choice but there weren't enough around. The new turbine factories set up by the Maritime Commission in 1941 were producing engines for the "C" type ships and some of the tankers. There simply weren't enough extras to power a new class of 500 ships. Even when design studies showed that only 5,600 horsepower was needed, it didn't help. The only available choice was the steam reciprocating engine (the workhorse of the Liberty).

The idea of using a steam reciprocating engine brought its own problems. A test engine had to be designed and built before production could start. This would take valuable time. There was on the market the Skinner Uniflow single expansion steam reciprocating engine. It had the right horsepower but turned at 160 RPM, much too fast for a single propeller. Another alternative suggested was the Sun-Doxford diesel which was used with some success on the C-2s. But this idea was dropped for a number of reasons.

Finally the decision was made to use a German diesel engine, the Lentz. There was one difficulty. No Lentz engine that size had ever been built. The American Shipbuilding Company of Cleveland was the only company licensed to produce such an engine. By November it was agreed that the new EC2-S-AP1 engine would be rated at 5,500 horsepower and turn at 85 RPM with a 59-inch stroke. A special company was created to do the drawings and the U.S. Navy agreed to test the first engine. Other designers produced new plans, based on the Victory concept. The designation EC2-S-AP2 was given to a variation of the basic design which used the 6,000 horsepower turbine from the C-2s. When equipped with the turbine used on C-3s which was rated at 8,500 shaft horsepower, the designator became EC2-S-AP3. AP4 was used to indicate diesel propulsion, but only one such ship was ever built.

On April 28, 1943 the ship's designator was officially changed from EC2 to VC2. The Victory ship was born. That same month, the first Victory contracts were given to the Oregon Shipbuilding Company in Portland, Oregon and the California Shipbuilding Company in Los Angeles. They were to build the AP3 type with the 8,500 horsepower engine. Contracts also went to Bethlehem-Fairfield in Baltimore, Maryland; Richmond Yards No.1 and No.2 in California; Delta Shipbuilding Company in New Orleans, Louisiana; the Houston Shipbuilding Corporation of Texas and The South Eastern Corporation of Savannah, Georgia. Each of these companies was to build the AP1 powered by the Lentz engine.

But production of the Lentz engine met one delay after another. There were legal problems in producing an engine licensed by a company located in an enemy country. The patents were under the control of the Allied Property Custodian. Adding to the problem was the ongoing battle between the War Production Board and the Maritime Commission. The War Production Board wanted fewer new types of ships. It also wanted more standardization with the C-2 serving as the model. It advocated building more Liberty ships. The Maritime Commission wanted to keep the number of designs at a minimum but at the same time build a variety of newer and faster ships.

The AP3-type Victory ship would have 8,500 horsepower and be capable of a speed of 18 knots. The ship in this photo is unidentified, but recognizable as the AP3 by the protruding whistle housing on the stack — the only external difference between the AP3 and the AP2. Courtesy Maritime Administration.

In an attempt to end the battle, the Combined Shipbuilding Committee (Standardization of Design) was set up in March of 1943. Representatives of both groups were on the committee. The dispute focused on two issues: 1) Should Victory ships be built instead of Libertys, and 2) What engines should be used for Victories and/or C-2s.

The Maritime Commission wanted to produce 524 Victorys during 1944, the first year of production. It planned for 347 AP1s and 177 AP3s. The AP3s were planned because suddenly turbine manufacturers had more engines than hulls to put them in. They, too, had turned the corner of "building them faster than they could sink them." Production levels on the C-2 engine were designed so as to create a surplus for AP-2 construction. It was thought the Lentz engine would produce 15.5 knots, the C-2 turbine 16 knots and the C-3 turbine 17 knots.

Meanwhile, the Combined Shipbuilding Committee continued its squabbling. The Maritime Commission gave Victory ship parts its highest priority only to have the War Production Board refuse to authorize facilities or materials.

The situation eased somewhat when turbine builders agreed on mass production of a standard turbine. With this development, the Commission agreed to drop the Lentz engine, providing enough turbines were available. At the same time, the War Production Board agreed to allow the Lentz engine if not enough turbines were produced. There was further agreement when the Maritime Commission agreed to drop C-1 cargo ship construction in exchange for authorization for Victory construction.

This common-sense approach was not to last. The problem then became how many yards should build Victorys and at what rate. The real issue was who had the greater authority — the War Production Board or the Maritime Commission. The WPB decided to stop production of C-2 turbines with the idea of using Victory ship turbines on C-2s. They argued that building two similar turbines in war time when one was far cheaper than the other couldn't be justified. They issued orders canceling turbine production. The Maritime Commission issued counter-orders calling for not only production, but increased production.

Finally the Joint Chiefs of Staff stepped in and forced a settlement. They decided that the battle between the two groups was detrimental to the war effort. Their findings were that there would not be a bottleneck in shipping in the near future because of the urgent need for the production of other types of war material. Building large numbers of Liberty ships was no longer necessary and the Commission's program of a great number of faster ships would better meet the strategic requirements for 1944 than would any of the alternatives offered by the WPB.

The overall effect of the long feud between the Maritime Commission and the War Production Board was that fewer Victorys were built. The contracts to the Southern states were canceled. The yards on the West Coast that were building Libertys didn't launch their first Victory until half-way through 1944. The spare turbines for the C-3 program (for use on the AP3) were finished before the ships were ready and had to be stored.

On February 28, 1944 the first of the new ships, the *United Victory,* was launched by the Oregon Shipbuilding Corporation. She made her inaugural voyage the following month. While it was a beginning, production was slow. By May of 1944 only fifteen ships were ready, eleven from the Oregon company and four from CalShip. Gradually the other shipbuilders eased out of Liberty Ship construction and into Victory ships. Victory ships were built by Bethlehem-Fairfield in Baltimore, Permanente Metals Corporation in Richmond, California and Kaiser in Vancouver, Washington. All the Kaiser production was modified to attack transports.

A total of 531 Victory ships were built. Of these 414 were cargo ships and 117 were transports. The cargo ships included 272 of the AP2 type, 141 of the AP3 and one of the AP4 type. The attack transports were designated AP5s. There were three ships redesigned and delivered in 1947 to the Alcoa Steamship Company, Inc. of New York. Bearing the modification number AP7, they brought the total number of Victory hulls produced to 534.

Of the 272 AP2 type Victorys, the California Shipbuilding Corporation of Los Angeles, built 69; the *Lane Victory* was No. 46.

3

BUILD THEM
FASTER . . .

As the deadly Battle of the North Atlantic sent ships by the hundreds to the bottom, the nation grimly set out to replace the lost tonnage. "Build them faster than they can be sunk," was the goal. But all the shipyards in the United States were operating at capacity and most of the experienced labor force was already at work. The only solution was to create more yards and operate them with people from other industries, whether they knew about ship construction or not.

The California Shipbuilding Corporation or "CalShip" began January 11, 1941 with the award of a facilities contract by the Maritime Commission. Three days later ground was broken on Terminal Island in Los Angeles Harbor. Responsibility for the new yard rested with Bechtel-McCone. Their engineers designed, built and managed the facility.

At first glance it might seem this was an unlikely choice for a group to manage a shipyard. Like Henry Kaiser, who was also building shipyards, they had no experience with ships. Like Kaiser, Bechtel-McCone also had an excellent reputation in building bridges, refineries and dams. They were well known for their ability to organize and accomplish any project. They were very much a "can do" organization. And because they weren't experienced in shipbuilding, they didn't have preconceived ideas about what would and wouldn't work. Beginning with a clean slate, they revolutionized the shipbuilding industry.

Steve Bechtel was the first president of the new yard. He was succeeded in later years by John McCone.

Bechtel-McCone and Kaiser did for shipbuilding what Henry Ford did for automaking. They brought the assembly line to shipbuilding. Ships were prefabricated in sections, the sections moved to the launching ways and assembled there. Total construction time was drastically reduced.

At CalShip ships were prefabricated in sections, the sections taken as needed to the launching ways where the ship was built. Here we see several double bottom and bulkhead sections stacked, awaiting the call. Credit San Francisco Maritime National Historical Park.

Eight months after the ground breaking, the first ship, a Liberty christened *John C. Fremont,* was launched. Construction escalated rapidly as new launching ways, cranes, rails, shops and fitting out berths were added.

Two of the *Lane Victory's* volunteer crew worked for CalShip at Terminal Island during the 1940s.

I. Roy Coats was the 106th person hired at the new yard. "I was a supervisor of transportation on the swing shift."

Don MacLean was also one of the first workers at the new yard. "I started there in the early part of '41 and I worked as a marine machinist."

I. Roy Coats, as supervisor, handled everything from steel plates to prefabricated sections. ". . . that entailed both the raw material, the plates, and the fabricated plates, and then the fabricated sections. We stood all of our plates on edge and we built

The Liberty ship John C. Fremont *was the first vessel launched at CalShip. Here she is caught just as her stern enters the water, the champagne bottle trailing from a ribbon on the bow. Courtesy Worldport LA.*

them up in sequence so when we filled an order we'd just take one plate out of each rack to make a section."

The only limiting factor to the size of the sections was that they had to weigh less than the capacity of the cranes at the launching ways.

I. Roy Coats: "The size of the sections were predicated on our lifting capacity, what we could lift aboard ship. We could lift anything out in storage because you could jack it up or anything else. But when you placed it aboard the ways, why, two cranes was all we could put on one section. And transverse bulkheads . . . 'course they were all one section because they went across and you can't split them in the middle. Those were really our heaviest lifts. And the sideshell and everything was all sub-assembled. You had your sideshell that went down to the turn of the bilge, I believe that was the "C" strake and then the turn of the bilge over to the keel and then the top one was the "J" strake and that included your bulwark rail and then your deck sections and your hatch combings . . ."

At its height, CalShip had thirty-four ships simultaneously under construction.

Don MacLean: "I can still see it in my mind's eye. I can still see them all lined up and sometimes you wondered which one you were working on, there were so many of them."

I. Roy Coats: "They had about thirty-some ships under construction at all times. We had fourteen ways and they had ten outfitting docks and then they were working throughout the yard on sub-assembly."

In June, 1942 the yard broke the world's production record for ships by delivering fifteen Liberty ships.

One of the larger pre-fabricated sections was the shaft alley. I. Roy Coats: "They were made up in about thirty-foot sections."

Working in the shaft alleys was considered one of the grittier jobs in the yard. In the earlier days, as people developed new skills and innovative techniques evolved, there were problems. Don MacLean: "I was a journeyman marine machinist in

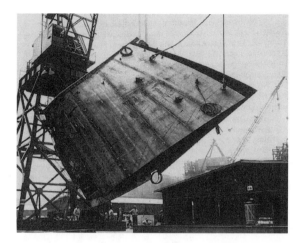

Above, a bow section (the stem is on the upper left edge toward the crane) is raised in final pre-assembly. Right, the same section now faces the camera while workmen rig it to "walk" it to the waiting ship. Credit both photos San Francisco Maritime National Historical Park.

the shaft alley setting the Joshua Hendy steam triple-expansion engines. To line up the [propeller] shaft with the engine you would use a feeler gauge to make sure all the flanges were exactly the same thousandths apart.

"First you'd set the bearing under the shaft. Using a feeler gauge you'd bring the bearing into position. Then you'd measure the distance from the bearing to the bearing plate and order chocks, four chocks for each bearing. The chocks were one or one-and-a-half thousandths oversized. Then you find the lowest point on the bearing and start from there and blue and scrape your bearings in. Well, you had a little hook that you'd

Prefabricated sections were limited in size to the capacity of the two cranes that carried them into place. Here we see the same bow piece as it nears the ship on the ways. This is a small lift, the transverse bulkhead sections being much more difficult. Credit San Francisco Maritime National Historical Park.

get under there and jerk them out after you fit them and I had my finger in the hole . . . You used to put your finger in the hole to see how far you was in, and I had my finger in there and I jerked it out and I took the end of my finger off!

"I had to get it fixed. They had a first aid station there, and I went to the first aid station. They were just lined up for about half a block, people trying to get in there and get fixed. So they had lots of accidents.

"After we lined the shaft all up and chalked it in we would bolt it up. That meant we had to re-drill the holes. We had the bolts made oversize. Then we would drive them in with a lead sledge. Then we'd pull on them with a hydraulic jack. The jack bolted right on to the threads of the nut and we pulled it through.

"It got pretty dangerous down there. They were drop-ping planks and people and wrenches and everything else on us down there 'cause the caps on the shaft alleys were open. The shaft alley on a Liberty ship is different than a Victory. They're open and they divide the hatch. They actually divide the hatch. So they decided they would put the covers on while we was working there to protect us. Can you imagine working where they're riveting on covers?"

Part of the earlier problems were due to the lack of skilled labor. Less then ten percent of the workforce had ever worked in a shipyard before.

Lucille "Bunny" Raymond started as a pool stenogra-pher, but ended up working for the Maritime Commission in the office of the Resident Auditor. She recalled some of the workforce had never seen a ship before. "I remember there was one letter of recruitment, it was either Arkansas or Kansas. Some state they were recruiting for workers at the shipyard, hiring welders, all kinds of shipyard workers. And that letter was forever being asked for when they would meet with the Cal-Ship officials. That came up so many times I kept that where I could find it."

There was training for every type of job.

Don MacLean: "I went to what you would call a timing school. It was for timing on your steam reciprocators. You set the spool valves and so forth and I got pretty good at that. About the time I left they were about to give me another job which would have been timing engines instead of setting them in."

CalShip's training facilities weren't simply schools, they were part of the construction process.

I. Roy Coats: "See, they didn't only teach them to work but they also did productive work. We had an awful large welding school and we did a lot of our assembly in welding school."

One of the welding school's jobs was to correct mistakes in the manufacture of the steel plating for the ship's hulls. Ac-

At first CalShip built Libertys. Here we see the sterns of two, the one in the foreground just prior to launching. The American flags are indicative of the war spirit that permeated the yard. The armed guard in the foreground demonstrated the concern for security. Credit San Francisco Maritime National Historical Park.

cording to supervisor Coats, "They didn't check for lamination in the plate shop or anything. The lamination — that's where the plate had separated in the mill — got an air pocket in it when they rolled it. That looked all right when it was sheared at the mill and set on the flatcar. So they put a bevel on it in the plate shop and didn't inspect it. We pulled probably twenty-five flatcars out of the plate shop every mealtime. The inspector waited until they were loaded on the gondola. Once they were loaded, the inspector could see the bright shiny edge and he'd go along and he'd paint it blue or red or something and that meant when we off-loaded the flatcar we sent all our laminated plate down to the weld school. They'd chip all that out and buff it out and

Don MacLean remembered there were so many ships under construction at one time, he was never sure which one he was working on. Here we see Libertys; in the foreground already launched, in the background still under construction. Credit San Francisco Maritime National Historical Park.

The CalShip yard as seen from the water. Tugs in the center await the launching of the Liberty ship nearest them. Courtesy Worldport LA.

then re-weld it and then buff it out again, and then they'd have it inspected and send it back to the racks."

Twenty percent of the workforce was women. "Rosie the Riveter" and "Wendy the Welder" weren't just catchy names, they were an important part of the workforce. I. Roy Coats thought highly of their abilities. "We had 7,000 women out of a workforce of about 45,000. I would say probably over half of those were in production, not in office work."

According to Don MacLean the welders had some of the hardest jobs, especially the women welders. "They got really good with them torches. I used to feel sorry for them welding on the side of the ship 'cause they were hanging in them bosun's chairs out there doing all that welding. Man I don't see how they could stay on them welders like they did. Hour after hour, welding."

Of course flat, horizontal surfaces could be welded automatically.

Don MacLean: "It used to be fun when I was on deck to watch them deck-welders, you know, them little machines that would run along and weld, you see them on this ship, beautiful welds right down there, them little machines just run down there, nobody watching them or nothing. . ."

In June of 1943 the construction record toppled again to the count of twenty ships.

Once things got into full swing there were fewer problems and fewer accidents. Confusion at learning a new skill and bewilderment at working in a new setting gave way to the demand for production, production, production. "Build them faster than they can be sunk," created constant pressure.

I. Roy Coats preferred the swing shift to any other. "Swing shift was the best shift to be on because it was the cool of the evening and you didn't get out of bed to come to work like the graveyard did. You didn't work in the heat of the day. Plus you didn't have all the bosses around you. In the day time we used to say we had to make a lift as many times as there was bosses around. They got criticized all the time. They even had a rule on the day shift that you were to keep your boom swinging whether you were working or not. So even while you were waiting on a trailer it looked like the yard was all working."

Don MacLean remembered other incentives for hard work. "We really worked. I mean, you didn't loaf because if you loafed they told you they would call your draft board and have you drafted.

"You really worked. No question about it. They had what you'd call bosses, I forget what you called them, but they had bosses that watched you pretty close. What they'd do if you didn't do your job, they'd put you off on another job. And they'd always try to find a meaner job for you so you had incentive to work. And there's no doubt that the people there worked hard."

CalShip provided its workers the right tools to work with. Don MacLean: "We had all our tools made. We'd go up and we'd get a cutter. They had cutters on board. All over the ship was a table with a cutter there. Any time you wanted something cut you'd just go in there and he'd make it. We'd make these wrenches, they had a loop in them to pull the chocks out and somebody was always stealing your wrench. Almost every shift you'd have to go get a new wrench made. They got pretty good."

The hard work paid off. CalShip became a well-oiled, smoothly-functioning shipyard. Resentment turned to pride, confusion to professionalism. There was a sense of accomplishment. Everyone was enthusiastic, high-spirited and proud of a job well done. In December of 1943, the yard set yet another record when twenty-three ships — nineteen Libertys and four tankers — were delivered.

I. Roy Coats: "No kidding. There was never a day that went by that I didn't wish that I had another two hours left on the shift so I could complete what I had started. I was constantly on the run and most of the other fellas were too."

Don MacLean: "It was funny . . . the shipyard was full of war effort. There was no question about it. And so was the merchant marine."

At peak employment the shipyard had on board a population of men and women equal to that of the city of San Bernardino, California.

With so many people working around the clock in one place, transportation and parking were problems. Trolleys and buses and even ferries ran to CalShip.

Don MacLean took the ferry. "What we used to do, we'd go to work in the morning. I had the early shift. We'd go over on the ferry. We had a ferry running between San Pedro and Terminal Island. It was an auto ferry with passengers. On the island side they would meet us with a bus and they would bus us to the turnstiles. We'd go into the yard and we would take our card and punch in. Then we would go into the yard and start our job."

Those that drove tried for the parking spaces closest to the entrances. Of course the day shift had the best spaces taken by the time the swing shift arrived. I. Roy Coats developed a creative method of getting a parking spot. "They encouraged you to share your ride. Our parking lot was a mile long. 'Course you tried to get by the gate you walked in at. With that many people the day shift had all the good spots by the gate. But four of us we'd get two on the back bumper and two on the front and we'd go down about six cars and jiggle . . . start jiggling them over and then jiggle them the other way and I'd get a spot I could squeeze into. We did that almost every night."

The pay was good and, as it was wartime, there wasn't much to spend it on. "There wasn't anything you could do with your money," Coats remembered, "because gasoline was rationed, shoes was rationed, everything was rationed. So you stayed home all the time. You didn't go anywhere."

Looking back more than fifty years later, it's interesting to see how things have changed. Life was different then.

Concepts were simple. The enemies were Hitler and Tojo. Hard work, rationing and enough ships would beat the enemy. It was as simple as that. Life in general was a lot less complex. People went to work and then went home. Families gathered around the radio to hear the news or conversed with their neighbors on their porches or over the back fence. There was no television. Radar was in its infancy, credit cards didn't exist, the atom had not been split, there were no laser beams nor ball point pens. People hadn't yet dreamed of pantyhose, dishwashers, clothes dryers, electric blankets, air conditioners, drip-dry clothes or man walking on the moon. Penicillin, polio shots, frozen foods, Xerox, plastic, contact lenses and the PILL were yet to come.

People got married first, then lived together. Closets were for clothes, not "coming out of." Bunnies were small rabbits and rabbits were not Volkswagens. Designer jeans were scheming girls named Jean, and having a meaningful relationship meant getting along with your cousin.

Fast food was what you ate during Lent, and Outer Space was the back of the local movie theater. There was no such thing as a house husband, gay rights, computer dating, dual careers and commuter marriages. The day-care center, group therapy and nursing homes had yet to be invented. No one ever heard of FM radio, tape decks, electronic typewriters, artificial hearts, word processors, yogurt and guys wearing earrings. Time sharing meant togetherness . . . not computers or condominiums (What was a condominium, anyway?). A chip meant a piece of wood. Hardware meant hardware and software wasn't even a word.

"Made in Japan," meant junk and the term "making out" referred to how you did on your exam. Pizzas, McDonalds and instant coffee were unheard of. There were 5 and 10 cent stores where you bought things that cost five and ten cents. Ice cream was a nickel for a single scoop, a dime for a double. For a nickel you could ride a trolley, make a phone call, buy a Pepsi or enough stamps to mail one letter and two postcards. You could buy a Chevy Coupe for $600 if you could afford it. Gas was eleven cents a gallon.

Grass was mowed, Coke was a cold drink and POT was something you cooked in. Rock Music was Grandma's lullaby and AIDS were helpers in the principal's office. Although not before the difference in sexes was discovered, it was before sex change. People made do with what they had and were the last generation that was so dumb as to think you needed a husband to have a baby.

I. Roy Coats: "Your shave cream came in a zinc tube then. They hadn't learned to make them out of plastic yet. So it was sort of a precious metal and they wanted you to save that. Then they encouraged you to take your trunk lid off and turn it in for the steel in it. I drove a Chevrolet without a trunk on it . . . I went to the junk yard and put an old seat back in the trunk. I had a two door, a Chevy, probably a '32 or something like that. I put that seat back there (in the trunk) and I had two riders that rode in the rain.

"In fact, they wanted you to conserve gas and stuff and rubber."

Don MacLean: "There was a lot of rationing, you'd ration your meat and everything . . ."

I. Roy Coats: "There was a shortage of leather shoes. The other day I run across the wife's application. I couldn't believe it. Application for a pair of shoes. She had to have her shoes examined by a doctor to say that she definitely had to have a pair of shoes or she was going to injure her feet or something."

A Liberty ship cost about $1.5 million to build in 1943.

CalShip production was valued at $919,000,000. Some of the financing came from the employees.

"They was constantly trying to get guys to buy bonds and they bought an awful lot of bonds," recalled I. Roy Coats. "They tried to pay for one Liberty ship a month. In other words they were delivering twenty ships a month, well they would try to pay for one every month with our Liberty bonds."

When CalShip employees bought war bonds in their children's names, the child was given this certificate to commemorate the occasion. Credit the Walt Disney Company.

I. Roy Coats: "I had bonds running out of my ears. The wife wouldn't go through my pants or my shirt pockets when she'd wash'em or they'd get throwed off in the trash. I'd ask her maybe a day or two later, I says 'Did you get the bond?'

"And she says, 'Well, no,' she forgot it. I'd go out and find it in the trash. They were Mickey Mouse bonds. See, to get you to buy bonds they did all kinds of things and they had the Disney Corporation design a bond with Mickey Mouse and all the characters on it and you'd buy'em in your kids' name. You bought them for $18 and at the end of so many years they were $25 bonds."[1]

---

[1] It wasn't actually a bond. The Walt Disney Company designed a War Bond Certificate which was presented to children when a standard U.S. Government bond was purchased in their name.

The war bond itself. Issued in denominations of $25, $50 and $100, they financed one out of every twenty ships built at CalShip. Courtesy Don MacLean.

With the war effort and ship production in full swing came a need for more workers. Shipyards from Puget Sound to the Mexican border worked around the clock. The labor pool on the Pacific Coast dried up.

I. Roy Coats: "They went down south and set up recruiting stations and hired these colored people. They guaranteed them a place to live and they started an auxiliary union. They had to join the union but the boilermakers didn't want them in

As the war progressed CalShip production changed from Libertys to Victorys. Here we see nine such ships in various stages of construction. Courtesy Worldport LA.

their union . . . the bulk of our union was Local 92 over here in Wilmington, the boilermakers. So they started a local 92-A and just soon as the war was over they did away with the 'A' so these guys were still without work. Long Beach had about 5,000 Negroes before the war and after the war we had 45,000. They even built a Red Car track right to Watts. Brought them right down to CalShip. They didn't even need an automobile."

There were no racial problems. The war was everyone's war. People worked so hard to get the job done there wasn't time for anything else. I. Roy Coats: "They did segregate to a certain degree but there wasn't any beef about it. I mean, they didn't care. They had a good job, or the best job they ever had. On a crane crew you'd have all black on a crane crew. You wouldn't have a couple of whites and a couple of blacks."

Labor problems were almost non-existent. I. Roy Coats: "We had no labor disputes. "Journeymen made $1.10 an hour, leadermen got ten cents more, and foremen got maybe twenty cents more than that."

Strangely, the only labor difficulties were with wounded veterans.

I. Roy Coats: "The only time we had any dissension or any talk against it was those veterans towards the last, in '45. From January until the war was over, they were released and we were starting to get fellas that had been injured, you know, and they weren't <u>beginning</u> to work. They figured they'd done their share, and they sat down and they wouldn't work. They just wanted the pay. They figured we'd been over here making the money while they were over there fighting, and by God they were going to get a piece of this money before the war was over. And they did give us a little trouble. It was the only time we had any trouble."

But production continued. Calship was the second largest emergency shipyard in America during World War II. At its peak it employed more than 55,000 people. On one well-remembered day four ships were delivered. The average time between deliveries was sixty-five hours. But there were periods that beat the average. I. Roy Coats: "We were delivering one ship to the Maritime every thirty-two hours, manned.

"And in 1944, the California Shipbuilding yard was building one-eighth of all the ships that were being delivered in the United States . . . of any sort or any kind. We were producing one-eighth of all the ships." By May of 1944 the total was 336 with another 131 yet to come.

Lucille Raymond: "We'd have to approve the [payment] vouchers. They came in on inter-office mail about every half hour. We were really kept busy."

With the end of the war came the end of the need for more ships. CalShip delivered its final ship on October 27, 1945 after four years and ten months of operation.

I. Roy Coats was there from start to finish. ". . . the last one was the *Council Bluffs Victory* and Earl Warren's wife launched it. That was the last ship we launched."

California Shipbuilding built 467 ships: Libertys, tankers, troop transports and Victorys. To do this they used 1,604,788

The last Victory built by CalShip was the Council Bluffs Victory. *Here she is prepared for the launching ceremony at which Mrs. Earl Warren broke the champagne on the bow.   Credit San Francisco Maritime National Historical Park.*

tons of steel. The steel was fastened with 131,275,025 feet of welding; equal to the distance from Los Angeles to Washington, D.C. Piping on these ships measured 18,240,025 feet while 17,102,000 feet of electrical cable went into them. This one shipyard created 4,814,260 deadweight tons of ships which, if placed bow to stern, would form a line forty miles long.

It was in this era, one of strong family values, and in this yard, with its sense of working together against the common enemies, Germany and Japan, that the *Lane Victory* was launched. She was the forty-sixth ship in the AP-2 class built by CalShip.

4

Isaac Lane's Victory

After the first ship in the new class, the *United Victory*, the next thirty-three ships were named after countries which were members of the United Nations: *Brazil Victory*, *Paraguay Victory* and so on. The next group of names came from cities and towns in the United States: *Des Moines Victory*, *Las Vegas Victory*, etc. A third group of names was taken from American colleges and universities. Lane College in Jackson, Tennessee was selected for the Maritime Commission hull #V-794 — the *Lane Victory*. It was an apt choice.

Isaac Lane, the founder of Lane College, was born into slavery on March 3, 1834 in Madison County, Tennessee. As was fairly common at the time, his father, Cullen Lane, who owned the plantation on which he lived, was also his owner. Isaac was one of twenty-seven slaves on the Lane plantation.

Slaves were not allowed an education. The white southern philosophy was that uneducated slaves were more easily subjugated. Lacking the ability to better themselves they would be more content with their station in life and less able to challenge the *status quo*. Isaac Lane proved the validity of this view. Against the odds he managed to educate himself and then set out to educate his people.

Although it was forbidden for slaves to use pencil or paper, Isaac Lane at an early age saw the advantages of reading and writing and determined to learn both. He knew it was a dangerous ambition but he decided he would somehow get an education. Committing the only crime of his entire life, he stole an old spelling book. It was daring and foolhardy but that single act changed his life forever. With determination he studied the book by candlelight after work, until he could read and write. With the development of those skills came the craving for other books.

On his one-hundredth birthday, he recalled, "In the evening hours when work was over I would read and meditate until my candlelight or pine torch flickered out. The Bible, *Binney's Theological Compend, Clarke's Commentaries, Watson's Bible Dictionary*, and *Ralston's Elements of Divinity* were among my first books."

At the age of 19, with his master's approval, he married Frances Ann Boyce of Haywood County, Tennessee. In the following years they had seven daughters and five sons.

Always a deeply religious person, Isaac Lane became a Methodist on October 21, 1854 when he joined that church in Jackson, Tennessee. About four months after joining the church, he was asked to give a sermon and two years later, in November 1856, he was licensed to preach. He remained with that church until after the Civil War. In 1865, now a free man, he moved to Salem, located about five miles from Jackson, and joined the Methodist church there. At the Methodist Conference of 1866 Isaac Lane was elected and ordained an elder in the church. In 1873 he was elected and consecrated as a bishop of the Methodist church.

As Bishop Lane preached to various congregations in the community he became increasingly aware of the lack of education in the congregations and even among his fellow preachers. He knew from his own experience that education was the key to success. But there was no source of common school education for his people or his preachers. He wanted to create such a source but the task was overwhelming. How could one man teach everyone? Where did one start? How could a black bishop in the deep south create educational opportunities for his people in a climate of oppression?

Realizing that it would be difficult to educate both the congregations and the preachers, he decided to concentrate on the preachers. They, in turn, would educate the congregations. He was determined to build a school whose mission would be to turn out educated preachers.

The Education Committee of the General Methodist Conference of 1874 said: "When the cry comes up to the Annual Conference, 'Send us a good preacher', it is generally understood that they mean an 'educated' minister, one that rightly divines their words of truth. We may not expect to do a great deal at present in educating the masses of our people, but we can educate our young preachers that may come into the ministry from time to time. An institution of learning under our control and manned by a competent faculty and well equipped, would act as a stimulus to the whole church."

With the spiritual, but not financial, support of the church, Isaac Lane began. Determination was his strongest trait. Once he decided to do something it got done. In later years he would be known as "the old Roman" because of his ability to complete a task once he set his mind to it. Despite the fact that he and his wife were raising and educating twelve children, he saddled his horse and set out. Canvassing the surrounding countryside he almost single handedly raised enough money to buy the land for the new school.

On January 14, 1880, he purchased four acres of land in Jackson, Tennessee for $240. As might be surmised, the land he could afford to buy was not in a prime location. Situated fifty feet from the Illinois Central Railroad Line, the site was noisy, but it was a beginning.

The first building was put up in the summer of 1882. A two-story frame structure, it measured thirty-four feet by forty-four feet and contained a chapel, a library and recitation rooms. The first class of the C.M.E. (Christian Methodist Episcopal) High School consisted of twenty-seven students. It was taught by Jennie E. Lane, Bishop Lane's twenty-year-old daughter.

In 1884 the school changed its curriculum and name, becoming Lane Institute. Bishop Lane was moved to write in 1888, "We assure the students who will attend Lane Institute in the hereafter that we will have a full faculty and competent teachers for every department of the school. We hope for Lane Institute a prosperous future."

In 1889 a large two-story building' was erected to serve as a girls' dormitory. A one-room building combining office, library and recitation room for the theological department shortly followed. In 1895 a main hall was completed. For many years this three-story brick and wrought iron building was the center-piece of the campus.

In 1896 the school was reorganized as a college and the name changed to Lane College. The Charter with the State of Tennessee was amended to read:

BE IT KNOWN, That Isaac Lane (Pres.). D. W. Featherston, (V.P.), W.H. Daniels (Sec.), W. M. Payne, and J. W. Lane, all of whom are over 21 years old and resident citizens of Madison County, Tennessee are hereby constituted a body politic and corporate by the name and style of "Lane College" and to empower said corporation, so as to support and conduct a literary or scientific undertaking as a college or university, with power to confer degrees and as an academy or college, debating society lyceum, the establishment and historical society and the support of same, the promotion of painting and arts of various kinds. "Lane College" to have its situs in the City of Jackson in Madison County, Tennessee. And a religious and literary undertaking, the successor of Lane Institute.

This was in anticipation of a gift the following year.

In 1897 Wyatt A. Taylor, who sold Bishop Lane the original tract of land for the college, donated an additional acre of land. Included in the gift were a boys' dormitory, a black-smith shop, a wood shop and an additional structure which housed offices and a printing press.

The College Department offered courses in Latin, Greek, German, Mathematical Astronomy, Ethics, Mythology, Analogy, Physics, English, History of Civilization and Rational Theism.

The year 1904 was one to test Bishop Lane's mettle. Early in the year he lost some valuable personal property in a fire. Then the family horse died, a serious problem in the days before automobiles. The difficulties multiplied. On November 2, 1904 the main building and two frame buildings of Lane College burned to the ground. Then a personal tragedy struck. On December 17, Bishop Lane's son, the Reverend Charles Wesley Lane, became ill and died while visiting his father.

Bludgeoned with one loss after another, a lesser man might have given up. Isaac Lane was not such a person. Sub-merging his grief, "the old Roman" immediately set to work rebuilding his college. Because the girls' dormitory was one of the buildings burned, the girls were moved into the boys' dorm. The boys were moved into town with family friends. St. Paul's Chapel, near the campus, did double duty as a classroom.

Plans for a new and bigger main hall were drafted. It would hold recitation rooms, classrooms, study halls, a chapel, a library and offices. One year after the fire a three-story brick building was completed.

Despite the setbacks, in 1906 the new college graduated its first class of two students. One graduate, John Henry Coleman, went on to become a pastor in the C.M.E. Church at Mt. Olive, Tennessee and the other, James Stuart Vaughn, became a Pro-fessor of Greek and German at Tyler College in Texas.

Even before the main hall was paid for, work began on a new girls' dorm. In rapid succession there followed a new boys' dormitory, steam heat for every building on campus, and an Industrial Arts Hall. By 1920 Lane College, like the mythological Phoenix, had risen from the ashes to become even more formidable than before.

As the years passed, the college continued expanding. By its one hundredth anniversary in 1982 more than 4,500 students had graduated from Lane College. It is now a fully accredited Senior Liberal Arts College.

Bishop Lane died on December 5, 1937. He was 103 years old. His early vision was realized. Lane College educates the preachers and the congregations.

In honoring Bishop Isaac Lane, who through courage and determination overcame poverty, ignorance, oppression and prejudice, the United States also demonstrated her determination to victory over the forces of oppression in World War II.

The keel for Maritime Commission hull number V-794 was laid on April 5, 1945. On May 31 Mrs. Florence Cleaves Evans, Bishop Lane's granddaughter, proudly christened her the *Lane Victory*. The ship was delivered to the War Shipping Administration and American President Lines in June of that year.

5

WORLD WAR II

Official trials for the new vessel were rigorous. After testing the engines at slow ahead and slow astern while tied to the dock, she left the pier for sea trials. Underway on her own for the first time she was "swung" to adjust the compasses and test the steering gear. The anchors were dropped and raised. Pumps, motors and electronic equipment were put through their paces. Finally, leaving the harbor behind, the *Lane Victory* was slowly brought up to full speed and beyond. Next came a "crash stop" — full astern — as the ship shivered and shook to a halt with the wash of her propeller boiling and frothing white around her.

Upon successful completion of her official trials, the ship returned to her berth with a broom flying at the mast indicating a clean sweep of all tests. At this point the official transfer took place. She was delivered to the Maritime Commission, the War Shipping Administration and the operating steamship company on June 27, 1945.[1] The *Lane Victory* was valued at $3 million at that time.

CalShip's diligence and pride in Doing The Job Right carried through the fitting-out berth to the actual delivery. Their vessels were received in immaculate condition. Vern Richardson joined the *Lane Victory* as a third assistant engineer when she was delivered to the Maritime Commission, her owners, and American President Lines, her operators. He remembered walking aboard and being impressed that the ship was ". . . spotless. They were getting on to the thing about finishing the ships up right, you know."

To third engineer Richardson, sailing on a Victory was a rare treat, like going from a Chevrolet to a Cadillac. "Oh, yeah. You know, from a Liberty into a Victory ship, you don't see anything moving on a Victory. Everything is enclosed and covered up. On a Liberty everything is going up and down and spraying and splattering everywhere. It was quite a change. About the time I took that Victory ship job I had a chance to go on a diesel, a C-1, the *Cape San Diego*. And I was debating at the last minute, should I? I don't know, I like steam. So I just stayed there. I never did go on a diesel ship."

The gun crew came aboard on June 29 while the ship was berthed at Pier 19 in Long Beach. Their task was to man the 5" 38 gun located on the stern, the 3" 50 gun located on the bow, and the eight 20mm machine guns, two forward, four amidships and two aft.[2]

---

[1] Although the ships were built for the federal Maritime Commission, they were operated by commercial steamship companies (unless they went to another branch of the government such as the Navy). Ships that operated commercially were leased to the steamship company under a General Agency Agreement. This agreement allowed for an expenses plus fee arrangement. Thus, the Maritime Commission was the owner while the steamship company was the operator for the War Shipping Administration.

[2] The numbers 38 and 50 refer to the length of the barrel, that is 38 times and 50 times the 3-inch or 5-inch diameter of the projectile fired.

The *Lane Victory*'s first trip to sea was a short hop up the California coast to Port Hueneme. At the beginning of the war many merchant ships were lost to Japanese submarines and aircraft. For this reason merchant crews were paid bonus money as soon as their ships left the safety of West Coast ports. The closer the ship got to the Far East, the larger the bonus. As the ship departed Los Angeles Harbor late on the night of July 2, 1945, the crew began receiving a partial bonus even while off the California coast. From the official logbook: "2340 at Los Angeles harbor light crossed boundary line between inland waters and high seas as defined by pilot rules. 33-1/3 % bonus effective."

John (Jack) Morrison was making his first trip as an ordinary seaman. "Shortly after we passed the Federal Breakwater, I, who had scarcely been in the wheelhouse, was put on the wheel. I did not know the slightest thing about steering a ship and we went way off course. The mate came over to me and said, 'What the hell are you doing?'

"I told him I didn't know myself. I was replaced immediately. The next day, during daylight I was taught about the compass and the wheel. I did fine from then on."

Approaching Port Hueneme on the morning of July 3, 1945, the ship was challenged by signal light from a small patrol craft. The following exchange by blinker light took place:

Small Craft: What is your war call?

Navy signalman on the *Lane Victory*: Do you mean our recognition signal?

Small craft: Negat. You have a war call.

Navy signalman: Regret we do not send such information by blinker.

Small craft: What is your name?

Navy Signalman: This is *Lane Victory*.

Small craft: Stand off one mile. Pilot and tug will be out.

Arriving at Port Hueneme, the next seven days were spent loading for an unnamed destination in the Pacific. On July 10, 1945, with just over 4,400 tons of military goods on board, the

This photo of the Bluefield Victory *captures the essence of official trials: an "economy haze" coming out of the stack with everything working the way it should. Courtesy The Los Angeles Maritime Museum.*

ship pointed her bow west on her first trans-Pacific voyage. As soon as she nosed out of the harbor the crew again qualified for the 33-1/3 percent bonus.

Wartime conditions were extremely strict. "Loose lips sink ships," was not just a catchy phrase. It was a religion.

"Oh, yeah," recalled Vern Richardson. "It was different because it was wartime conditions right to the teeth, you know. You never knew where you were going. Absolutely. In fact, half the time, the captain hardly ever knew where he was going until he opened the orders out at sea. So you couldn't even tell your relatives where you were going 'cause you didn't <u>know</u> where you were going.

"Letters were always censored. And the mail would get nine or ten months late. And then you'd get a whole bunch of letters maybe at the end of the voyage. They never caught up with the ship."

One requirement unique to the wartime conditions was the standing order for scuttling the ship. Each merchant vessel was issued a letter of instructions.

CONFIDENTIAL

From: The Secretary of the Navy.

To: Master - S.S. LANE VICTORY

Subject: Instructions for Scuttling Merchant Ships

   1. It is the policy of the United States Government that no U.S. Flag merchant ship be permitted to fall into the hands of the enemy.

   2. The ship shall be defended by her armament, by maneuver, and by every available means as long as possible. When in the judgement of the Master, capture is inevitable, he shall scuttle the ship. Provision should be made to open sea valves, and to flood holds and compartments adjacent to machinery spaces, start numerous fires and employ any additional measures available to insure certain scuttling of the vessel.

   3. In case the Master is relieved of command of his ship, he shall transfer this letter to his successor, and obtain a receipt for it.

FRANK KNOX

   At night ships ran without running lights and all portholes covered. Exterior doorways held double doors so that the inner one was closed, blocking off any light behind it, before the outer one was opened.

   "Everything was blacked out," recalled Richardson.

   John (Jack) Morrison: "All doors and portholes were covered over, so as to keep the ship completely dark. It made it very hot and muggy and we found our way around deck by moonlight and phosphorus tape stuck on the walkways."

   As the ship proceeded westward and into more dangerous waters, the bonus increased. From the Official Log: "July 13, 1945 1234 crossed 136 W. proceeding in Westerly direction 66 2/3 % bonus effective at 0001 this date."

   On July 16 in Longitude 152 degrees West, the ship began steering a zig-zag course. This was a standard tactic in enemy waters to make it more difficult for submarines to sink a ship. By changing course every few minutes the sub wouldn't have

time to plot the ship's course and speed and calculate an inter-
cept course for her torpedoes.

The war bonus increased again on July 21st: "0337 (W.
Longitude date and time) crossed 180th meridian in westerly
direction. 66-2/3 % bonus ceases. 07/20/45 2400 West time
100% bonus plus $5 a day begins. 0001 7/21/45 West time (i.e.
7/22/45)."

Like an automobile, if a ship is "broken in" properly, she
gives years of trouble-free service. The *Lane Victory*'s chief
engineer babied her during the early months.

Vern Richardson: "It was really, really great. I think
one of the reasons why, the first chief engineer that was on there
was a night trial chief at CalShip. The yard was closing down
and they asked him if he wanted a job on there, he said 'Sure,
I'll take the job.'

"Jimmy Scott was his name. He took the ship on our
first trip, I think it was Manus Island. But he never opened up
the speed nozzles. He said 'The gears gotta be worn in right,
gotta take it easy on the first trip.' Which is good, you do that
with a new car, you know.

"And that's why I think we never had any trouble with
the engines. Nor much with the other machinery."

Even the most carefully crafted of ships has a few break-
ing-in problems. One difficulty the *Lane* did have was with the
fresh water maker. The water simply disappeared. "That was
the fault of the manufacturer of the distilling plant," recalled
Vern Richardson. "He didn't finish a weld on the inside in the
collecting tank. The water that was being made was falling right
back down into the boiler section again. And nobody could find
out why that rascal, brand new, would not make water. So we
finally had to cut it apart and looked in there and they forgot the
finish welding."

When the official orders were opened it was discovered
the ship's destination was Manus in the Admiralty Islands.

Junior Third Mate Don Runyon remembered, "Captain Cramer left the mates alone to run the ship. He very seldom came on the bridge. A John Wayne-type man, strong and silent, very efficient."

Because malaria was common in the South Pacific, it was standard practice to have the crew take quinine (Atabrine) as a preventative. Beginning on July 27, 1945 Captain Cramer ordered all hands to take one grain of Atabrine every day until further notice.

Don MacLean, the marine machinist from CalShip, shipped out late in the war. He recalled receiving Atabrine on a different ship in a different manner:

"They put Atabrine in our beer, when we could get it, which wasn't very often. It tasted terrible. It ruined the beer."

There is a sterility to the business of war. Behind the red, white and blue star-spangled battles, the military atmosphere is dull grey or olive drab. Maintaining supply lines, stockpiling goods, establishing bases — everything that occurs away from the front lacks luster. The war machine grinds on. When in gear, the supply side of war is efficient, overwhelming and dehumanizing.

A merchant ship has only one job: to deliver the goods. Military ports are typically far from the gin mills, houses of ill-repute and other "attractions" the merchant seaman usually finds in his off hours. There is little to see or do in a military port. This makes voyages to military ports rapid, boring and colorless. The *Lane Victory*'s first voyage was a quick one. After anchoring for two days in Seeadler Harbor she went alongside Nabu Pier. Speedily discharging her cargo she sailed from Manus, Admiralty Islands, on August 13.

Don Runyon: "We were there several days unloading Army equipment and supplies. The Navy Seabees were very nice to us inviting us to their movies and beer parties."

On August 15, two days after the *Lane Victory* sailed from Manus, the war in the Pacific ended.

John (Jack) Morrison: "On the way home, we had all our lights on — doors all open, wind finding its way through the ship. Occasionally we would see other lights at sea and it just seemed marvelous. Seemed like another world."

When people are in contact with one another for long periods of time such as on board ship, they get to know each other very well. Like it or not, they learn things about one another that they would never know ashore.

Vern Richardson: "I remember this Bernard Gunn, the first assistant engineer on the first trip when I first come on there. He would never wash any clothes. You know, he would go and buy some more clothes before he'd wash any. Put those clothes on and then he had a giant pile of dirty clothes four feet high in his cabin. Then when we'd get into port he'd get the people from the port who pick up the laundry."

Overall it was a happy ship. Don Runyan: "The crew got along very well, good cooks, great weather."

The voyage ended on August 29 in San Francisco. Tradition and Coast Guard regulation require that one voyage end at midnight and the next start one minute after midnight the following day. Normally this would be the case. But there was a month of inactivity while the country went from war to a post-war posture. To the *Lane Victory* this meant two weeks of refitting and minor repairs at the Hurley Repair yard in Oakland followed by two more weeks of idleness at Pier 44 in San Francisco. Voyage 2 didn't commence until October 8, in San Francisco.

On board a merchant ship all important matters in the ship's existence are entered in the official logbook. This includes the names and ratings of each crew member as well as a report of their character, dates of departure at each port, draft readings, damage, collision, births, marriages and deaths, and any violations of the law committed by a crewman including: desertion, failure to join the ship before sailing from a port, quitting a ship after arrival at a port, willful disobedience of a lawful command, continued willful disobedience, assaulting an officer, willfully damaging the vessel or embezzling from the cargo and smuggling. Punishment for offenses can be anything from forfeiture of pay to imprisonment. The official log is turned in to the Coast Guard at the port in which the voyage terminates. Any disciplinary incidents are dealt with by that agency. Punishment may vary in magnitude from a severe warning to imprisonment. If serious enough, they can revoke a seaman's papers — his "Z-card" — thus depriving him of his profession. Revocation can be for months or years or permanently, again depending on the seriousness of the action. Being "logged" is not a desirable thing to have happen.

The sailing board was set for 1400 the 24th of October. At 1055 the day of sailing one of the cooks told the captain he was quitting. The cook felt he didn't have enough help in the galley. Packing his gear he carried it down the gangway and left. It was impossible to get a replacement on such short notice. Captain Cramer, who normally might overlook minor problems, considered this one serious; a disciplinary matter. His entry in the official logbook reflects his anger: "Left the ship of his own will and volition and is hearby classified as a deserter inasmuch as this action took place less than four hours prior to ship's departure." The ship sailed short one cook.

With the war over, the captain and crew were now told their destination, in this case Guam. Bonuses were still paid, but at a reduced rate. From the official log: "11/2/45 At sea. At 1630 vessel crossed the 180th Meridian in 32 53 N. Lat. vessel westbound and using west longitude date and time area bonus effective commencing on this date."

Pay on a merchant ship is handled differently than in any other profession. A seaman receives credit for a monthly wage. After the normal deductions and withholding taxes he is permitted to send an allotment to his wife or next of kin. The allotment is monthly and can be up to 100 percent of the amount of money he has coming to him. As the ship arrives in port, the seaman can "draw" against the wages he has earned (if there are any left after withholding taxes and allotments) up to that date. Although technically not required, some pursers or masters allow sailors to draw against their overtime. In addition, the crew is entitled to a draw every five days the ship is in port.

As the ship arrived in Guam on November 9, 1945 the purser gave advances to those of the crew that wanted them.

November 10 found the ship tied to buoy No. 5 awaiting a berth. On the 16th Berth R opened up, she went alongside and started discharging cargo.

With the war over, the war machine slowed to a crawl. There was a long delay while discharging at Guam. The island was recovering from its capture and recapture during the war and there were few diversions for the crew ashore. At first there were parties aboard ship.

Vern Richardson: "I remember crewmembers had gotten cases of beer and they were having a party there. And they were throwing the cans over the offshore side, but there was no tide. All of these empty cans were all clustered around the ship in this huge ring, and the authorities, the military police, came aboard to stop a fuss or something. The crew said, 'We're not doing anything.'

"And the MPs said, 'What is that all over the side there?' You know, this huge pile of empty cans."

Manuel Medina, an AB on voyage 2 remembered it as ". . . a happy ship. We all got along on there."

With so much idle time on their hands, the crew got into more trouble. The next incident was one on which Capt. Cramer was forced to act by the shoreside military authorities. A military police officer came aboard on November 21st. He was a Navy Lieutenant Commander and Assistant Provost Marshal of the island. Informing the captain that three men from other ships had purchased whiskey from someone in *Lane's* engine department, he insisted that something be done. Of course, this was a surprise to the captain. The shipping articles which every seaman signs at the start of a voyage specify that "no grog shall be allowed aboard." (Grog is interpreted to mean any alcoholic beverage). Mustering the entire crew he found everyone was on board except one man. The Provost Marshal then brought aboard the three men who bought the whiskey so they could identify the crewman who sold it to them. They couldn't find him. Dismissing the crew, the three men were asked to point out the room from which the whiskey was purchased. The room they selected was the one inhabited by the missing man. An immediate search revealed nothing. But the missing man's lockers were locked. The captain ordered the lockers broken open. Inside were several bottles of "Paul Jones" whiskey, the same brand sold to the three men. The contents of the locker were confiscated. Later, when the missing man returned to the ship he was questioned by Capt. Cramer. He admitted selling the whiskey to the three sailors. One quart of "Paul Jones" fetched him $15, not a bad profit in 1945 dollars.

Vern Richardson remembered that the seaman was punished severely. "I think this fella that was selling the liquor, he was put in the stockade, the Marine stockade and they let him go when the ship actually was leaving the dock."

The entry in the official log concluded with the statement, "For willful disobedience of a lawful command, i.e. bringing grog aboard the vessel, you will be turned over to the U.S. Coast Guard upon arrival at the first continental U.S. port for hearing or trial as they may deem circumstances warrant."

Before sailing from Guam there was one other crewmember to deal with. On December 8, 1945 one of the Fireman Watertenders returned after an absence of fifteen days. He was logged for being AWOL. Fifteen days is a long time and his punishment was proportionately stiff. Fined two days' pay for each day he was absent, he was also charged $100.50 — a substantial amount in 1945 — to defray expenses incurred in hiring a substitute.

It was with a sense of relief that the *Lane Victory* sailed from Guam on December 9, after a month in port.

A few days later she arrived at Peleiliu Island in the Carolines. Upon her arrival, on December 12, she was immediately assaulted by a Navy tug that tried to assist in tying the ship to a mooring buoy. The official accident report reads:

At Barnum Bay, harbor of Peleiliu Island, Palau group Caroline Islands. Nature of accident hull indents in shell plates. Upon this date the USN tugboat Abinaco while under the command of ---- -- and while engaged in assisting the SS Lane Victory in mooring caused damage to the SS Lane Victory. At 1045 the said tugboat while attempting to get her prow against the port bow of the Lane Victory approached at excessive speed and contacted the Lane Victory at right angles in such a manner as to puncture a hole of approximately 24 inches by 6 inches through the shell plating of the Lane Victory between frames 18 and 19 with the exposed upper part of her metal stem. Said hole was approximately 9 feet above the tank tops of #1 lower hold and approximately 10 feet above the present draft.

The tugmaster probably hoped to make up in perseverance what he lacked in skill. He tried again.

At approximately 1350 the said tugboat while approaching the starboard bow of the Lane Victory again contacted the Lane Victory at right angles with the exposed upper part of her metal stem making a deep dent in the shell plating of the Lane Victory between frames 26 and 27. Said dent is approximately 10 feet above the tank tops of number 1 lower hold and approximately 11 feet above the present draft.

After the second hole in the hull plating, perseverance gave way to dogged determination.

A few minutes later the tugboat shifted her position somewhat and made another small and deep dent to the extent of causing a break in the shell plating of approximately 4 inches parallel and adjacent to the forward side of frame 38. Said dent and break is approximately 3 feet above the deck at #2 lower hold at the forward starboard bow at approximately 11 feet above the present draft.

Three holes were not sufficient to discourage him. The tugmaster set his cap, gritted his teeth, and made another attempt. Determination had become grim obsession.

At approximately 1527 the said tugboat while approaching to port to assist once again contacted the Lane Victory at near right angles close to the stern. At this time the exposed upper part of her metal stem slightly gouged the shell plating approximately 5 feet on sternwards then made a small and deep dent in the shell plating between frames 121 and 122. Said dent was approximately 10 feet above the tank tops in number 4 lower hold at the lower port side approximately 11 feet above the present draft. Weather conditions small easterly sea, no swell, wind easterly force 3-4, no cargo on board, no injury or loss of life. Repairs are contemplated.

The logbook from the armed guard carries the laconic entry: "0900 Attempted to tie to Bouy at Peleiliu."

Seven hours later a second entry states, "1600 Finally tied up to the bouy after several attempts."

There was no place to repair the ship at Peleiliu. The holes and dents had to stay until the ship returned home.

Battered but intact, the *Lane Victory* was finally secure to her mooring. Cargo operations could begin.

Throughout the Pacific there was a tremendous surplus of equipment. Vehicles, parts, weapons, ammunition, machinery were stockpiled everywhere. The military was more than willing to share with merchant ships in the harbor.

Vern Richardson: "The Navy, we asked for some valves. We wanted to get some valves and some odds and ends, some bar stock and everything. And they said, 'Well, you fellas, we'll get a big six-by-six truck here. You go up there to that storage area and help yourself. Anything you want in that area.'

"So we went up there and we got about three six-by-six loads of rags, valves, bar stock, tools . . ."

With almost nothing to do aboard or ashore the crew developed their own diversions. Swimming, trips in one of the ship's lifeboats and walks ashore were about the only entertainment at Peleiliu. Even with the war over, however, these could be dangerous activities.

Vern Richardson remembered the gun crew was especially frustrated by idleness: "There were about twenty men and one ensign. All they did was just clean and service and occasionally fire . . . and practice putting the ammunition down, all that kind of thing. They always would fire a few rounds of the five-inch gun and a few from the three-inch, and fire some machine guns off and then clean up the guns.

"I remember another thing in Peleiliu. We were anchored out, during the loading and unloading and I decided to go for a swim . . . just swim out away from the ship a ways and then come back again. And I was out four or five hundred yards from the ship and the gunners were back on the stern with automatic rifles. They were shooting down in the water. What they had done is they had taken some meat and hung it on meathooks and dropped it down in the water. They were pulling the sharks around there and then they were shooting at the sharks. When I figured out what they were doing, I was the fastest swimmer in town. I hastened my way back to the ship real quick."

Idle hands, idle time, nothing to do. A member of the Navy Armed Guard remembered just how close he came to killing one of his shipmates because of idle time.

"We was on watch, we wasn't doing nothing. I was on a victory ship. I was on the stern, Yorkavitch was on the topside and Scott was on the bow. We were at anchor, you know, and each one had a thirty-eight. This is the twelve-to-four in the morning. Everybody's asleep.

"So Scotty called up, 'Hey, we go down in the mess hall and play cards. How about you, Baca?'

"I say, 'It's OK with me,' I say, 'How about you Yorkovitch?'

"So went down in the mess hall. Pretty soon that got boring. We had nothing else to do and then we started talking about that stupid gun. It didn't have a safety on it. It had an

Chief Engineer James E. Scott, in white hat, with crew of Lane Victory.
Courtesy Vernon Richardson.

empty chamber. That was the safety. And I could have sworn the damned cylinder would rotate to the left. And he said, 'No. It rotates to the right.'

"I said, 'Well, hell,' I says, 'I'll show you.'

"And I pulled it out like that. And I pointed it [at his head].

"'Now, tell me Yorkavitch, which way is it turning?'

"And luckily, thank God, that I pointed it above his head.

"He says, 'You're right.' He says, 'It turn to the left.'

"I squeezed it like that. All of a sudden that mother went pow! Right in the bulkhead. Made a hole about that big in the bulkhead. The gun smoked up and the mess hall got smoked up. The only guy that was on duty was the cook.

"He opened the window like that, he says, 'What the hell you guys doing, playing cowboys and Indians in there?'

"I tell you I was petrified. So pretty soon, Yorkavitch, the guy I almost shot, he came around first, he started cussing me, 'You stupid . . .' like that. 'You idiot, you stupid . . .'

"'Yorkavitch,' I said, 'let it all hang out, you can call me anything you want. I'm just glad to hear you talking.'

"I could just see a big hole . . . right between his eyes. And I said, 'Oh, shit. I'm dead. This is a court-martial sure as hell.'

"We sat there waiting . . . I was stupid. And I just sat there and I says, 'What can I do, face the music.'

"We just sat there . . . We thought somebody had heard it. The only one heard it was the cook. So nobody came. So I told that cook, I said, 'Seems like nobody heard but you. Please,' I said, "don't say shit . . .""

On another occasion Richardson and some of the crew went for a ride in one of the lifeboats. "We had taken the lifeboat and gone for a tour around the lagoons. It was a beautiful spot. And you know you could see down very deep and the white sand. But we were in one lagoon and directly underneath the lifeboat was a shark and that rascal was as long or longer than the lifeboat. [The lifeboat on a Victory ship is 24 feet long.] We could look down there and see that . . ."

"We were invited over to another island," remembered Richardson, "to go and see this banana or coconut plantation, whatever it was. So I went with a native guy and an oiler who was an Australian guy about six-foot-three. We went on a dugout canoe over to the other island. And we got almost to the island and the dugout canoe began to come apart. And it did come apart. The lashings came apart. I think it was too much weight. I really do. I think it was made for two men and there were two men and one big heavy guy in it. And the outrigger went one way and the canoe upset. This Australian guy, the oiler, was hysterical. I said, 'Hang on.'

"I could swim. Swim pretty good. And the native guy could swim pretty good, but the oiler was hysterical. I said, 'Hang on to that wood thing. It's not going to sink.'

"The other, the native, he hung on, and I pulled the center, the main section with the two guys hanging on to that thing until we could touch bottom and we scampered out."

In the months to follow it would be cheaper to drive trucks and equipment into the ocean rather than ship them back to the States. But with the war just over, there was a tendency to continue "business as usual" and there was some effort made to ship damaged equipment back to be repaired.

Vern Richardson: "We had taken brand new boxed jeeps in the cargo down to Peleiliu and we took old battered jeeps and trucks, loaded them for shipment back. I don't know whatever happened with all that new equipment, you know, but that was the end of the war there. And they would pile up the trucks and the vehicles on the deck, all damaged and throw a big wire over them and put a turnbuckle on them and pull them down like that. They were salvageable equipment, but, you know, put a wire across them like throwing it over telephones poles, didn't do them any good."

A few days before sailing and still bearing the scars from her previous encounter with the Navy, the *Lane Victory* was again assaulted by a Navy craft. The incident took place on January 11, 1946 while a landing craft was coming alongside to work cargo. The official accident report reads:

> At 1810 this date the USN LCT-999 when coming alongside the Lane Victory struck the shell plating causing a small deep dent. This dent was made by the sharp corner of the LCT's ramp. This dent located between frames 60 and 61 starboard side of number 3 hatch about two feet below the overhead of the lower 'tween deck. Lane Victory moored to buoy. Heading easterly, LCT heading NE'ly at the time of accident. Wind easterly force 3, slight easterly sea with small westerly swell. No injury or loss of life. No repairs contemplated, no protest filed.

Just before sailing on January 13, there was a request to carry some passengers to Honolulu. A freighter can legally carry no more than twelve passengers (a doctor must be on board if more are taken) but the military authorities wanted the *Lane* to carry twenty. The captain refused to carry them unless the port authorities issued a waiver. The first of the twenty passengers to board delivered the waiver, signed by the port director.

Captain Cramer then had to decide where to put the passengers. A Victory ship has just enough rooms for the crew. The twenty military passengers were berthed out in the open. Fortunately, the run from Peleiliu to Saipan, the next port of call, and from there to Honolulu was in pleasant weather. According to Vern Richardson, "They just slept on deck."

The *Lane Victory* spent several days working cargo at Saipan where she arrived on January 16, then sailed on February 8 for Honolulu, Territory of Hawaii.

The entry in the official log shows how the war bonus had been reduced by this time. "On February 15 crossed 180th meridian eastward bound at 0430 in Lat. 21 08 N, using east longitude date and time crew bonus of $2.50 per day stops at 2359 this date."

In Hawaii, tied to Pier 39A, the ship discharged her passengers, took on bunker fuel and stores and, on February 21, 1946, sailed for San Francisco.

Voyage 2 ended February 27 at Pier 6 in San Francisco. During the next two weeks the ship's guns were removed. The armed guard packed up their gear and left. The *Lane Victory's* involvement with the military was over with — for this war. She was about to embark on a career as a tramp, going wherever the cargoes took her. Her adventures were just beginning.

Early March, 1946. Alongside a pier in San Francisco. The Lane Victory's hull and stack have just been painted. The guns will be removed in a few days. Courtesy Fred R. Hicks.

6

To The Far East
and Beyond

Once again, as in 1919, the end of the war brought about a surplus of merchant ships. "Build them faster than they can be sunk" suddenly became "What do we do with all these ships?" Laying them up all at once would have a devastating effect on shipyards, suppliers, seamen. The entire industry would be virtually out of business. Instead, the government allowed steamship companies to time charter the ships they operated during the war under General Agency Agreement. This enabled the industry and the government to ease their way from the frenzied struggle of war back to peacetime commerce.

In simple terms a time charter is a lease for a given period of time, usually defined in months or years. This type of charter is also called a "bare-boat" charter, because the vessel owner does not provide a crew, fuel or supplies. He leases the ship to the operator, "bare" of these items. It benefits the owner of the ship because his vessel is working and earning money. It is useful to the operator because he needn't worry about construction costs, amortization or replacement. American President Lines chartered the *Lane Victory* from the government at a flat monthly rate.

Voyage 3 began on March 5, 1946. Capt. Ralph Moon, replacing Capt. Cramer, headed up an almost entirely new crew.

Capt. Moon: "I had sailed with Cramer before when I was chief mate aboard the SS *Bernardo O'Higgins*. Very, very fine gentleman. He had taken a leave of absence from the Los Angeles Police Department to serve in the merchant marine and he got his license and so forth; a very scholarly and very efficient man."

Loading general cargo in the San Francisco Bay Area, Capt. Moon found himself immediately thrown into international intrigue, albeit of a benign nature.

"I was approached by a group of Chinese doctors who had heard that we were going to Shanghai and asked if I could do them a favor. It seems that they had gathered a small quantity of penicillin culture that was dearly needed in China at this time and if I could deliver it for them they would be forever grateful. I recall going down this dark alley in San Francisco's Chinatown to pick up this package and taking it aboard ship with my personal belongings."

The ship sailed for Wilmington (Los Angeles) on March 22. Topping off with cargo there, she departed for Shanghai on the 25th.

The voyage across was uneventful. Three weeks were spent discharging the cargo in Shanghai. During that time, the captain delivered his contraband. "I do not know if we were breaking any laws or if we were actually smuggling or not, but the doctors in Shanghai were sure happy to see this box of penicillin. They wined and dined me and presented me with two pieces of Ming dynasty jade carvings."

After the war, many Victorys, including the *Lane*, had passenger rooms added. Located on the bridge deck aft of the skylight, they were a welcome source of extra income to the steamship company. Ralph Moon: "The Victory ships at this time were fitted with two or three cabins for passengers. APL [American President Lines] and all those steamship companies were going to make every dollar they could. And if they could haul a few passengers . . . They were not very luxurious but adequate for someone wanting a less expensive means of transportation. They had their own bath facilities and the passengers ate with the officers in the officers' mess.

"On the return voyage from Shanghai one of the passengers, Byron Summers, and I became very good friends, he being a good chess player and I considered myself fairly good at the game."

The *Lane Victory* sailed on May 3 and was back in San Francisco fourteen days later. As the ship pulled in to the dock at San Francisco, Capt. Moon was surprised to see a complete stranger being overly friendly with his wife. "My wife and year-old daughter were on the dock to meet us. With them was a total stranger (to me) with his arm around my wife. Needless to say, I was very curious and anxious about this. As it turned out, Janie (my wife) had met this man on the train from Fresno to San Francisco. Sitting next to each other he mentioned that he was going to meet his brother who was coming in on the *Lane Victory* and she said it was a small world as she was going to meet her husband who was Master of the *Lane Victory*. The man and his wife subsequently became our lifelong friends."

The voyage ended on May 18, 1946.

Once again there was a wait for cargo. With so much surplus tonnage to carry cargo and the government no longer booking war materiél, it was difficult to locate a profitable load. Voyage 4 finally commenced with the first draft of cargo coming on board June 18. Taking a full load for the Philippines, the ship sailed from San Francisco on June 24, 1946.

Peacetime brought about many changes in seafaring. The guns and gun crews were gone and the logs no longer mentioned the various war bonus rates. The entire dateline entry for this voyage reads: "July 2, 1946 West Longitude time (July 3, 1946

East longitude time) 0330 at 21 01 N. Lat. vessel crossed 180th meridian in westerly direction."

In the first port, Manila, there was a long wait. It was less than a year since the war ended and Manila was a long way from recovering her pre-war efficiency as a major world port. The harbor was filled with sunken ships, their masts sticking above water. Berths were few and facilities badly damaged. Even after the ship was finally alongside, the cargo was discharged slowly.

As always, idleness had a bad effect on the crew. The chief cook on this voyage was a problem from the start. He was unkempt, unsanitary and didn't seem to care. For someone handling the food for the entire ship, this was difficult to overlook. By the time the ship was alongside the dock in Manila the officers and crew were complaining. The chief steward finally had enough. He expressed his feelings to the captain both verbally and in writing. Capt. Moon attached the steward's letter to the official log, an unusual step.

Dated August 12, 1946 it states:

> Subject demotion of Chief Cook to messman. As you know the chief cook has been warned and admonished repeatedly by yourself and by me as to his personal cleanliness and as to sanitary conditions in the galley, meat box and ice boxes. He has failed to pay any attention to any of this. This morning he was told that it was his duty to clean the meatbox below. He replied that if he had to clean it it would never get cleaned. You know from both your personal observation and from comments from the crew and officers of the man's unsanitary condition, particularly while preparing the food for meals. Not only for the health and safety of the ship's crew but also to obviate a cause of criticism by the crew and to maintain sanitary conditions in my department I must ask that this man be demoted.

In the steward's department the chief cook is second in rank only to the steward himself while messmen are the lowest rating. Nevertheless, the chief cook was demoted to messman.

Capt. Moon: "There were very few problems with the deck crew and the engine gang was well run by the chief and his assistants. The steward's department was another story. One problem after the other."

A different type of problem arose when the ship's guns were removed at the end of Voyage 2, the tubs and platforms in which they were mounted remaining on board. The after guntub measured about twenty feet in diameter by four feet deep. Some of the crew thought it would make a dandy swimming pool.

"The after gun tub," Vern Richardson remembered fondly. "We appropriated lumber and cement, and closed up the openings on the forward side and we had a swimming pool. And it really worked fine except that it always was lousing up the draft. That weight was way back on the stern and it would make the stern go down and they were trying to figure the right draft for it. And it would leak a little bit and it was making rust stains on the guy's paintwork and everything."

Ralph Moon: "I remember that. The bosun that I had was on a ship with me before, on a Liberty ship. And he built a swimming pool out of lumber on the side over by the guntubs. And it was a work of art. It was a beautiful thing. How he ever managed to scrounge all the lumber to build the thing with I don't know, but he did. When we went aboard here why he said, 'Hey, we got a natural swimming pool here. We don't have to build one. We can just fix up that guntub back there.'"

Unfortunately the swimming pool didn't last long.

Vern Richardson: "We were at a dock in Manila. We had rigged up floodlights over the top of the pool. Our crew was not having any trouble . . . but some of the crew from the ship across the dock, they were watching over there and they saw us jumping in the pool. So several of them came over and wanted to know if they could jump in the pool, too. Well one of those guys had too much to drink and he dove in the pool and split his head open. And he was bleeding like a stuck pig. He didn't crack his skull or anything . . . But the captain said, 'That's the end of the pool, take it apart.'"

The after guntub as a swimming pool. Note the cargo light rigged above the pool for night swimming. Courtesy Vernon Richardson.

Capt. Moon: "I knew that I was living on borrowed time as far as the swimming pool goes. Permitting them to build a swimming pool aboard ship is not quite what APL would have in mind. It had me worried. So when that incident happened I guess I found a good excuse to tear it down."

The day before the *Lane Victory* sailed from Manila, a more serious incident occurred. From a letter to the ship's agent written by the chief mate:

August 26, 1946 at Manila. Subject, death of crewmember. Coming ashore in an emergency business matter in our ship's lifeboat on the afternoon of Sunday, August 25, 1946, I decided to secure the boat to the offshore side of the *General Meigs* at pier 15 for the night so that it would not be stripped by thieves. Chief engineer and deck maintenance were in the boat. Another deck maintenance and myself were aboard the *General Meigs* to secure the lines. After securing the boat I ordered the two men in same to wait there until I had obtained another boat to take them to the dock. Returning I saw the deck maintenance climbing the line from the lifeboat to the deck of the ship. At this time he apparently became tired and started slipping down the line and when about 6 feet from the water he fell landing in the water astern of the lifeboat. He did not return to the surface so the chief engineer immediately began diving to locate him, being joined by myself and an unidentified U.S. Army enlisted man. Due to the muddy nature of the water and the depth of 30 feet we were unsuccessful in our attempts to locate the man though we dived from the time of the accident at 6 pm until 6:45. In the meantime the Provost Marshall had been contacted and crash boat dispatched to the scene to aid in the search with grappling equipment and three members of the crew of the *General Meigs* aided in diving. An U.S. Army ambulance crew with pulmotor stood by until seven thirty at which time the search was given up for the night. After the accident I learned from the other crewmember that the man did not know how to swim and in addition was wearing a pair of boots weighing several pounds. The combination of these, added to the fact that he probably had the breath knocked out of him by the fall into the water, I believe were the reasons for his drowning.

Capt. Moon: "Kenneth Rambo, the chief mate, worked his butt off. He was wiry and small, tough. You wouldn't want to meet him in a dark alley, even at his size. He'd tear your head off. And that man must have dove for hours trying to find the crewman"

Vern Richardson: "His body slipped underneath the bilge keel of the ship. And then when the ship backed down, it surfaced."

The mood on the ship was subdued when she sailed on August 26 for Legaspi on the southeastern tip of Luzon, the largest island in the Philippine Archipelago.

Mooring at Legaspi was a difficult and intricate maneuver. The only facility consisted of a narrow, rickety "finger" pier too weak to support a ship. Capt. Moon had to moor with both anchors and run lines from his stern to the pier. "You went in and dropped one anchor and ran on it clear to the end of the chain. Then you dropped the other anchor. Then you backed down and pulled in on the first anchor and let that second anchor go out until they were even. In the meantime you threw the stern around, slow ahead or dead slow, so it just started moving around in the direction you wanted. At the same time you took up on the two anchor chains and got them tightened up. When you got around near the dock with your stern, you got the heaving line on the dock. The secret was to get those anchors far enough out from the dock. If you were in too close you couldn't get the right angle on them and you'd end up crashing into the dock. Or if you were out too far, you couldn't reach the dock. It was quite a tricky deal. If you didn't do it right you could just annihilate that dock. I had three tries before I made it.'

With so much time and temptation ashore in Manila, some of the crew spent money faster than they earned it. Now that they were in Legaspi, a few of the more enterprising ones tried going into business for themselves to supplement their finances.

On August 29, one of the crew was stopped by a Philippine customs inspector as he went ashore. In his possession was a large case of assorted goods from the vessel's food supply. When the customs official returned the man and the stolen goods to the ship, the third mate on watch identified him as a crewmember. The chief steward was called out and took possession of the food. Returning the goods to the reefer box he found the lock broken and the door open. The food was replaced, a new lock installed and the man logged. Capt. Moon held the matter over to be dealt with by the Coast Guard at the ship's first port of arrival in the United States.

After a few days working cargo in Legaspi the *Lane Victory* sailed on August 30, 1946 for Bulan, Sorsigon Province, Luzon, Philippine Islands.

The problems in the steward's department continued. As the ship approached the Bulan anchorage the third cook and a messman got into a fight. Angry, drunken words were exchanged, knives drawn, a scuffle followed and the third cook was stabbed by the messman.

Capt. Moon: "The Filipino messman knew his way around the port, had the prettiest girls, and made the rest of the crew very jealous. This messman was very small in stature and when a big 250-pound assistant cook made advances and slurring remarks to the messman's girlfriend a fight ensued that carried over to shipboard where the messman was waiting for the cook. At the first opportunity he used his knife. The messman was confined to a spare cabin and kept under guard until proper authorities could take charge. The messman was so small that he was able to crawl through the porthole and try to escape. He was caught by the gangway watch and kept in irons for his own protection 'til sailing."

As the ship came to anchor at 0120 August 31, a doctor was summoned. Boarding at 0250 he took one look at the victim and recommended immediate hospitalization. The *Lane Victory* was now down to one cook with the chief steward doing triple duty as chief cook, third cook and chief steward.

Capt. Moon: "The victim was hospitalized in Bulan and showed up aboard the ship six months later when the *Lane Victory* once again called at Legaspi. He was down to skin and bone, from about 250 pounds to about 150 pounds.

"The Filipino messman returned to duty after sailing and was exonerated by a Coast Guard inquiry at San Francisco; the finding was Self Defense.

"This little messman, a Filipino boy, he was very well liked. Everybody just loved this little kid. And, of course, to see him get into trouble like that. I think we all went to bat for him. The other guy finally died from the stab wounds. They just didn't have the facilities for taking care of anybody there in the Philippines."

Overwhelmed with work, the steward's problems continued. On August 31, he discovered that the linen locker had been broken open with a fire ax. When Capt. Moon heard of this he ordered an immediate search of all officers' and crew quarters.

Nothing was found. But at 1230 the same day, the third mate on watch caught a Filipino leaving the ship with a bundle of linen: eleven sheets and one bedspread, all from the ship's linen supply. After questioning by the captain he claimed he paid twenty-five pesos, fifty centavos for the articles. He offered to point out the room where he made the purchase. He said the linen came out of one of the lockers in that room. The locker he indicated belonged to one of the ABs. The AB denied knowing anything about it. To find the culprit, the captain mustered the entire crew on the afterdeck. There the Filipino pointed to an ordinary seaman as the guilty party. The ordinary said he was innocent, claiming he only had about ten pesos in his pockets. A search revealed he had twenty-five pesos, fifty centavos in the same combination of coins and bills the Filipino paid for the linen. Case solved. Further action was held in abeyance until arrival in the United States for "action by appropriate Coast Guard authority."

According to Capt. Moon, "That was a favorite trick — to take linen. Especially if you could short sheet it and pull it over so it looked like your count was right. Of course, what happened in return when the linen came back from the laundry, why we were short-changed."

It was with a great deal of relief to the captain that the ship sailed from Bulan on September 3 for San Francisco. Hopefully, a new voyage would bring a fresh crew and fewer problems.

Voyage 4 ended in San Francisco on September 21, 1946. Once again there was an idle period. Post-war cargoes were increasingly difficult to find and competition for them was keen.

After more than two months of idleness, the *Lane Victory* was once again activated. Voyage 5 commenced on December 4, 1946, with Ralph L. Moon returning as her master. Vern Richardson had progressed to Chief Engineer.

Sailing from San Francisco on December 11 the ship made an uneventful crossing to Manila. As usual there was a lot of idle time awaiting discharge.

Seamen are always interested in other ships and willing to help out if a ship is in need.   Chief Engineer Richardson recalled one such incident In Manila.   "We had to make some repairs on a passenger ship's big lifeboat which was along the dock.   They had come in and the ship was out in the anchorage in Manila.   They came in there with a bunch of passengers. From the passenger ship they brought the boat in with people that wanted to go sight-seeing.   The boat was alongside the dock which was right in front of the bow of our ship.   They couldn't get the diesel engine started.   They had two men, two big Dutchmen, and they had the type of diesel where you cranked this big flywheel and then you throw the compression thing . . .   You'd get it going under centrifugal motion . . .   You'd throw the lever and it shuts them off to get compression to ignite.   It wouldn't start.   So they came desperately and they said 'Does anybody know anything about the diesel?   Come over and help us get that motor started.'

"There was very few people aboard . . .   I was there and another man and I said, 'Well, I'm not doing anything, I'll go down there and see if I can help them get it started.'

"So this boat had water in the bilges and I said 'Maybe water got in the fuel and it's in the injector lines and everything.'

"I began cleaning those lines, get a clean system again and I dropped a part of one of the injectors, a little ball, down in the bilges.   I had to feel around there until I found that piece, put it back together again.   And after working on it for two or three hours all the passengers are standing on the dock there in pouring rain.   Wet from top to bottom.   We were working in the rain, too, to try and get it going.   This Dutchman, this great big man, was getting so tired of cranking this thing while we adjusted it.   Finally it started off, bang.

"The *Bantam*.   That was the name of the Dutch ship.   So then the first engineer and the chief invited us, all the engineers involved in fixing the boat, over for a big dinner on their ship. And they served us an Indonesian dish, ricestaffel or something like that.   It was really good.   And they had a servant behind each chair with white linen and silverware and they really did it up fine. We invited them over to our ship for a complimentary return dinner but it wasn't anything like that."

One of the oilers vanished on January 3, 1947. Twelve days later when the ship sailed, he missed the ship and was logged for "failure to join."

An assistant engineer also missed the ship. The entry in the official logbook regarding him said, in part,

> January 15, 1947 ---- having knowledge of vessel's next ports of call absented himself January 15, 1947 without leave in Manila evidently with the intention of rejoining the ship at a later date. A letter authorizing an advance to the amount of his transportation and subsistence was left with the company office in Manila with the supposition that he would join the vessel at the next port of call. Disciplinary action pending his return to the ship.

Sailing from Manila on January 15, the ship began a series of short runs to small ports in the Philippine Islands. Referred to by some as the "jungle run," this type of voyage is favored by those sailors who enjoy tropical climates and calm seas. Palm trees, warm sandy beaches and placid lagoons are the rule. In addition, the island women are attractive and cheerful. In the port area many could be found who were willing to entertain foreign visitors.

The next port was Cebu, on the island of the same name. Departing on January 21, the *Lane* then went to Jiminez, from which she sailed on January 26. Her next port was Legaspi.

Capt. Ralph Moon: "Once again we ended up in Legaspi to take on a cargo of copra (dried coconut). It was very tricky maneuvering the ship's stern to the dock. I was complemented highly by the port officials for doing such a fabulous job of ship handling to do it right the first time, especially at night. Little did they know (and I didn't tell them) that six months prior it took us three tries before we got moored. I wasn't going to make the same mistake twice."

In Legaspi hundreds of stevedores carried bags of copra aboard. Crossing on planks at the stern of the ship, they looked like ants marching in a line. Courtesy Vernon Richardson.

Vern Richardson: "Legaspi. Now that was another interesting port. But there's no real dock there, so the ship drops both anchors offshore and backs into the shore. They take the stern lines out. They run the stern lines out ashore. There's a little rickety two-lane, two-person dock made out of timbers. It runs up and they put some big mahogany planks between the end of this dock and the stern of the ship and we loaded bulk copra which came in about three hundred pound bags.

"Each one of the stevedores has one of these bags on his head

Each bag of copra weighed 300 lbs. Carrying it to the edge of the hatch the longshoremen dropped it in the hold. Courtesy Vernon Richardson.

Copra shells were loaded from a barge tied alongside. Courtesy Vernon Richardson.

and he walks up the plank like an ant. Hundreds and hundreds of them, so they dump the bag in the hold and he walks back down the other side. Up one side and down the other. And we had pretty near a full load of that copra."

Capt. Moon: "They looked like ants going up there. They had to keep in step because they had that thing bouncing up and down so they had to stay in step or else they'd have fallen overboard. It was very interesting.

"Copra, of course, is dried coconut. The coconut meat which is dried and then they put down the mats and the husks were used for making fuel of some sort.

"Copra is a very dirty cargo. The ship becomes infested with copra bugs, a very small beetle type bug that gets in your food, clothing, bedding, everywhere."

Vern Richardson: "There's some precautions with that copra because it's packed in — spontaneous combustion. In fact, when we unloaded the copra in Los Angeles, the top of the hatches, when they took the hatch boards off, it was probably 130 or 140 degrees and they couldn't even go in there until it cooled down.

"Mount Mayon is a volcano, active volcano, right behind Legaspi. And it was blowing off and a really spectacular show, the lava rolling out of the top of the thing and down the hill. The brightness of that lava from where we were, it was so bright that you could read a newspaper at nighttime."

It was in Legaspi that the missing oiler turned up long enough to be logged for being AWOL (Absent WithOut Leave) and failure to turn to from January 15 to January 29, 1947.

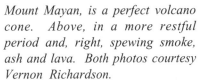

Mount Mayan, is a perfect volcano cone. Above, in a more restful period and, right, spewing smoke, ash and lava. Both photos courtesy Vernon Richardson.

The missing engineer also returned. Apparently he found something better to do ashore. He was logged for failing to join the vessel when it sailed on January 30. He had last reported for duty on January 29, packed all his clothing and gear, and left the ship.

When the *Lane Victory* sailed to the next port of call, Tabaco, on February 2, 1947, it was without one of the messmen. He, too, was logged for failing to join.

The next and final foreign port was Donsol, and there one of the cooks was logged for being AWOL on February 3. The ship sailed on February 5, 1947, short several crewmembers, but homeward bound once more.

It was an era of strong unionism. Capt. Moon found the crew difficulties more and more frustrating. "During this period [end of World War II and beginning of the Korean conflict] discipline became a bigger and bigger problem aboard U.S. Merchant vessels. Each department had a union representative who was supposed to act on the behalf of any crew member that got into trouble. The problem was that, in their eyes, the master was being unfair. 'Boys will be boys' was their attitude. 'We'll see what the Union has to say when we get home,' was a stock reply.

"It became harder and harder for the master to run a tight ship. I doubt that most loggings for discipline were ever upheld. Only severe cases ever made it to a Coast Guard hearing.

"Since there was no more 'war zone' bonus the big word was OVERTIME. Everything was overtime, going aloft, painting over the side while in port, etc. There was a list a foot long of what constituted overtime work. Whenever two or more ship captains got together, the conversation always got around to these two subjects: discipline and overtime. During that time the skippers or officers had no control of the ship. The unions ran the ship. You couldn't discipline anybody, I don't care what you did to them. You didn't dare lock them up or put them in irons or, Jesus, they'd have your ticket."

Arriving in Los Angeles, February 23, Capt. Moon had one other problem: "The only way to rid your ship of copra bugs is by fumigation. When the copra was unloaded at Los Angeles I thought we would get rid of the copra mats before they fumigated. This was not to be. The copra mats were stored in the after gun tub and the fumigation did absolutely no good. APL thought we might use the copra mats at a later date on another voyage to the Philippines."

Sailing from Los Angeles March 2, 1947 the ship arrived in San Francisco a day later to have the voyage terminate at midnight.

Voyage 6 began on March 7, 1947 with still more crew problems. Sailing from San Francisco March 11, one man was logged for failure to join on departure. Fortunately it was a coastwise voyage and additional crew were easy to get out of the Portland, Oregon hiring hall. Arriving in Longview, Washington on March 18, the crew was filled out and a cargo of bulk grain loaded.

Capt. Ralph Moon: "Voyage six was to be a short trip, taking a load of grain from Longview, Washington, to Karachi, India, and return to San Francisco. Little did we know that it would be a four months' voyage to eight different countries and the worst shipload of dysentery ever to sail the seven seas."

An interesting characteristic of grain cargo is how quickly it's loaded yet how slowly it's discharged. Vern Richardson: "All of that grain was put in in bulk. But the Indian stevedores [at Karachi] were down in the hold and they sacked every bit of it and they brought it out in sacks."

Knowing they would spend several weeks discharging, Chief Richardson and some of the other engineers thought it would be fun to have their own transportation. "A couple of us went to Western Auto Stores and bought two little motor scooters called Hiawatha Doodlebugs. We brought them back to the ship and the other engineers went up there, right up there and bought four more, so we had six motor scooters on the ship."

After only ten days the ship cleared the Columbia River Lightship on March 28, outward bound for the far, far east.

The first leg of the voyage was routine, uneventful. Arriving in Karachi they began discharging the grain. It was a tedious process with the Indian stevedores shoveling it into sacks, sewing the ends shut, and slinging the sacks out of the cargo holds.

The first problem in Karachi was again due to one of the crew trying to supplement his pay. On April 27, 1947 one of the wipers was logged at the rate of four days' pay for each day of work. His crime was pilferage of ship's property. Broaching the ship's linen locker he helped himself to linen and towels which he tried to sell ashore. He was caught and brought before Capt. Moon for questioning. The seaman admitted he intended selling the linen. He was logged for direct disobedience and fined.

There was a good market for linen in India. A different wiper was logged later during the same port stay for selling ship's bedding.

Meanwhile, the engineers put their motor scooters to good use. "When we went ashore in Karachi we'd jump on those things and they were supposed to have been licensed and they were supposed to be cleared with customs and we just went zipping out here and there. Every day the taxi drivers were getting madder and madder and were jumping on the customs and all. There'd go twelve people and they would get beat out of fares. We went all over town. They just parked them and they were really quite a novelty everywhere. We were worried that they were going to be stolen but there was never any problem."

Capt. Moon: "They had a ball with those things."

Vern Richardson: "And then one of the junior engineers was showing off how he could jump the thing by running down the dock. There was a ramp, and he jumped that motor scooter and he got a lot of rash, and bent the handle bars. There wasn't anything that we couldn't fix and straighten out on the ship. He did get a real bunch of injuries from that.

"Needless to say, we were using some of the spare lifeboat gasoline which was in drums and we were just about out of gasoline and I told the captain, 'I think we're getting low on gasoline, you better order a couple more drums.'"

Capt. Moon: "I didn't know they were using the lifeboat gasoline. I was a little bit upset at that."

Fresh fruit and vegetables are a treat on board ship. After the first two or three weeks of a voyage all the fresh produce is gone and everything that is served is canned. Even milk is reconstituted. Whenever possible a good steward will buy fresh local produce — papayas, mangos, lettuce, tomatoes, etc. There are some ports in the world, however, where this isn't done because of the conditions under which the produce is grown. Karachi is one such place. But the chief steward let his desire to make the crew happy override his judgement. Just before sailing, and contrary to warnings from the company agent, he bought vegetables from a local market.

Vern Richardson was one of those to suffer the consequences: "The ship bought prohibited greens in Karachi, against the regulations — lettuce, vegetables — and the crew began to get deathly sick with dysentery."

Capt. Moon recalled the problem as being water rather than vegetables. "I think it was contaminated drinking water. In either case it was very serious and we all lost a lot of weight. I went from 225 to 175. In fact I was a trim, thin-looking guy when we got to New York.

"I never got really ill. I just lost weight and couldn't eat. You just don't feel like eating. I never got bedridden or anything of that nature. But there was hell to pay over that incident."

The dysentery was debilitating, so much so that the ship had to make an unscheduled stop in Colombo, Ceylon [now Sri Lanka]. Capt. Moon: "We had to pull into Colombo because the chief mate was so sick. That's why we had to stop. The crew, many of them, were coming down with amoebic dysentery."

From Colombo the *Lane Victory* went to Singapore, to load rubber. Capt. Moon: "The stevedores were all women. These women up there throwing these bales of rubber around. They handled those 200 pound bales of rubber like they were nothing."

Transiting the Straits on May 13 the ship sailed from Singapore on May 21.

The next port was Davao, in the Philippine Islands. Vern Richardson: "At Davao we loaded pineapple. From Del Monte, cans of pineapple. That was a big pineapple port then."

Sailing from Davao on May 26, the ship next stopped at Cebu.

Ralph Moon: "I recall that Cebu harbor was full of sunken ships. There were so many that they were making a breakwater of anything they could move."

From Cebu on May 28, the *Lane* then returned to Manila. Sailing from Manila on the last day of May, the ship was short one messman, who was arrested by local authorities, one electrician and one oiler.

There was a quick call to Hong Kong for general cargo. Departing that port on June 4, 1947 the ship sailed for Shanghai. A full month had passed since Karachi and the crew was still suffering the effects of the ill-advised vegetables and/or water. Chief Engineer Richardson was bedridden. "Finally it got to me in Shanghai and I was in bed and couldn't get out of bed and was partly delirious from it. The port engineer came in there and was needling me, 'Get out of bed and get to work, quit belly-aching.' I couldn't even get up."

From Shanghai on June 7 the ship went to Jinsen, Korea where she loaded briefly and departed on the eleventh for Pusan [at that time called Fusan].

Different ports mean different things to seamen depending on the experiences they have in them. To Isaac Givens, the *Lane Victory*'s cook on a later voyage, Pusan was always the place he got gypped.

"In Pusan, I seen them guys out there picking up all the paper, cottons and things. We was throwing them over the side, you know. The ship'd throw them over the side. And I wondered what they was doing with those things. I found out thirty dollars worth. I went ashore there. Boom, boom, boom, boom. 'Tooled leather, tooled leather, thirty dollars, thirty dollars!

"I done bought that suitcase on the ship. Guys seen it, 'man I should a bought me one of them, I'll give you forty dollars.'

"'No, no, you should of bought you one, I ain't gonna take you money for this. I ain't going to take you money . . .'

"We got to Seattle, and here ain't never go to Seattle if ain't raining and we all gettin' off the ship. I had that thing loaded, and god dang got in that . . . rain hit it and that suitcase get wet, all that paper swelled to pieces . . . (laughter). Made out of paper, made out them papers. You'd be surprised.

"And another thing I got gypped. I'se sellin' cigarettes over there. You know they had a lot of nice silk over there and you sell cigarettes . . . you had to bootleg the cigarettes out there . . . and these kids they just . . . oh they count money like that brrrrrrr [noise like a money roll being fanned]. Here it is . . . and this guy switch, he done switched bales on me. Nothin' but paper. And I give him the cigarettes, I looked around, the kid was running. I didn't see nobody or nothin'. I take it out I ain't got but one bill and all the rest paper. Yeah, yeah, yeah, changin' money. That's the only time I got gypped going to sea. That's the only time, was right there at Pusan, them two things I got gypped there. Yessir, I got gypped all right, oh boy."

Sailing from Pusan on June 15 the crew continued suffering the repercussions of the Karachi lettuce. This time the effects were bureaucratic.

"We were quarantined in Kobe because of that," remembered Vern Richardson, painfully. "And they went and they took stool tests of all the people that had been sick to pinpoint what the trouble was and that's what they decided."

Sailing from Kobe on June 19, the ship's next port was Yokohama. Amazingly, the engineers recouped more than the cost of their motor scooters in Japan. Vern Richardson: "By the time we got up to Japan and the ports that we'd been, those motor scooters were well worn. They'd been fixed over and over again. We got up to Japan and the Army guys were drooling over these things. They wanted to buy them at any cost. One of them started to sell his and he went ashore and he told another guy and a whole bunch came down and these guys bought them for anything that they would take for them. They were all worn out, total wrecks. But the guys wanted them and they just took them off our hands."[1]

Departing Yokohama on June 26 the *Lane Victory* finally headed home again. The voyage ended in San Francisco on July **7,** 1947 after four months.

Her next trip would place some of her crew among the select few who have circumnavigated the globe.

---

[1] At the time Japan was occupied by American servicemen and dependents who guided that nation as it made the transition toward democracy.

7

EUROPE AND

AROUND

THE WORLD

The awe-inspiring feats of shipbuilding in World War II are legend. In addition to military vessels, over 500 Victorys and more than 2,700 Liberty ships were built during the '40s, with one Liberty ship, the *Robert E. Peary* setting the construction record at four days, fifteen and one-half hours. Because they were so numerous, most seamen of the period had at least one Liberty, or a series of them, in their background. The transition from a Liberty to a Victory was akin to trading in your "Tin Lizzy" for a Model "A." When Gil MacMillan joined the *Lane Victory* in San Francisco for voyage 7 on July 8, 1947 he considered himself fortunate.

"Their quarters were much better. Those Liberty ships were pretty primitive. And as an officer, the Victory ship was much nicer. We had a pantry on those ships. Officers' pantry. And a nice saloon. They rode better. I figured the Libertys were rollers and the Victorys didn't roll so much. I think they

Taken on July 14, 1947, this photo shows the ship in San Pedro. Note the liferafts still in place, two years after the war. Credit Capt. Harold Huycke.

were smoother because of their engine system. You don't have the thumping of that reciprocal engine going all the time. The bridge was definitely better. You know, you got a better view. Definitely a better ship to be on.

"There's no question the added speed made a lot of difference, fourteen to fifteen knots. That speed was almost twice as much speed if you really averaged it out. And I think fuel economy too. I've seen some of my work papers of the barrels per day that we consumed and it was amazing. When I tell people how many barrels of oil it takes to move one of those things at 20,000 to 30,000 tons . . ."[1]

The next major cargo was waiting on the East Coast. A partial load was taken for New York and the *Lane* sailed from San Francisco on July 11, stopping in Los Angeles for fuel and additional cargo. Departing Los Angeles on the 14th, she proceeded toward the Panama Canal.

Capt. Ralph Moon: "The APL office says, 'Capt. Moon, how would you like to take a load of coal to Finland.'

"Of course, this sounds like a luxury cruise, little guessing that we would not see the Golden Gate again for nine months.

"We left San Francisco and headed for New York via the Panama Canal."

---

[1] A capacity load of fuel for a Victory ship is 2,883 tons or 19,117 barrels or 802,900 gallons.

Second Mate MacMillan found Capt. Moon very easy to work for.

"I liked Moon mainly because he didn't interfere or bother you at all. He wasn't a yeller or a screamer, very quiet spoken. And he never came on the bridge and shot a sight. The whole ship was run by his officers and I kind of liked that."

The Canal transit was uneventful as was the trip through the Caribbean and up the East Coast. Discharging her cargo in New York, the *Lane Victory* proceeded to Baltimore to load coal.

The coal went in quickly and the ship sailed for Finland the next day. As it was summer and the weather relatively calm, the Atlantic crossing was uneventful.

Gil MacMillan: "We picked up a North Seas pilot when we entered north of Denmark there at Halsingborg [Sweden]. As we slowed down the pilot boat came out and loaded a pilot. He took us to Finland. You know, you don't go up through there without a pilot in those days, too many mines left from the war. It was no pressure on us, no hard schedule. They probably had a good path laid through and that's the way they knew what it was."

The coal was destined for the power plant at Rauma.

"We went to a little village north of Abo, in Finnish, or Turku, in Swedish, for the same city. We unloaded there, it seems to me, two weeks. It was quite some time."

Vern Richardson was chief engineer on this voyage, too. "We took a load of coal to the power plant. Lots of men and women there all blond hair, light complexion, all of them blond, every direction."

Bordered by Norway in the north, Sweden to the west and Russia to the east, Finland extends partially above the Arctic Circle and fronts the Baltic Sea. Gil MacMillan remembered it as a clean, attractive country.

"We were surrounded by forests, clean air. It was cool. Sharp, cool nights, which was very nice. It was a pleasant place to be."

Capt. Moon: "It was just a beautiful place. It was lovely. You'd go through all these fjords and things."

Gil MacMillan: "I met a Finnish student who spoke a little English and we made our way around to some of the bars. And I remember the Finnish national drink which gives you the most horrible hangover the first night or two and then you're immune to any further damage. It has a very, very, very strong . . . I always call it a kerosene flavor, and much like the Russians . . . If you've been in Russia you always drink straight vodka. Vodka is drunk just like wine and this aquavit is the same way. You drink it out of a smaller glass and it's a powerful thing. But I do remember we all had terrible hangovers and then after a while it disappeared."

The local drink made an impression on the entire crew. Vern Richardson: "It was the only strong drink that was available . . . I don't remember now what it was, but it was some kind of strong drink. It was something unusual, and that was the only thing that was available."

Capt. Ralph Moon: "There was another Victory ship there and a friend of mine was skipper of it. So we were invited to come out, the whole gang of us to come out to his ship. We'd all been out partying and we were having a good old time. I guess we were feeling no pain. So he says, 'Come on, let's go out to the ship.'

"I guess we ran out of booze, or something. He says, 'I got a bottle aboard the ship.'

"So we got in the lifeboats and headed out to the ship. The party proceeded from there. It ended up that we were making too much noise. And, jeeze, I guess we woke up the whole ship. So this guy goes down to his cabin and he gets his captain's hat with the scrambled eggs on it. And, by golly, he's drunker than hell. But that captain's hat, that was his badge of authority. 'Get the hell off of my ship, all of you.'

"He kicked us all off the ship. That was a funny incident."

Second Mate MacMillan: "For a seaman it was a good place. The girls were all fun to be with and all pretty.

"One of the nice things though . . . I would have to look in my book to remember the chap's name, but he took us down to Turku to spend the weekend with his parents. I think it's the second largest city in Finland.

"What I remember most about it is going in the car through the apparently planted forests, which are small trees. Not like the California forests which you have big and little and all. It's funny how you remember, that the trees were all about the same diameter.

"We had lovely dinner at their home on a Sunday afternoon. The men ate in the dining room and the women ate in the kitchen. I think there was the father and the son and another son and another one of my shipmates and myself. I think there was five of us sat at the dining table and there was three women that sat in the other room and had to eat after they served us. Now, I don't know whether that was because there was no room at the table or whether that was Finnish custom. But I like to remind my dear California girlfriends who are fighting so much for equality, that's what I remembered there."

Capt. Moon: "I was with him. That was a fantastic thing. Going to this country home and having dinner with them. I recall going with him and having this dinner with these people and the women eating in the other room. They really treated us fantastically, beautifully.

"A few of us visited a fox farm in the country. Minks, sables, silver foxes, and all kinds of fur-bearing animals were being raised for their pelts. I bought six beautiful silver fox furs for my wife. She still has them. First made into a coat, then a jacket, now a stole."

Sailing from Rauma on September 10, the *Lane Victory* returned through the North Sea to Grangemouth, near Edinburgh on the east coast of Great Britain.

Gil MacMillan: "It's in Scotland, the harbor for Edinburgh, a refueling spot. We stayed there during the day."

Capt. Ralph Moon: "We couldn't get any fuel up there in Finland at all. Of course, they were hurting as it was, that's why we were taking coal up there. So we just stopped at Glasgow to get fuel. It was the first port that we could get fuel in."

Second Mate MacMillan invited a former girlfriend over from Glasgow while the ship was in port. "I remember I got in trouble with Capt. Moon because, during the war, I was on the Murmansk run. And when I was in Glasgow, I met a girl, Barbara McKay. So this now is two or three years later and I wirelessed her and she came over in a tug from Glasgow to meet me on the ship. And she was a very attractive blonde, and we went out and had dinner and a few other things."

Capt. Moon: "Nobody went ashore because there just wasn't anything to go ashore for. You didn't have time to go anywhere. All we were going to do was take on fuel. We didn't know when we docked how long it was going to take. Whether it would be six hours or eight hours or four hours or what. He must have just taken off the ship and said, 'I'll be back before you're ready to sail.'"

Gil MacMillan: "I didn't know the exact time to come back. But the problem was the ship was ready to sail. I wasn't aboard."

Capt. Moon: "We had all the lines singled up and no second mate. Waiting, ready to sail. Whether we took on the fuel faster than he had anticipated or what . . . We had to put the gangway back out again because we were going to leave. Here he comes up the dock. We were all singled up ready to sail and here he comes driving up the dock."

Gil MacMillan: "Capt. Moon was young and not a terrible 'Bligh-type' skipper so he growled a little bit about me but it was more jealousy at me having this gal than anything else. But we didn't spend overnight there at all. It was in in the morning and we were gone."

Capt. Moon recalls his reaction somewhat differently. "And, well do I remember that incident. You don't expect that out of one of your mates. A seaman or something like that . . .

"I did a little more than growl. I was pretty upset. I didn't log him or anything, but I chewed him out a little bit."

The Lane Victory *in Venice with a full load of cargo, awaiting discharge.*
Courtesy the Lane Victory.

With the second mate safely on board, the *Lane* sailed September 14, 1947 for Norfolk, Virginia and another load of coal.

Capt. Moon: "Norfolk did not have much of a customs crew. They only had one customs officer there and he didn't bother to check anything. So a lot of items, including my furs, did not get declared."

Voyage 7 continued, for the articles specified the voyage wouldn't end until the ship reached its first port of loading, San Francisco. Departing the United States East Coast on the first of October, the *Lane* once again crossed the Atlantic, this time bound for the Mediterranean. Her destination: Venice, Italy.

Capt. Ralph Moon: "We took a load of coal clear up in there. It was quite a drive from the harbor down to Venice. You had to take a cab or a bus."

Gil MacMillan: "There wasn't a lot of tourists 'cause it was after the war. That was quite a trip. I would say we were there a couple of weeks.

"I was raised a very strict Presbyterian and my top contact was the world's prostitutes through sitting in the bordellos

As the Lane Victory *approaches the pier in Venice, a tug maneuvers into position to aid in docking. Courtesy Capt. Ralph Moon.*

with my shipmates and drinking rum and coca-cola. I remember the tremendous number of prostitutes in the Grand Palace there, the court yard. We had trouble walking because they just pestered you and pestered you and pestered you. They were grabbing your arms constantly. It was kind of interesting. In the fact, they were generally good looking. My dilemma was the desire, the physical desire, but the mental prohibition had been built into me.

"It was the heyday of black market. You know, cigarettes, which I don't smoke. So a carton of cigarettes, it'd bring real big prices there in Venice. I think we were issued a carton of cigarettes a week, and, of course, on a long voyage I might accumulate eight, ten cartons — sixty cents, I believe, in those days. Then the smokers sometimes got upset because here a non-smoker goes ashore and gets twenty to fifty dollars a carton and they smoked theirs up."

While some of the crew dealt in small quantities of cigarettes, others went to extremes.

Vern Richardson: "The thing in Venice was the ship had to pay a fine because of smuggling of cigarettes there by one of the crewmembers. And that fine had to be paid before we could leave the port. Then there was a big fuss about that. That crewmember had bought a case of cigarettes. He was taking them ashore by the cartons and giving them to the customs and everything and he would get all kinds of money for them. He was a real wheeler-dealer, but then somebody squawked there around the port area, and they nabbed him and came and took the rest of his stuff away. Then they fined the ship and the fine had to be paid before we left the port, and of course the fine was deducted from his wages eventually."

Gil MacMillan: "Capt. Moon . . . He was a mild sort of a skipper, and he would probably just be disgusted and argue and try to get the agent to help us. But you know the Italians were shaking everybody down in those days."

Capt. Moon: "I think cigarettes were number one. I think soap was number two. Silk stockings, oh, if you had silk stockings you had it made. A lot of guys did take stuff like that. Used for bartering. The black market in those days was a way of life. Nobody thought a thing about it. If you gave one of these customs officers down on the dock a carton of cigarettes or a pair of silk stockings . . . you could have the whole world. He'd turn his back all the time. Let you go. So it was not uncommon.

"But somebody got carried away and took a whole case. That was just getting a little too much. I suppose the customs boys could get into trouble themselves. They had to look out for their own hides. I had to go up to the customs office and try to get the ship off the hook. We were in a problem there because we had a big fine slapped against us. Finally we said the culprit involved will have to pay the fine. We did log him for it and deducted it from his pay. I don't think it was that great of an amount, a couple of hundred dollars."

Italian craftsmen are world-famous for the quality of their work. Venice was becoming a major shopping and tourist city and the crew took advantage of their stay to buy Venetian wares.

Gil MacMillan: "I remember we bought gloves. Gloves were the big items to buy. There was a lot of ceramic things that were supposed to be the thing to buy and take home but ceramic is very difficult to transport. It was a good shopping port considering the black market exchange and the value of the dollar versus the lira at that time.

"Venice had these original glass blowers, all the artisans. We went to a shop to watch them do that sort of thing. Yeah, they had that. I do believe that I did buy a few little brandy crystals, something of that nature."

Ralph Moon: "Venice at that time was such a paradise for merchandise. You could buy anything there. I bought a beautiful Rolex Oyster watch, I think I paid fifty bucks for it. If I had it today it's worth thousands of dollars. At home we still have the Venetian cut glass and Venetian glass leaded with silver that I bought."

In many ports of the world native people make a living acting as guides to merchant seamen. They take the sailor wherever he wants to go and usually receive a percentage of any purchases the seaman makes. The thinking is that the guide has brought extra business to an establishment by steering the sailor there, so he is entitled to a commission. The seaman benefits because he has a translator and someone familiar with the area. He doesn't waste a lot of time searching, or, if the guide has scruples, end up in a bad part of town. Because the guide leads the sailor around unfamiliar areas in just the way a ship's pilot steers a ship around the unfamiliar waters of a foreign harbor, he is called a "pilot." Unfortunately this type of pilot is not always scrupulous.

Gil MacMillan: "I had befriended an Italian kid who was our pilot. He was our guide and translator and a good kid, but a few days before we left he stole us blind. Which was something you had to be aware of. They could be so friendly but they would steal from you when they knew you were leaving. He also tried to sell us guns, pistols and things which we didn't buy."

Italy, of course, is the seat of Roman Catholicism. Priests and nuns are seen everywhere — on the streets, in the cafes, at markets and sometimes even aboard ship.

Vern Richardson: "In Venice, the Catholic nuns came aboard the ship to solicit funds for the church."

Gil MacMillan: "Not on my watch they didn't. I was a fanatic. I would kick them off. I wouldn't allow any of the church people on board the boat. I'd never let the nuns come up the gangway and be on the ship. We used to discuss that and the hotshot Catholics would be a little bit offended. We had quite a discussion, but hey, it was my watch, in port, and I had generally the day watch. I wouldn't allow them aboard the boat. I said they had to be down at the dock, I couldn't control that. And there was a little controversy but nobody ever countermanded me. And Moon, you know, he could care less."

Vern Richardson: "We had a Kanaka [Hawaiian] junior engineer. He was very heavy set, good, good worker. The Catholic nuns were going up and down the passageway to all the cabins, 'How about helping the church.'

"And this Henry Fern said, 'I'm going to give you some funds and I'm going to give you a carton of chewing gum, a carton, not a box or a package, a carton of chewing gum, if you take that headdress off and show me that you're bald.'

"And they were having a hard time conversing and one in Italian, but she got the message. She peeled it right off and she was bald as a billiard. He laughed. He thought that was the biggest joke, you know, he said, 'O.K. I believe you. Here it is. Here's some money. That's all I wanted to know.'

"And she thought it was a big joke, too."

Departing Venice empty, on the 22nd of October, the *Lane Victory*

Junior engineers Richard Coleman, Richard Pennington and Henry Fern. Courtesy Vernon Richardson.

stopped at Naples for a return cargo.

Second Mate MacMillan: "But when you see the poverty in those days in Naples, if you were there and you go out to Pompeii and you say, 'My God, what's happened here!'

"I was going through one of those typical church tours with this priest and he was showing me the jewels. I remember I said, 'Well, why don't they sell some of this jewelry and help the poor?' "And he says, 'My son, we do not give to the poor. We take from the poor.'

"To this day I wonder, was he being religious or was he being a little bit cynical about the system. 'We don't give to the poor, we take from the poor.'"

From Naples on October 26, the ship sailed for New York.

Gil MacMillan would be transferred to another American President Lines ship. But he enjoyed his time on the *Lane*. So much so that he would return to it a few years later. "It seemed to me it was a laid back ship. It's peacetime. This is early peacetime, you know. And we've all been accustomed to wartime. As I remember it was a great ship. I enjoyed the trip. I was on my own. I was navigator and I got to shoot my sights and do all the navigating and it was fun."

Like all visitors from foreign shores, merchant seamen must declare their purchases to customs officials when they enter the first American port from a foreign voyage. Occasionally someone will try sneaking their curios ashore. In New York several of the crew were fined by customs for trying to sneak souvenirs in without declaring them.

Capt. Moon: "The ship was loaded [with souvenirs]. We were supposed to go back to load another load of coal. Well, of course, the crew had been in this coal harbor before and they knew there was only one customs officer and he couldn't be bothered. One day out we get this message to divert to New York instead. We get into New York and put out the anchor and here comes a whole boatload of customs officials. They knew every trick in the book. You didn't fool those boys.

The Lane Victory *anchored at Tocopilla, Chile, loading nitrate for Alexandria, Egypt. Courtesy Vernon Richardson.*

"Now one of the favorite tricks used to be to take a piece of black thread and hang stuff down in the oil tanks. They'd wrap it up in plastic or whatever and hang it down below the oil so it couldn't be seen, even with a flashlight. You didn't fool those guys. They found every one of those. Or they'd take the emergency lights in the alleyways and take the batteries out of them and stuff their contraband in there. They found every one of those. They'd take the tile off some of the cabin ceilings and load that up. They'd load the ventilation ducts full of contraband. These guys knew every trick in the book. They didn't miss a bit.

"The crew paid dearly. They got in line. I'm just lucky I didn't have my furs then."

The nature of tramping is that you go where the cargo is. The only cargo available at this time was at the opposite end of the globe. Sailing from New York City on November 18, 1947 the *Lane Victory* headed south.

Vern Richardson: ". . . down to Tocopilla, Chile to load nitrates, bulk nitrates."

It was a long voyage; south along the United States East Coast, south to the Panama Canal, south along the West Coast of Chile. Once the ship arrived in Tocopilla, some of the crew

Loading nitrate at Tocopilla, Chile. The stevedores are resting between loads. The white powder on the deck is spilled nitrate (bird guano). Courtesy Vernon Richardson.

either celebrated their arrival more than they should have or took more time off than they were entitled to. On December 4 one of the ABs was logged for failing to turn to. He was too drunk to work. An oiler was fined for being absent without leave and failure to turn to.

The need to let off steam extended to the upper decks. Capt. Moon was invited ashore by Mr. Boyington, the ship's agent. From the captain's "guest log:"

> There was a dance at the Club Reunion and the Lord said let there be thirst. And the next day throughout all the land there was suffering.
> (signed) Art Boyington,
>   a fellow sufferer.

From Tocopilla on December 15, the ship reversed her previous course running north along the West Coast of South America.

Chief Richardson: "We took it back through the canal to Alexandria, Egypt."

Clearing Cristobal in the Canal Zone on December 22, the crew spent Christmas day somewhere in the Atlantic, bound once more for the Mediterranean. The year 1948 was welcomed in at Alexandria. One of the third assistant engineers celebrated too much and had to be logged on New Year's Eve for being drunk and disorderly.

Capt. Moon and some of the officers took advantage of the opportunity to do some sight-seeing. "A group of the ship's officers took a two-day tour to Cairo to visit the pyramids and be real tourists for a couple of days."

The captain (Ralph Moon) of the ship aboard a "ship of the desert." Courtesy Capt. Ralph Moon.

Having discharged the nitrates, the ship sailed from Alexandria on January 15, took on bunkers in Port Said and departed the same day.

Vern Richardson: "And from Egypt we went up to Sardinia to load salt for Japan."

Capt. Moon: "It was a great big pile of salt, just a big a mountain of salt. They shoveled the salt into these baskets and put aboard ship. It came aboard in pretty good shape, as I recall.

"When they took it off it seems to me they had

To leave the ship and visit Cairo and the pyramids took a special pass from the Egyptian government. Here Capt. Moon appears at the age of 27. Courtesy Capt. Ralph Moon.

to sack it. The Japanese were down in the hold there sacking that salt."

While at the salt dock at Cagliari, Sardinia, the ship's slop chest, the store where the crew buy their cigarettes, candy and other incidentals, was broken into. The padlock was broken and the door jimmied open. The thief wasn't caught.

Capt. Moon and a few of the officers took the opportunity to visit Rome. "A bunch of us flew over and the damn plane, I didn't think was ever going to make it. A little Italian two-engine job, it was falling to pieces and shaking. Rome healed its war wounds pretty rapidly but there was still a lot of damage and bombed-out buildings to be seen on the edge of town. No damage was visible to any of the churches or historical landmarks."

There was so much salt on board, the ship sat on the bottom at low tide. As Chief Engineer, Vern Richardson had to transfer ballast to get the ship off the bottom. "We were picking up, I think around close to 9,000 tons of salt. Well, somebody didn't figure the tides right and we were sitting there on the bottom and we can't get off the bottom. So I had to transfer fuel and tip the ship way over so it came off at an angle, deep loaded you know. And then once we got fully afloat, I transferred it back and straightened it up a little bit. But we had just enough oil to get to Japan from Sardinia."

Leaving Cagliari on February 2, the *Lane Victory* made her first trip through the Suez Canal.

Clearing the northern terminus, Port Said, on February 6, the ship eased her way toward Suez which she cleared the following day. The passage through the Red Sea, the Gulf of Aden and the Indian Ocean was calm and uneventful.

There were no difficulties until the ship reached the Singapore Straits. There the crew found some extra people on board. Capt. Moon thought they might have come aboard in the Suez Canal. "Either in Port Said or Suez, these young stowaways managed to ship aboard and tunnel under the copra mats stowed in the after guntub."

Vern Richardson: "Back in that gun tub, there were stored cocoa mats, extra cocoa mats to line the holds to carry bulk copra which we had done previously. And those were all piled up in rolls, big rolls clear to the top of it."

Vern Richardson thought they boarded in Sardinia: "We got three stowaways, boys about seventeen and fourteen, somewhere in that age group. They scampered aboard thinking the ship was going to the United States. Nobody spotted them until we had passed Singapore Straits. Then one of the night crew was up and they saw this guy in there helping himself to the night lunch in the icebox. You know, 'Me no speaka da English.' And he took off.

"The fella went and told the mate, he said, 'There's a stowaway on here.'"

Capt. Moon: "The first we suspected stowaways was when food started disappearing from the crew's night lunch. Then strange people were seen and strange noises."

Vern Richardson: "They went looking for him and they found two guys buried in these cocoa mats. That's where they were hiding. So they put them to work. And then, lo and behold, a third one shows up. He was hiding in another part of that pile of mats. So the mate put them to work and they said, 'We're going to have to take you off when we get to Sasebo, Japan.'

"They disappeared for a second time. The crew was out looking for them, can't seem to find them. Well, there was some friction between the mates and the captain. And the captain had wired to San Francisco that the stowaways that we found are now missing. And then some of the crew told the captain, they passed the word to him that some of the other crew didn't like them [the stowaways] and they threw them over the side. Well that was not the case. That was only to needle the captain. And sure enough they showed up when they got hungry, because they came out to get something to eat. They'd been hiding down in one of the hatches. Well then the captain wired back to San Francisco, 'Found three stowaways.'

"So we all thought, boy, what does the company think of this? What's going on in that ship?"

According to Capt. Moon, the friction was caused by his mates' careless attitudes toward the stowaways. "The mates said, 'We'll get them out of there captain, don't worry.'

"The next thing I know, I see the mates heading aft with their sidearms. 'A few rounds fired into the mats will bring them out.'

"I got into a fight with my chief mate. I said, 'No way are you going to shoot any bullets or shells into those . . .'

"I was fairly easy going. I like to run a tight ship, yet if a man does his job I'm not going to interfere with him. It's when he doesn't do his job, that's when I step in. Anyway, as I recall, that was the only time I ever got mad at my chief mate, or any of the mates as far as that goes. But I just would not agree to that.

"Needless to say, I put a stop to that in a hurry. I could see nothing but trouble ahead if one of the stowaways was struck by a bullet."

The authorities in Singapore wanted nothing to do with stowaways. When the ship sailed, after fueling, on February 21 they were still on board.

Being used to the warm waters of the Mediterranean, the stowaways had no idea just how cold the sea was in Japan in February.

Vern Richardson: "We got out at anchorage at Sasebo, and waiting to go to the docks and these guys had put on life jackets and shed their pants and they were just in their underpants and they were going to make a swim for it. The stowaways. In that icy water. And of course they were caught there and the authorities came and took them ashore. But they would never have made it, even if they had their lifejackets on."

Capt. Moon: "They were put ashore in the custody of the U.S. Army in Sasebo, Japan."

Sasebo was under the control of American military authorities. Rules and regulations that apply to Army and Navy personnel are applied to merchant seamen as well. Some seafarers consider themselves civilians and not under military authority. Others simply choose to ignore the rules. In any case, the voyage from Sardinia was long, the desire for feminine companionship strong.

On March 2, one of the crew was apprehended for being in an off limits area. Enjoying the pleasures of a geisha house in "Geisha Town," he was taken by the military police and thrown in jail. As the cargo was unloaded during the next few days, two other crewmen were restricted to the ship due to being caught in geisha houses.

If the crew had a difficult time, the officers were treated royally. Capt. Ralph Moon: "We were treated like conquering heroes by the Japanese. It seems that the *Lane Victory* was the first non-military vessel to enter Sasebo Harbor after the war. The Japanese couldn't do enough for us.

"We were dined by city officials at a banquet for all the officers and given gifts and generally treated royally. I was presented with the key to the city and made an honorary citizen."

Sailing from Sasebo on March 6, the ship was short on fuel. Normally the law requires that a ship carry a reserve of twenty-five percent of capacity in case of accidents or bad weather. APL convinced Chief Engineer Richardson to bend the law a little in order to make the next port without having to go out of the way for bunkers.

Fuel was Vern Richardson's responsibility, and one he took seriously. "We had an argument. I was responsible, and I said, 'We don't have the twenty-five percent safety margin of oil leaving Japan.

"The company tried to get us some oil, and none of their other company ships that were there would give us any. When you have to figure that you might get into a big typhoon or whatever, you got have a good supply of oil. So they prevailed on me to go at standard speed, no more. I said 'If we go right on the block, I think we can make it. We won't have twenty-five percent left but we'll still make it.'

"So we went, not any speed at all and we made it OK. We get into Honolulu and I said, 'A thousand barrels of oil is what we need to get to Los Angeles with a twenty-five percent safety margin.'

"There's a whole line of ships on the dock there. They're all fueling. So I put all the oil into one tank. Then they shut the oil off on me and I gauged it. I said 'No, I don't have enough here, I'm short, couple a hundred barrels.'

"I can't make a mistake in one tank. I know exactly that I'm short about two hundred barrels and I said, 'That's really our safety margin.'

"And the guy says, 'I don't care what you say, that's what you've got.'

"I said, 'Well I'm going to sign it under protest. And give me two hundred more barrels.'

"So he put on two hundred more barrels and then I had the right amount."

With what should have been a comfortable margin of fuel on board, the ship sailed from Honolulu March 19 with no more than the usual crew problems. One of the wipers missed the ship and was logged for Failure To Join. One of the ABs was too drunk to work and logged for failure to turn to.

Vern Richardson: "We took off. I had a shortwave radio in my cabin, a Hallicrafters radio and I was always tuning it in, listening to whatever sounded interesting. I happened to come in on a frequency that was abnormal. It was a 'Notice to Mariners,' a warning to stay out of a missile range, from out here in the Channels (Channel Islands). I told the radio operator and I told the mates, and I said 'I heard something about stay out of this missile range, they were gonna fire missiles.'

"'You engineers, you don't know what you're talking about, mind your own business.'

"I said, 'I heard it on a radio.'

"I said, 'I'm from this area . . . I know where Port Hueneme is.'

"'WE didn't hear it. WE didn't get any notice.'

"I said, 'I heard it.'

"We started into the missile range and a twin engine plane flies right over the top of the mast with a loudspeaker and said, 'Reverse your course 180 degrees and steam out to sea.'

"Well then I had to needle the guys there, I said, 'You guys won't listen to the engine department for 'Notice to Mariners.''

"So then, you know, we're there, low on the oil as it was. To make San Pedro, I said, 'You know, we had to steam out fifty or sixty miles and turn around and come back again.'

"We got back but I thought, that's all I needed is to run out of oil out there in the channel because of something like that and have to be towed in. We made it back and that was a real nightmare, I'll tell you."

From Port Hueneme the *Lane* sailed once more to San Francisco where her around-the-world voyage finally ended on March 29, 1948. Traveling some 56,700 miles it took almost nine months to complete the trip, crossing the Atlantic five times, transiting the Panama Canal three times and sailing the Suez Canal once.

Never a company to stand on ceremony when a profit was to be made, American President Lines put a new crew on board and immediately loaded for the Far East. Voyage 8 commenced on April 6, 1948. Edward C. Dumouchelle was her master.

Capt. Moon: "I was relieved in San Francisco by Capt. Ed Dumouchelle who immediately had the copra mats put ashore and destroyed, something that I tried to do for over a year."

Sailing from Oakland on April 9, 1948 the *Lane Victory* took the quickest route, a great circle course, to Yokohama.

Isaac Givens, second cook and baker: "Well, the *Lane Victory*, I made one trip on her. I generally make more than one trip on a ship.

"I made a trip in '48 on her. You know how I found that out? I happened to go down my discharges and I looked there, I say, 'My God I was on there. I was cookin' in there, 'bout five weeks. I was on this ship. Yeah, I was on this ship.'

"The galley's kind of different on her, 'cause they have the steam table in the galley. This the first one I seen. With the steam table in the galley, the cooks had to serve the meals. You see the other ships, the steam table was in the pantries. But this was in the galley."

For a black man, going to sea was difficult. But the war opened new doors for Isaac.

"First I tried to get in the longshoreman. They had a big line out there. They started a fight 'cause this guy was first or this guy was next. The guy come out there and say, 'Get on with it. I ain't gonna hire nobody.'

"Well I go away from there. Then I went to the Marine Cooks and Stewards and they had jobs everywhere on the board. So they asked me, said, 'Am I a cook?'

"I said no, I can't cook, but I can wait tables, I can do this. So the first job I had was a messman's job."

Even with strong unions, it was difficult for blacks to overcome the prejudice of white West Coast crews.

Isaac Givens: "Well most of the ships . . . you know you catch a couple of guys on every ship that's unhappy. Well that's his problem, you see. He may have left home unhappy, you know. But you can't go along with that, because I remember the ship I went down on, during wartime. They had a German steward there, and he say, '. . . the deck gang don't want no Negroes here.'

"I said, 'Well, that's all right, I'll go on back to the hall.' So I went on back to the hall. They told me, say, 'You go back down there and let the captain turn you down. You go back and tell the captain this and you let the captain turn you down.'

"So when I got down there they was signing and the captain and the commissioner heard the commotion in the hall so they come out, they say, 'What's wrong?'

"The steward says, 'The deck gang don't want no Negroes.'"

". . . deck gang don't run . . . Come on. You got your papers?'

"I say, 'Yes.'

". . . come on. Sign on.'

"I went on there, sign on. He say, 'They don't run my ship. I run this ship.'

"But they would had him fooled. They didn't want this on here and they didn't want that on there. That was forty-two. And it was an old 'hog island.'"[2]

"So I went on out there. They had a few on there, but in that length of time they changed. I was the only black sailing on these ships for over two years, two-and-a-half years. You had some on there was out of the way and you had some on there was all right. In the length of time at sea, get in them storms and things, regardless of how prejudice a guy was, that sea changed him. He changed. When he come back he is a changed man."

One can't help thinking that Bishop Isaac Lane would have understood.

The great circle course across the North Pacific passes through or just south of the Aleutian Islands, depending on the whim of the master. In either case the weather is almost always rough with grey skies, icy winds and froth-covered blue-grey seas topping long, rolling, mountainous swells. Sometimes it was so bad the cooks could only serve sandwiches. Pots and pans rolled off the galley range or dumped their steaming contents on the deck.

Isaac Givens: "It's a funny thing what that sea do to you. Waves out there high as this ship. Sometime you didn't think you was going to come back. 'I get out o' this, I ain't coming back out here.'

"It was a lot of times you couldn't sleep for three or four days at a time. The crew get all upset. The whole crew gets upset, you know, you in them storms and things. Then after it calm down, everybody's happy again."

The only port was Yokohama. The cargo was off-loaded faster than it came on board in Oakland. Although Japan was

---

[2] Toward the end of World War I, the federal government embarked on a massive shipbuilding program to revitalize the American merchant marine. Of the ships built, 122 were constructed on the same basic plan, a design first fabricated at the American International Corporation's yard at Hog Island, Pennsylvania. These ships were nick-named "hog islanders."

impoverished after the war, Isaac Givens was impressed with the industry of the Japanese people.

"Japan come up quicker than any country I ever seen in my life. You could go out there two, three o'clock in the morning. These Japanese just like a bunch of ants. They working, they working, they working. And they work and they work and they work.

"Truman. These businessmen got on Truman to move MacArthur from over there. MacArthur said, 'Long as I'm over there they won't build so much as a rowboat.'

"Truman got on MacArthur and fired MacArthur from over there. He got rid of MacArthur. These businessmen went over there with that money, looking for cheap labor. That's what they was doing, looking for cheap labor. These businessmen lookin' for cheap labor and then it got so high in Japan they had to leave Japan, see? They had to leave Japan. Then they went into Pusan. Now they tell me Pusan is got too high for them, see? They was all looking for cheap labor. After the war, we was in Japan. I was in Japan three days after the war, when MacArthur was reading the roster to Japan, 'You can't do this, you can't do this, you can't do the other.'

"What he didn't know, when he got through saying that, they bowed, and say, 'Well, we want the world.'

"We didn't understand that then, but we understand it now. They got all the money and we got the glory."

To the crew's thankful relief, when she sailed from Yokohama on April 26, the *Lane Victory*'s next port was Honolulu. That meant no Alaskan weather to deal with. The warmth of Hawaii was left behind on May the 5th as the ship made her way home again. But this time she was headed for the lay-up fleet in Suisun Bay, California.

The voyage ended on May 11, 1948. The crew was discharged except for a small "riding crew." Taking the ship to Suisun Bay, they tied her in a row of several other Victorys. There she would wait, like her sisters, mothballed until needed again. But it would be a short wait. The Korean conflict was already taking shape.

8

THE KOREAN WAR

Suddenly the United States was again battling an enemy on the other side of the Pacific. The war machine kicked into gear and took off at full throttle. The business of war with its ever-important supply lines must be kept running. At the eight National Defense Reserve Fleets across the country ships were yanked out of their mothballs, dusted off and thrown into action. Victory ships, finished almost too late for World War II, were ideal. They were fast, could unload their own cargo, and were small enough to negotiate the shallow waters and dramatic tides of Korea. From Suisun Bay came the *Lane Victory.*

Ray A. Fullbright joined the vessel as purser on October 9, 1950. "The ship was operated by American President Lines and we were the first trip out when it was brought out of mothballs."

Gil MacMillan: "I was third mate. I don't know why, but they threw me on this boat. Try to figure it out. There was a lot of deals going on there. I was trying to make a quick buck I guess. I just got off the *President Wilson* as third mate, I was senior third on the *Wilson*. They had this ship and they needed mates. There was a shortage, a war, so I went out on that. I could have had a different ship but I figured because I was only out there for a short time, let's make all we can."

After a quick shake-down, Voyage 9 commenced October 10, 1950. The ship loaded military supplies at the Oakland Army Base.

Fullbright: "We had an old seadog for a skipper by the name of Marinus Olson."

Gil MacMillan: "Old Capt. Olson. He was an old-time, hard-type skipper."

Sailing from Oakland on October 15, the ship had a quiet crossing and arrived in Yokohama, Japan on October 29. On arrival, some confusion arose stemming from the captain's old-fashioned use of the command "starboard your helm."

Centuries ago, the first device used to turn a rudder was a tiller bar. Extending horizontally from the top of the rudder, it was pushed in the opposite direction of that in which the vessel turned. For example, pushing the tiller to starboard caused the rudder and the ship to go to port. If a captain wanted the helmsman to turn to port he ordered, "Starboard your helm." This tradition was so strongly ingrained that when steering wheels first came on the scene in the 1700s, they were rigged so that turning the wheel in the opposite direction of the way you wanted to go produced the desired result. In this way, captains could continue ordering, "starboard your helm" for a left turn. The tradition lasted longer in Europe than it did in the United States. Thus, the Swedish-trained Capt. Marinus Olson sometimes forgot and went back to the old ways.

Third Mate MacMillan: "I remember coming into Yokohama, trying to dock the boat. We had a Japanese pilot. Capt. Olson, when he got stressed he would revert to the old

days where you would starboard the helm. Starboard and larboard.
So the helmsman would be going the wrong way, 'cause he'd
think starboard and it's really the opposite, you know. So I
would correct the helmsman each time 'he means right wheel,
left wheel.'

"And, God, he had a fit. He just threw a fit at me one
time . . . 'Ah, *ja*, you don't correct my order. You leaf my
order alone.'

"He was really stressed out. So the helmsman knew he
gave the wrong order and he looks at me and he says 'Hey,
mate, what do I do.'

"I says, 'I don't know.'

'He says, 'We're going to hit.'

"I said, 'I know it.'

"So we hit the dock real bad coming in to Yokohama.
I'd always corrected his wheel 'cause I know what he meant and
I would do it. But this time he heard it, see, and he had a fit.
And the helmsman, I remember him saying, 'Mate, what do I
do?'

"And I says, 'You better leave the wheel the way it is or
the captain's gonna chew me out again.'

"And we're almost laughing and pow! We tear the dock
up. So there was big damage.

"But he was not a vicious man, the captain wasn't. Course
he was pretty old, too.

"That was the biggest joke ever, you know. I don't think
Olson changed a bit that way either. He wasn't aware of the
confusion he was causing by 'starboard your helm.' And as long
as the mate on the bridge and the helmsman translated it to the
correct deal it was no problem. It was just that he was jealous
of his command. And he shouldn't have been."

The Japanese were beginning their post-war recovery and
American dollars were greatly in demand.

Gil MacMillan: "I remember again the thing that bothers
you in Yokohama was from the minute you went through the

At first post-war recovery was slow and difficult for Japan. These shoe shine girls are in a prime location — outside a bar catering to American servicemen and seamen. Courtesy Gil MacMillan.

gate at the dock there were prostitutes everywhere. It was better to have two or three of you walking together. Mainly because they're grabbing your arms. It's hard for a people that haven't been molested that way if you just want to walk downtown and have a drink someplace. I recall at least 200 women would be after you and pawing you. These prostitutes were rather desperate. Those were poor days for the Japanese. And these girls would hound you and follow you and hound you. You know, you could ignore them, you don't say a word, but they were there and they were grabbing your arms. I thought it was a nuisance. I thought it was really a bad nuisance. Of course, you're always torn between maybe the desire to pick one out. But in those days it was just not in my morality to do that.

"It's just like I was in Shanghai before it fell to the communists. We learned real quickly that if you took a rickshaw back to your boat that the way to get rid of the rickshaws which would be all around you would be to take the money and

Taken in the 1950s this photo captures the drabness of Japan at the time and the guarded attitude of the people. Courtesy Gil MacMillan.

throw it on the ground and head for the dock. Because otherwise the rickshaws would be around begging for money and they wouldn't let you through. But the minute you threw money down on the ground, everybody went for it.

"That's funny how I remember Yokohama. I remember there wasn't too much to buy, except the traditional things like silk kimonos and dinner jackets, which we don't wear, and silk pajamas that I

Second Mate Oupe ashore in Japan. The ever-present military police could be a thorn in the side to fun-seeking American seamen. Courtesy Gil MacMillan.

still have. Beautiful silk pajamas that are very nice. And, of course, the china . . ."

"I went out one time trying to find somebody that a friend said to look up, that she spoke English. But I don't think that he realized that it wasn't good for her to fraternize in any way with Americans. And in my attempt to find her address, I found nobody . . . They were all polite but nobody was helpful. I thought we were always treated with respect but not in any way friendly. Whether it was a taxicab, a bar, I don't think anybody was friendly. It was cold. You'd feel uncomfortable. The poverty that was there at the time . . . You know things were tough in those days. And they were probably a little bit respectful but that was about it. Not like today I imagine, they'd be waving and smiling . . ."

The war in Korea was not going in a predictable manner. When the ship sailed from Yokohama on November 16, she had no cargo. She was sent north for an unknown purpose. It was like going into another world. Once more the log entries included the word "bonus." From the official logbook: "November 19, 1950 vessel crossed into area V, 100% bonus at 0640 ELT (minus 9 zone time) or 2140 GCT November 18, 1950 Lat. 32 16 N. Long 126 50 E."

Korea in winter is bitter, dank, barren and grey. The country looks almost as if there is no vegetation and never has been.

Gil MacMillan: "That's Korea. It was always cold and miserable. And it's always overcast, kind of foggy, damp and freezing. I call it the San Francisco weather with thirty-two degree temperature. Moist, penetrating, cold wind, freezing. The whole trip."

The *Lane Victory* arrived at Inchon on November 20.

Third Mate MacMillan: "We went to Inchon and we sat around for some time while MacArthur was going to end the war. The next thing we know we had 3,000 prisoners of war being put on board the boat."

Loaded with POWs, the *Lane* sailed from Inchon on December 3, 1950.

Gil MacMillan: "We're taking the prisoners of war from Inchon around to Pusan. I was in charge of feeding the prisoners of war. They were in the upper 'tween decks. We had barrels of rice. They gave me some military armed guards that were all shell-shocked and really wild guys. What I did, I went down in the hold with a couple of armed guards and rifles. And I had them put in blanks and we went down there and made them sit down, 'haunch,' I guess was the term in those days. Then one of these armed guards who was really a nasty son-of-a-bitch . . . If anybody stood up he was ordered to go over and hit them with a rifle butt. A lot of people think it's cruel, but the Koreans in those days, they whipped them with whips and that they understood. The minute you hit them and maybe knocked him out nobody would move. But if you didn't establish discipline, which happened on other boats, then there were food riots in those holds and it became dangerous.

"They could have grabbed us, you know, maybe there was a hundred-fifty or two hundred. It's almost dangerous to be down there with them. Even though I was down there in uniform and they did respect officers, they could have killed me instantly. But we maintained discipline and we did it in every single hold. The minute one person broke ranks this guy was right on top of them with a rifle butt. As I say, I thought it was cruel, but I used to watch how the Koreans treat each other. They believe in physical punishment. And they respected force like that.

"Then they came by and they put food, if they had something [to put it in], or they put it in their hands. They put big hunks of rice. That was all they got. I saw that everybody on the boat was fed. We fed them twice. Now there was a couple of other ships out there that had riots and then half of them didn't get fed because of those problems. But anyhow the point was everyone [on the ship] was fed and they were fed twice.

"I think it was two or three days from Inchon to Pusan. And I always figured that we were the only ship that didn't have any problems with feeding.

"We had three dead. I think it was malnutrition. These people had been brought down in terrible shape. It was cold. This is winter time. Most of them didn't have shoes. They were barefooted. They had khakis and some of them would stuff newspapers around them and button it up to stay warm. I just think it was lack of food and the cold. When they died we just pulled them out of the hold and put them in the guntub."

The ship arrived in Pusan on December 5, unloaded the prisoners and sailed the following day.

On December 6, the *Lane Victory* was at Wonson and on December 7 they began loading Korean civilians, many of them women and children.

Ray Fullbright: "We were assigned to evacuate Wonson. We eventually were bringing them aboard in slings and carried people between Wonson and Pusan. It was winter and very cold."

Gil MacMillan: "We were ordered to come in and take off a few thousand. We put on 7,000 refugees. Well, you can imagine if you were skipper on that ship. What are you going to do with these people? And they keep coming. They're coming out in these LSTs."

Ray Fullbright: "During the process of loading the refugees they would come aboard in slings and we would have an officer or crew member at each hatch to get a count on how many we had and to get them to go down the ladders into the holds. They would go down one end of the hatch and try to come back up the other ladder. It was dark down there and they were naturally afraid. In the process of going back and forth trying to keep them from coming back out I fell off the top of a hatch on to the deck and broke my leg which had to wait to get put back together when we reached Pusan at a MASH hospital."

At Wonson the city was attacked and dynamited even as refugees were brought out to the ship. In this photo the smoke is so thick it blots out the sun.   Courtesy Gil MacMillan.

Gil MacMillan: "The city is blowing up and these barges come up and they're coming along the gangway, and Olson is screaming. He's calling the command, whoever's in command. I think there's a cruiser in charge. They were bringing all these

Landing craft were used to get refugees to the ships at Wonson. With tens of thousands of people wanting to get on the few ships available the situation was chaotic. Being under attack added to the confusion.   Courtesy Ray Fullbright.

people in and once they got on these boats they don't want to go back. And they're blowing the city. You can see them blowing the whole place up. And they had dynamited and all the explosions and these people were coming on and he couldn't get them stopped."

Ray Fullbright: "We were trying to get the refugees aboard and we were being shelled from shoreside."

Gil MacMillan: "He's screaming, he's screaming at them, 'Hey, hoist the gangplank. Ve don't vant no more. Ve don't vant any more.'

"He'd hoist the gangplank and then some Army official would come by in his boat and order him to put it back down, you know . . . He'd tell him, 'Hey you're in charge of the Army now, the Army's got to be in charge.'"

Ray Fullbright: "The most frustrating thing was the Navy continually changing our orders so that from hour to hour we didn't know what to do and they would not let us leave until all the refugees were on board."

Gil MacMillan: "And poor old Olson, he's screaming 'Vhat are ve going to do vid all dese people?'"

Ray Fullbright: "Finally the skipper disregarded the orders and we sailed anyway."

Gil MacMillan: "We disarmed all the refugees coming on board. Anybody that had a weapon, we took it away and piled the weapons up.

"I also think that there was a range of wealthy people. You should see the clothes that some people wore. I'm talking about the refugees — which had to mean that they were the upper class. And they're in with the rest of them. These probably had education. They had businesses and so on and they were running from the communist system."

With her human cargo, the *Lane Victory* sailed from Wonsan on December 8. The final total embarked was 7,009 refugees. But she arrived in Pusan the following day with 7,010.

Gil MacMillan: "We had one baby, one born. When she was delivering they brought her up and put her in a stateroom.

The woman's having a baby and we Americans are becoming unglued. The Koreans, when it comes time, the women that have pants, they just drop the pants and they squat down and they have the baby. And the women that are around help, and there's no big deal about it. But it seems like we had to get this woman into a private stateroom and into a bed and so on. And Korean women don't give birth to babies in bed. They squat down. And that was the thing that I thought was funny, because here we are, the captain . . . Everybody's trying to get this woman into a nice American medical environment. And, of course, she had the baby and the next morning she's off the ship carrying the baby with her and walking off the ship, you know. It's not considered a big deal.

"I remember a few prostitutes, they were beautiful, beautiful . . . And we were eyeing these girls, you know. God we'd like to get some of them up in our cabin . . ."

Caring for more than 7,000 refugees on a freighter can be a formidable task.

Gil MacMillan: "We put the empty rice barrels in the corner and these people, they put a plank on it. To go to the bathroom, supposedly they would crawl up on top of there and go in these barrels. Well, when they filled the barrels, those things were overflowing. Many people did that and many just went in the corners of the whole ship. By the time we got back to Pusan it was unsanitary. Unbelievable. It took us a long time. We had to get that out and the poor crew were with masks on, scooping out and then they had to steam the whole hull. It was a terrible mess, really a terrible mess."

Departing Pusan on December 10, the ship was ordered to Hungnam where she arrived on the 14th.

As the cruiser *St. Paul* and the destroyers *Charles S. Sperry* and *Zellars* laid down a covering fire, the *Lane Victory* embarked 3,834 troops, 1,146 vehicles and 10,013 bulk tons of cargo. She was one of seven merchant ships to aid in the evacuation in addition to twenty-one Navy vessels.

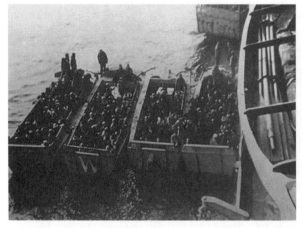

Once alongside the ship, left, the refugees had to wait their turn getting on board. Courtesy the Lane Victory.

At first the process of loading refugees was systematic. The ship's officers counted them and directed them into the cargo holds for warmth and safety. Courtesy Ray Fullbright.

The situation grew confused. Those refugees on board, frightened of the dark cargo holds, came out the other end of the hatch. At the same time more and more boats came alongside loaded with those seeking sanctuary. Courtesy Gil Macmillan.

The decks became crowded with cold, shivering, confused people. Some exhausted, some forlorn, all seeking escape. Courtesy the Lane Victory.

Carrying their only possessions, with the future uncertain, some refugees still managed a smile. Perhaps the future would be better than what they left behind. Courtesy Gil MacMillan.

As more and more refugees crowded aboard with their meager possessions, there became room for little else. Courtesy Gil MacMillan.

Eventually the Lane Victory *carried a human cargo of more than 7,000 from Wonson — literally a sea of people. Courtesy the* Lane Victory.

Ray Fullbright: "We also evacuated a Marine outfit, or what was left of it."

Gil MacMillan: "When we picked up the Army coming off the line, that was heavy cruiser fire right beside us. They were using eight-inch guns and the concussion off those things . . . I would say a hundred yards. The army was coming off the line and they were leapfrogging down. I guess a company would come down, hold position and the next one would pass through. We on the ship could look up at the fire fight going on at the top of the hills surrounding us. When you could see the heavy fire coming from the top you know the Chinese were over the top. That's when the cruiser would start its barrage. It could lay down one hell of a barrage. All night long it was firing, heavy fire on those ridges. I was in the Normandy beachhead, but you don't have a cruiser right beside you, firing all night long. The concussion off of those things can shake the ship. It was just constant all night long. Then we'd see the fire fight stop and then they'd start and the cruiser would open up again. I guess they were holding the Chinese from crossing down the ridge and the Army was coming down. There was combat fire and we loaded, I don't know how many. But we loaded them and we loaded their jeeps and their ammunition carriers and their trucks. These guys were coming. I heard a sergeant reported he lost two men. And we let the officers sleep in our beds and take hot showers and eat in our mess.

"We're at the dock and those ships are standing off. We take our turns coming in and combat loading, you know. Combat reloading and then as soon as you got your

At Hungnam the Lane Victory *helped evacuate the remaining military. Here trucks and equipment are lined up prior to loading on board. Courtesy Gil MacMillan.*

load you cleared the dock. All these ships were standing by to evacuate. It was sort of an emergency situation. It wasn't like a planned invasion where you have all the LST boats and so on. This is an emergency, where they were moving fast to get these troops out of there.

Here a jeep is loaded during the Hungnam evacuation. Note the vehicle is lifted with a wire sling where normally canvas or rope belly bands are used. Courtesy Gil MacMillan.

"We were handling the vehicles with nets, you know tire nets. The crew was running the winches. In fact some of the officers on watch would run the winches sometimes. And the coordination of running those winches on there. You couldn't just get anybody."

Sailing from Hungnam on December 15, the ship brought the battle-worn troops and their equipment to Pusan, arriving the same day. Then it was back to Hungnam, arriving on the 18th. The temperature dropped below freezing, the winds reached forty knots and the sea became rough.

Fullbright: "Our crew did take parkas and jackets for cold weather from the Marine supplies which were being blown up to keep the North Koreans from getting them."

MacMillan: "I know we went up to load the army and they were blowing everything up. There was a warehouse with clothes and we were allowed to go out. We had a lot of army clothes and we got all these fancy clothes because they were torching the whole place. Fur-lined khaki stuff, like long coats. I tell you this is warm and I tell you it's cold."

The second load from Hungnam departed on December 20 and was delivered to Pusan the following day. On the 21st, the *Lane Victory* finally pointed her bow south and out of the

War Zone. Although it had been only a month, to the crew it seemed forever.

But the whole operation was a great achievement. Working with the Navy, the *Lane* had done her part and could take pride in the commendation that followed:

> The Navy at Hungnam performed with spectacular skill although they received no banner headlines for their evacuation by sea of the entire X Corps and its equipment. But to take out from unfriendly territory, 105,000 troops, 91,000 Korean refugees, more than 17,000 vehicles and several hundred thousand tons of cargo was in itself a military triumph of no small dimensions. Equipment and supplies that could not be outloaded were destroyed on the beach, so nothing was left to the enemy.
>
> General Matthew B. Ridgeway.

The official log entry for December 23 reads, "Crossed boundary line out of bonus area at 34 N lat 129 E. Long. at 0245 (135 E. Meridian time)." That same day the ship arrived at Sasebo, Japan.

Gil MacMillan: "That's a Navy port. We went ashore there but that's just the grog shops. You just go ashore and sit and drink."

It was a relief just to get off the ship for a few hours. It was a short break but it was a break. The return to a quiet port had a calming effect on everyone.

Gil MacMillan: "Having prisoners of war and then having all those refugees and then the army, it was a sad environment. It wasn't a happy ship, 'cause how could you be happy with all this misery around you. Basically starvation and hardship, this stuff. We had no idea how long they were going to hold us there. I don't think anybody cared too much, but most of us never thought we were going to be gone six months. About three months, most people thought."

There followed a series of shuttle runs, ferrying troops and supplies to and from Korean ports and Sasebo.

Ray Fullbright: "The ship called at Inchon, Pusan, Wonson and Hungnam. "We were on a shuttle service between these ports of call carrying supplies. We carried general cargo at times."

Departing Sasebo on Christmas Eve, 1950, the ship returned to the war zone.

Official Log, *Lane Victory*: "December 24, 1950 Crossed boundary line entered bonus area V at 38-18 North 128-08 East at 1238, 135 East Longitude time."

Christmas Day was spent at Inchon. The steward's department went all out with turkey dinner and the usual trimmings. A bowl of nuts and hard candy was placed on each table to mark the occasion.

Gil MacMillan: "I know they sure did a great job at Christmas time and Thanksgiving."

There was some entertainment. MacMillan recalled, "They had an engineer that liked to dress up in women's clothes and put on a Christmas program. Which, you know, by American standards it's a little bit weird, but under British standards it's done all the time. And I think the Europeans, they do entertain themselves by putting on skits and plays of a little more cultural nature than what we have."

The ship stayed at Inchon until January 7, 1951. After a brief stop at Taechau, Korea on the 8th, she sailed out of the war zone for the final time on this voyage. Her destination was again Sasebo.

Lane Victory, Official Logbook: "January 9, 1951 passed boundary line out of 100% area V at Lat 33-15 N. 128 06 E. at 1152, 135 East long. time.

Arriving in Sasebo the same day, Capt. Olson was told to stand by for further orders. From the military point of view it probably seemed like good planning. Hold the ship in reserve in case it was needed again. Who knew which way the war would go? There might be more evacuations, further invasions. One more ship held in "hot" reserve made good sense. But from the point of view of the ship itself, and the effect on the crew, it was another case of that constant problem — idle time.

By the time the ship was routed back to the States at the end of the month, the effects of "nothing to do" were showing.

On January 25, one of the crew went ashore although he was supposed to be on watch. At 1245, an hour after he was told to stand his watch, he was discovered ashore without permission. He was logged two days' pay for being absent from his duty station. When questioned by the captain as to why he disobeyed, he refused to give a reply.

When sailing time approached, the crew had to be rounded up ashore.

Gil MacMillan: "We had some drunken crew we had to bring back in bumboats. And I know we had some pretty young ABs there. They were drinking an awful lot and there could be discipline problems. I got in a fight with one, in fact I got a hit on the face. I hated to hit a drunk, but I did and then I think the old man logged him about that. Hitting an officer. But I considered that was just a drunken kid. I saw my duty was to make sure the crew got back safe on this launch and that was when he took a swing at me. Well I hit him one back pretty hard and even when I did that I didn't know whether I was doing the right thing. Whether I had the right to strike a sailor."

Some of the crew took advantage of the low prices to buy souvenirs in Japan. MacMillan bought a set of Noritake china which he uses to this day. "I went ashore in Sasebo and had all this money. At the last minute I bought a 150 piece china set for about $50 and that's my best china at home today. And they brought it down to the ship in a huge carton, with excelsior and all that stuff."

The crew was happy to leave Sasebo on January 27. They were finally heading home. Quickly settling into the routine of operating a ship at sea, with a purpose and a destination, they put the war behind them.

With the coming of electronic navigation — radar, loran and radio direction finders in the 1950's few captains used the taffrail log. Those that did were reluctant to give up the old ways, and hadn't learned to rely on modern navigation methods. Swedish-trained Capt. Olson was such a person. He insisted on the taffrail log being streamed and read at every opportunity.

The taffrail is the upper railing on the main deck at the stern of the ship. In sailing ship days the "chip log" was streamed or run from this location. Consisting of a small wooden partial circle tied at the end of a piece of line, it was used to determine how fast the vessel was going. The piece of wood acted as a drag, pulling the line out. The line was knotted at intervals and by counting how many knots passed in the time it took a sand glass to run, speed was determined. With the coming of the industrial age this device was replaced by a mechanical log, called the "taffrail log." The wood chip was replaced by an elongated propeller. The knotted line became braided cotton without knots. The propeller turned the line which was fastened to a series of dials at a gauge mounted on the taffrail itself. By reading from the gauge how many revolutions the propeller made during a given amount of time, speed could be determined. The problem with chip and taffrail logs is that they give you speed through the water, not speed over the ground. For example, if you stream either log while you are traveling four knots in a body of water that is traveling four knots in the opposite direction, the log will show you doing eight knots when in reality you are making zero in relation to the land under you. In short, a chip or taffrail log is not very accurate.

Third mate Gil MacMillan on the starboard bridge wing. Courtesy Gil MacMillan.

Gil MacMillan: "We cut it loose, we got so sick and tired of it. We just cut it loose one night, got rid of it. Told the captain that it tore off during the night.

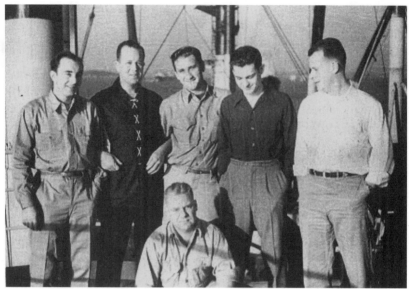

Some of the crew of the Lane Victory *on voyage 9. From left to right standing, Purser Ray Fullbright, Chief Mate William Chilcoat, Third Engineer Lloyd Trembly, Chief Electrician Karl Wasenius and Radio Operator Arti Aro. Seated, Second Mate Paul Oupe. Courtesy Gil MacMillan.*

Chief Electrician Karl Wasenius and Radio Operator Arti Aro during voyage 9. Courtesy Gil MacMillan.

Captain Marinus Olson, probably the most colorful skipper to command the Lane Victory *during her career. Courtesy Gil MacMillan.*

Purser Ray Fullbright somewhere in Korea on Voyage 9. Courtesy Gil MacMillan.

Olson was an old-timer, you know. He was one of these old squareheads that came up and the taffrail log, he wanted it. I remember he did shoot meridians, but, you know, he loved that log. The trouble with the taffrail log is you got to put it out. It's always getting seaweed. It's always getting crap. And it never was accurate, never. And we were getting sights all the time, what the hell, you know."

Without the war to distract them, petty incidents became the focus of the crew and officers.

MacMillan: "Chilcoat [chief mate] was always upset when I'd smoke a cigar on the bridge. None of his business, but he had an aversion to it."

Fullbright: "Olson. He saved every penny to send home to the family. He even would repair his shoes by taking odds and ends and nailing them to the soles of the old shoes. All in all, he was a good skipper."

The voyage ended in San Francisco on February 12, 1951.

Fullbright: "It was in the main a happy ship. All in all the *Lane Victory* was a good ship and I personally enjoyed my time aboard."

There was one thing to be settled after the ship arrived: the cold-weather gear taken from the warehouses in Korea.

Ray Fullbright: "On our return to the States, they [the marines] were waiting for us on arrival San Francisco and took them all back."

Gil MacMillan: "The military intelligence boarded the ship in San Francisco and made us give everything up. I thought

Third Mate Gil MacMillan dressed in some of the cold weather gear the crew liberated at Hungnam and was forced to give back in San Francisco. Courtesy Gil MacMillan.

it was dirty pool myself. I thought, God Damn it. It was going to be burned up. And it seemed to me that they should have issued it to us anyhow. But I guess they had their rules and regs and the guy had a job to do. So he come on the boat and right away he notified me. I was in charge of making sure it was all collected. They notified the customs too, to check us for any military stuff going ashore."

9

KOREA —
THE AFTERMATH

Voyage 10 commenced on February 23, 1951 from San Francisco with Marinus Olson as master. The next cargo waited in New Orleans. Sailing on February 24, the *Lane Victory* pointed her bow once more toward the Panama Canal.

With a full load of military goods for Korea, the ship sailed from New Orleans on March 20, stopped briefly at Los Angeles on April 3 for bunkers, then headed west. April 12, 1951 found her crossing the International Dateline at 29 degrees 14 minutes North Latitude.

Arriving in Ulson, Korea the ship discharged her cargo and began one of the most tedious periods of her career.

On April 26 when the ship sailed from Ulson, several of the sailors were intoxicated and unable to stand their watch. More than one was logged for being AWOL and many of them were fined one and two days' pay, for various offenses. It was just the beginning.

For weeks the ship shuttled between ports in Japan and Korea. Never staying more than a few days in each port, the crew felt as if they were constantly tying up and letting go: Pusan, Korea; Ulson, Korea; Moji, Japan; Pusan, Korea; Moji, Japan; Pusan, Korea; Moji, Japan; Pusan, Korea; Sasebo, Japan; Pusan, Korea; Yokohama, Japan.

Because the Korean conflict was still on, the crew received 100% bonuses for their time in the war zone. Traveling in and out of the zone so frequently made for pages of log entries. Ten days at one period, four another, here two days, there three — the total time was twenty-seven bonus days in the zone. But this did not alleviate the tedium.

Some of the crew showed their frustration in true seafaring fashion. There were more loggings for drunkenness, failure to turn to and missing the ship.

The ship finally got a respite. From Yokohama she sailed to Okinawa where she loaded ammunition for the Philippines. From the official log:

> June 21, 1951 ---- was smoking on the open deck port forward end of #5 hatch while stevedores were loading explosives in #5 'tween deck from barge LSU 1105 made fast on port side of #5 hatch. Cautioned about smoking he threw his lighted cigarette over his shoulder into the barge. Severely reprimanded for carelessness, became abusive. There are not less than 5 "No Smoking" signs visible from his position.

From Okinawa the *Lane* went to Subic Bay in the Philippines, where she discharged the ammo at anchorage. Sailing from Olongopo (the port for Subic Bay), on June 26, it appears the ship was released from military charter. Her remaining ports of call were those typical of a ship on American President Lines' "jungle run."

She loaded and sailed from Manila on June 30, Saigon, (in what was then French Indo-China) on July 7, Rangoon, Burma, on July 16, Kohsichang, Siam (now Thailand) on July 23, Saigon again on July 27, Manila again on August 4 and Guam on August 12.

The disciplinary entries for the crew on this voyage read as if there were a competition to see who could get into the most trouble.

"Absent 6/28/51 without sufficient reason.

"July 23rd, FTJ [Failed To Join].

"July 26 absent from duty, failed to turn to, etc . . ."

On this voyage twenty-seven incidents of AWOL, FTJ and other disciplinary matters were entered in the official log.

Manila seemed to have a particular effect on the crew. Several men were still ashore when the *Lane Victory* sailed on August 4. But one of the crew didn't want the ship to leave without him. The day before departure, he returned to the vessel after being in the hospital for several days. Stating that he would not stay at the hospital because he had been insulted by the doctor, he returned to work.

Crossing the International Dateline on August 17, 1951 at 1530 in Latitude 33 North, it was with hope for a better future that the ship sailed for San Francisco.

The voyage terminated in San Francisco on August 24 at midnight with Voyage 11 commencing one minute later.

John Mena and Phil Laudenschlager joined the ship in August of 1951. They had just graduated from California Maritime Academy and were getting their first taste of life on a merchant ship aboard the *Lane Victory.*

Phil Laudenschlager: "We were on the list in the [Union] hall and I think the only reason we got it, we were the two on the bottom. We had just gotten out of school. And this Marinus Olson had a reputation and the rest of them didn't want it. It was one of the charter ships that was government. They were long cruises. A lot of times that wasn't so interesting to some of the older people who just wanted to go out for three months and come back."

John Mena: "The first time I ever heard of the *Lane Victory* was when I got on her. We both took off and went down

Junior Third Mate John Mena on board his first ship out of California Maritime Academy — the Lane Victory, Voyage *11. Courtesy John Mena.*

to the union hall and got hired by APL who was the general agent for operating the ship with MARAD. It was a pierhead jump. We got on the ship in the middle of the night."

Phil Laudenschlager: "I signed on first. I didn't know John was going to be on there until later in the evening. It was sailing sometime late that night. As I recall it was eleven o'clock at night. So I was almost moved on when there I see John coming up with all his stuff.

"That's why I was signed on as the third and John was signed on as the junior third. He was a little after I was, as far as signing on was concerned. He had the 8-to-12. 1 had the 12-to-4."

"John and I were the only ones that were under fifty, I think. Almost all of them were much older."

Sailing from San Francisco on the 28th of August, John got his baptism under Marinus Olson. His first watch on his new license was something that he remembers to this day.

"The crew we had was raw. The deck hands had just got their seaman's papers. The first watch I stood, you know you come up ten or fifteen minutes before the hour. Midnight was going to be eight bells. So I was standing there and the guy goes one, two, three, four, five, six, seven, eight, nine . . . He rang twelve bells in succession and they weren't paired off. The guys were just totally green."

Phil Laudenschlager: "I'm not so sure that they were green so much as they just hadn't sailed in a long time. They were old, old sailors and they were just coming back because the jobs were available. The chief mate hadn't sailed for, I don't know, two or three years, and then he got this ship. The chief engineer, I don't think he'd sailed for a couple of years before."

John Mena: "I had the watch when we left. We had no radar and the gyro compass wasn't working well so we had to use magnetic. We got to the pilot station in the fog. The pilot had gotten off and the old man brought her around to the course he wanted. Called the engine room and said, 'O.K., Hook'er up.'

"Then he said to me, 'All right Mister Mate, I'm going down and turn in. Keep her on course.'

"Then I realized he hadn't told me to blow the fog signals. Of course we were going full speed in the fog. So I said, 'The least I could do, I guess, is blow the whistle.'

"So I started blowing the whistle. The phone rang. The old man said, 'Knock it off, I can't sleep.'

"So there I was going full speed in the fog, not even sounding the signals. I was scared to death."

The trip south to the Panama Canal was relatively quiet.

Phil Laudenschlager: "We were just light, in ballast and that was a pretty uneventful trip. The old skipper wanted the hands to get out there and paint every day and all this kind of stuff. And they really weren't ready to do all that."

John Mena: "We went to Gulfport, Mississippi to pick up pilings, creosoted pilings, and railroad timbers and that sort of thing for Korea."

Phil Laudenschlager: "Railroad ties in the hold and creosote pilings on deck. That was my first experience with southern stevedores. Those guys worked their tails off, boy. Most all of them were black. It took them six days to load the ship and then when we got over to Pusan it took over a month to unload it.

"It was a very typical southern town, more southern in the sense that the town itself was dry and all the way around on the city limits were all these dance halls and stuff. No drinking at all within the city limits. That was our first experience with that kind of stuff too."

With a full load on board, the *Lane Victory* departed Gulfport, Mississippi on September 18.

This trip might be called the Voyage of Groundings. Where a ship may go through her entire life without touching bottom, the *Lane Victory* grounded twice on this voyage.

John Mena: "While we were coming out they lost the plant and we went up in the mud. That was no great problem. They backed off all right when they got the plant back on the line. We took off and went around to Pusan."

Phil Laudenschlager: "What happened was we were in the channel, sand channel. Down there . . . big sandy long stretches where it's very shallow. Sand just drifts out from the runoff of the Mississippi River there. So the channel was narrow and as we was going along there we were brushing the sides of the channel and the sand was getting in the condensers and that's why they had to shut down. The engine was heating up. More than they really grounded, we had to stop and wait until they could flush the sand out of the condensers.

"We just sort of sat there. It was a flat day. We could see for miles. It was kind of warm, the humidity down there, but there wasn't any wind at all. It was just like glass out there."

Underway again, the ship left the Mississippi, transited the Panama Canal and pointed her bow northward. As the voyage progressed John Mena developed a grudging admiration for the captain.

John Mena: "I liked the old guy, but, you know, there was nothing very sophisticated about him. He would lean up on the porthole and tell sea stories.

"We were going by Acapulco. He was ready to stake me to an endeavor in Acapulco if I wanted to set up a restaurant. He was ready to give me the money. I'd only been with him a short while. I didn't know anything about the restaurant business."

As the ship approached Wilmington, California for fuel, one of the crew was injured.

Phil Laudenschlager: "The purser slipped in the damn shower. I guess he was filing suit because he was claiming it wasn't kept clean; slick and slimy in the shower. This happened at sea on the way from Gulfport to Wilmington, in that trip back around from the canal. We were coming up the West Coast and we transferred him to some boat out there that we met. He was strapped into that wire stretcher thing. He did something to his back and they took him to the hospital."

"We stopped in Long Beach for fuel and the bosun left, the original bosun left. This Ed Lewis, Bosun that came on, they were all upset with Marinus because he was pretty strong on running the ship the way he wanted it and wanting things done when he wanted them done and no questions asked. The bosun that left was just fed up with him and this guy was a member of the union that really didn't sail a lot but he came on because the union wanted to check into what was going on.

"The biggest thing that I remember in Wilmington was when we were trying to leave. We were trying to leave in the middle of the night and everybody had to get back by nine or ten o'clock in the evening. There wasn't a sober hand on deck. There wasn't a single one. The radio operator had to man the wheel. I know I had the watch going out and the bosun and Al Saar the maintenance man . . . The bosun took the stern and Saar took the bow and brought in the lines all by themselves. They were the only ones sober enough to do it. Then after we finally got out of the harbor, out off the point there, we got one of the ABs, an old fellow, he could barely see, but anyway at least he could stand up, so he took the wheel from the radio operator. It was not long after that the second mate came up and took over. But about four of us took the ship out."

After a few days the ship settled into a normal routine. It lasted until the onset of the first bad weather.

Phil Laudenschlager: "We were on government routing which was the long way around. Anyway, we did hit some weather on that last leg. With all that damn piling on deck we were sitting pretty low. That creosote stuff is pretty heavy anyway and we had a lot of water all over. At times a few of them would go clear over the top of the wheelhouse. I guess it was one of those typhoons, coming up from southern Japan marching over into the North Pacific. So we just slowed way down and took it on the quarter for a while until it calmed down a bit."

From a letter Phil wrote to his mother,

The Pacific isn't very Pacific out here. So far we have run into two typhoons and a gale and haven't seen the sun for more than four hours at a time since we left San Pedro. The sea keeps breaking over the bow and all besides keeping everything wet and salty. And everybody inside. You may have heard of the one we just went through the edge of. It's one that came up from the China Sea with winds up to 120 m.p.h.. We got some 50 m.p.h. winds and had water breaking all over the place. So far we haven't lost or broken much except the catwalk built over the deck load was broken up once and my lifeboat got shifted in its chock. Otherwise nothing. It's kind of pretty to see the bow go crashing down into the water and dip out a couple of tons of it splashing spray all over for the wind to catch and blow out into a wall of foam. So think that if it hit you it would knock you over and soak you to the skin. I just stand on the bridge and look out at the nearest swell which at times is above my eye level, which is 37 feet above the water line, and hope that we can come up to go over it before it crashes and breaks. The ones that break over the ship are the ones that do the damage as you can understand if you look up at one as it's coming at you.

John Mena: "We went through a hell of a typhoon. It was abating and he [the captain] brought the ship around and rode before the storm. He was right out there crawling over those logs checking the lashings. He was around seventy-eight at the time. He was quite a guy.

"We were in a storm one night and the able-bodied seaman was sent back to do something or other. He came back in the wheelhouse. The ship rolled as he stepped in. He ran right into the [engine order] telegraph. It had a pole that went up to the flying bridge. He ran right into that sucker and knocked himself out. It was darker than heck. We're in a storm and this guy's passed out on the deck."

The first port of call was Sasebo, to await further orders.

Phil Laudenschlager: "We were anchored pretty much in the north of the bay up by the city. I went ashore there a couple of times but we weren't there long. There wasn't much going on at all that I recall in that port."

From Sasebo the ship went to Pusan.

Phil Laudenschlager: "We were laying on some buoys and they had all these barges, lighter barges come around and they fill them up and haul them away. It took us over thirty days in that port to unload all those pilings. That was our first experience with the twenty-four hour shifts that they worked over there."

"And that stuff that they [the stevedores] ate. We called it Kim Chee but now I know it wasn't Kim Chee. It was really just fish heads. They'd have twenty, twenty-five maybe thirty stevedores on board. They ran twenty-four hour shifts. So probably three or four of them are sleeping somewhere all the time. They would come on at meal time and I think they'd feed twice during that twenty-four hours. The guy would come on with like a shoulder yoke and two of these big pails about that big around and they'd be full of rice. And then this pot, about a quart pot of this stuff that stunk terrible. But, anyway, then they'd all get up and bring their little shingle or whatever they had and that was for their scoop of rice and a little bit of this on top. To eat. They were always hungry and skinny as rails. That was just part of the reason it took so damn long to get the stuff off of there. They just were undernourished. Sometimes it would take fifteen or twenty minutes just to bring a pallet out, with those ties.

"About half of the crew, especially at night, about half the crew would just curl up in a corner of the hold some place. Loading would stop. Eight in the morning was when the shift changed. In many respects it was a pretty good deal for them because nobody really kept after them. I don't think anybody really expected them to work twenty-four hours straight through a whole shift. So at least they had a dry, warm place to sleep.

"Somebody said out of all the lighters that we filled up with those ties, only about two-thirds of them made it to where they were going. The rest of them got sidetracked, stolen. Disappeared along the way."

Stealing barge loads of railroad ties was but one type of enterprise.

John Mena: "They stole fire nozzles, hawsers."

It seemed that everyone had a "deal" of some type going on.

Phil Laudenschlager: "There was a guy who was one of the foremen, or he worked in the agent's office. Anyway, he was trying to buy clothes. I had an old double breasted suit, I sold them that. They'd take off their clothes, put that right on, put their clothes on over the top of that. It wasn't cold, it was pretty warm, so they could get off the ship. And they'd pay primarily military script for it. That damned double-breasted suit I'd had for two or three years, and he paid eighty dollars for it, something like that. And I know that the crew sold quite a bit of stuff there too."

The refugees the *Lane Victory* helped evacuate from Wonson on its first voyage had settled in.

"The living conditions, where those people were living at that time, were really, really, really bad. They had all those little shack cities that they just put up. It was really just loaded with refugees. That's what it amounted to. It didn't look in the least bit inviting to me. I remember one time we walked up on a hillside, and this gal had these kids up there and she was teaching them how to use the abacus. Sort of a sunny afternoon. But just downhill of them was acres of these little shacks made out of pasteboard boxes and anything they could make them out of. And, of course, no sewers, just ditches for sewers. And they'd come by with those insecticide planes and spray insecticide over the city. Spray everything, especially over these little refugee areas. Just to try to keep some of the disease down. Of course the enterprising ones were making money but the run of the mill people weren't."

Some of the officers and crew found diversions other than the typical wine, women and song, not much of which, in any case, was available in these ports.

Phil Laudenschlager: "Pete Kelder was a real artistic type. He wanted to go up and see the temples that were outside of Pusan. We went in the morning. He talked the agent into driving up there in the jeep they had. We had to go up over the mountains to get there.

"We visited some of the temples and they'd been just raided and stripped by the northern people or the Chinese or whoever it was that was in there. What was left, they were trying to organize and get back into shape. As we were coming back on the road the Army stopped us and told us 'Hey, you guys better stay here cause we're having trouble with guerrillas out there.'

"The agent and Kelder decided it couldn't be that bad so away we go. The agent knew the road real well, so he says, 'We'll go. We'll make it through.'

"We took off on down. We never saw a thing or heard anything, but we ran into some other Army patrols that were out there going around in the bushes and off the road. But we got on back without any problem."

Sailing on November 8, the next port was Masan, Korea.

Phil Laudenschlager: "Masan, yeah, it's maybe a hundred miles, seventy to a hundred miles south of Pusan. There's a whole lot of islands and it's protected inside these islands. We were at a dock there.

"We picked up a whole bunch of old shot-up tanks, trucks, junk. That was pretty hairy there, too, because the pilot really wasn't a pilot. He had a job as a pilot, but he didn't know anything about being a pilot. And so we had gone in there and they had a tugboat. The tug just banged into the side of the ship. The bow, of course, had a big pad on the front but they put a fairly good size dent in the side of the ship. But this is because they didn't know how to operate the darn thing. I guess it was an army tug but they had a Korean crew. Something that the army just threw in there for them to use. They knew they were going to load this equipment out of there."

Unskilled labor wasn't limited to tugboats. Phil Laudenschlager remembered stevedore problems. "That's where they dropped a damned tank with the heavy gear. It landed on deck or on the edge of the hatch combing. It seems to me the guy let the topping lift come down and then he tried to stop it. He was so low he couldn't stop it. The weight was too much and it just pulled it right on down."

From Masan on November 12, the ship sailed for Yokohama.

Phil Laudenschlager: "It was a real clear day when we came into Tokyo Bay and you could see Fuji, sticking up over there."

John Mena: "We were anchored out there in Tokyo Bay for three or four days waiting for dock space. We were full of all that stuff we brought from Masan and waiting for dock space to get in to Yokohama to offload and load up again and go out."

Phil Laudenschlager: "Offloaded the stuff there. They were going to rebuild it in Yokohama. What we did then was reload rebuilt stuff to take back.

"We backloaded repaired vehicles. That was our first experience with the Japanese stevedores. Boy, that was really something to see. They'd pick those huge, great, big D-4 bulldozers and set'em right down within inches of all of the gear and stuff on deck and really set them in there, get them all chocked in, tied down. And really a treat to see them handle cargo after seeing those Koreans. Of course, when they were loading that junk they were essentially just throwing it in the hold. They just put it down, shoved it over in a corner, blocked it up and just left it. Smash the next one against it. The tighter they could pack them in the less they had to tie down. We took back a lot of tanks, but what we brought from Yokohama was primarily the bigger gear, heavier equipment; bulldozers, graders, construction equipment rather than military stuff."

From a letter Phil wrote home on November 27, 1951: "We've been sitting in Tokyo Bay for about 20 days now . . . Japan is pretty nice, I went up to Tokyo last weekend. I was surprised at how modern and big it is."

Pat Barham, a war correspondent for the *Los Angeles Herald Express* devoted a column to her impressions of Japan at the time:

> The streets of Tokyo remind you a little bit of Michigan Avenue in Chicago when an iced wind winds itself around your neck and face and makes your teeth chatter like a whistle stop. By way of contrast however, there are other nights in Tokyo too that are almost balmy, its a strange land of shadows and contrasts. And great natural beauty . . .
>
> Where else can one see the scenic beauties of a land surrounded on five sides by the sea; the waters of the East China Sea, the Japan Sea, the Pacific Ocean, the Inland Sea, and the Okhotsk Ocean. Where one can lose himself in such retreats as Nikko. From here stems a city of golden temples, running rivers with fresh trout, snow-capped mountains and skiers and sledders breathing the frosty air with flushed red cheeks and matching noses. There are winding streets with antique dealers inviting tourists in to view old world treasures begging to be bought . . .
>
> Aside from all this scenic splendor, I enjoyed knowing the people themselves. Their cooperative attitudes are refreshing in a world that seems to boast of jaded tastes.
>
> The things I didn't like in Japan begin with the way everyone says "yes" in an effort to be over polite even when they didn't understand what you mean at all. Rather than hurt your feelings, they pretend they understand and it's usually an extra 10 blocks out of your way in a cab as the penalty for this politeness. If they'd only say I don't understand.
>
> I didn't like the plumbing system either . . . In this land of the honey bucket which although is caricatured in typical funny-land fashion throughout Japan on postcards or on ashtrays is, to me, actually "unfunny" possibly due to the peculiar construction of the bowls themselves . . . And along these lines, I did not like the

aroma either . . . If only some one would import quantities of chlorophyll . . .

I didn't like to see the prostitutes who must of necessity flaunt their charms, on the streets, day and night. These are girls who can't get jobs in Japan and so they have turned to this. They got the vote under General MacArthur but they can't eat it — they say . . .

I didn't like the heating system, on the whole, in Japan. The Japanese house or hotel is built for soft lights, sukiyaki and sake. Baby it's cold outside but in Japan, it's cold inside too. The halls always remain unheated even though the hibachi gives spare warmth to a tiny bedroom . . .

I didn't like the buckwheat husk pillows either. But then I've always had a hard head and the combination of a hard pillow and a hard head is not conducive to sleeping on a cloud . . .

I didn't like the some 5,000 orphans left here by our own GI's registered with the Japanese police department in Japan. Any soldier should be compelled by law to provide for his own progeny. If she isn't good enough to take home to mother, then she shouldn't be permitted to share his bed and board while in Japan either . . . even if it's here."

Phil Laudenschlager: "Olson loved fish. He'd buy that ashore. We didn't have a lot of fish on there. He'd go to the fish markets in Japan, you know, and that was fresh fish. I don't know what he would do with it. He probably talked the steward into cooking it for him."

John Mena: "He was always eating fish. Fish in the morning, fish at noon, fish at night. He always had a toothpick in his mouth, picking his teeth."

Fully loaded and with orders to return to Korea, the *Lane Victory* sailed from Yokohama on December 3. The shortest route was through the Inland Sea and Shimonoseki Straits, between the islands of Honshu and Kyushu.

Phil Laudenschlager: "We were taking it back there. That's when we went aground in Moji."

John Mena: "They had two pilots. They'd pick you up when you entered the Inland Sea. Pick up the first pilot and drop him off before you enter Shimonoseki Straits. Pick up the other pilot. We got as far as picking up the second pilot.

"You know how the third mate is the guy that gets the coffee. The pilot came out, I says, 'You want a cup of coffee, Pilot?'

"He says, 'Yeah, I want coffee,' and immediately asks for his binoculars. He couldn't locate his binoculars.

"'They're around your neck,' says the old man.

"And I went down and I got the coffee. We approached the entrance to the Shimonoseki Straits and the old man came in. I'm not taking bearings. I'm just listening for orders and handling the telegraph. The old man was on the starboard wing. He comes in and he says, 'Hey, Pilot. That buoy was awful close. Aren't we supposed to be making a left turn?'

"'Oh, yeah.' The pilot says. 'Left easy.'

"The old man says, 'Left easy, my ass. Hard left.'

"And you could see the bow coming around. I didn't know what the hell was going on. All of a sudden you see this flashing light up ahead of us. And every once in a while it would flash into the wheelhouse. I figured, well that's what we're trying to clear. And then the old man says, 'Stop the engines.'

"The pilot says, 'No. no, no. It's dangerous here. Strong current. Don't stop.'

"The old man says, 'Get out of here. You got me in enough trouble already.'

"About that time you could see this light dead ahead. The ship went up and bang, it just stopped. Fortunately it was a sandy to gravel bottom. The old man stopped the engine."

Phil Laudenschlager: "I was going to have the watch at midnight so I had gone to bed right after dinner. We were going through the Sea of Japan and the we hadn't picked up the pilot yet. John had just gone on watch to relieve the second and they picked up the pilot to go through Moji straits. I was laying in my bunk and all of a sudden I felt the ship sort of lurch. 'That doesn't sound right.'

"I got up and I looked out the porthole and the lights all looked awful close and so I says 'Oh, my gosh.'

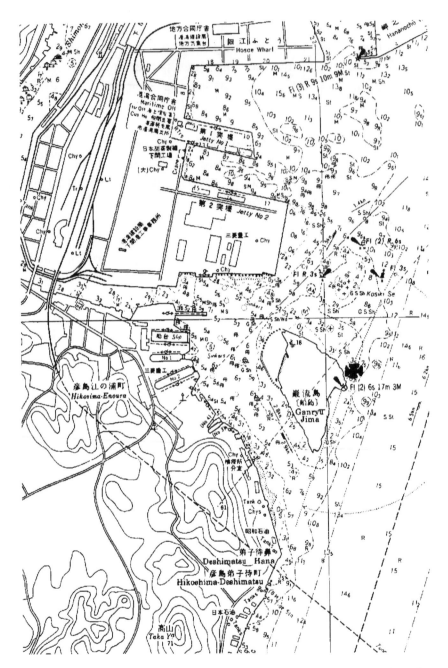

Ganryu Jima where the Lane Victory *went aground on Voyage 11. Note the current vectors of 6.2 and 6.5 knots adjacent to the island. This is a very difficult area to navigate. Courtesy Capt. Pat Moloney.*

The Lane Victory *aground at Ganryu Jima. Note the lighthouse dead ahead and the absence of water on the starboard side. Courtesy John Mena.*

"So I says, 'Well I'm going to have to go on watch pretty soon, maybe, maybe it'll be all right. Maybe it'll be over by then.'

"Then I got called up and went up there on the bridge and here's the lighthouse right over the front of the bow."

John Mena: "The pilot came in and said, 'Why did you stop? These are dangerous waters.' Then he went over and sat down and went to sleep.

"The old man says, 'By God, man, we are aground!'

"The pilot was over there snoring.

"I was scared to death. I could see visions of my license going out the window. He called the company (American President Lines) in Kobe. A guy by the name of Capt. O'Hara came out. The Coast Guard was notified. They were out there for twenty-four hours taking affidavits and then they bailed out.

Nobody was cited, even. They said that Shimonoseki was the hotbed of communist pilots and there were ships going aground there like they were going out of style. There was nothing new about a ship going aground in Shimonoseki. They took off. Never saw them again."

"The island was named Ganryu Jima. It was an historical island where the best samurai swordsman from Kyushu met the best samurai swordsman from Honshu. The guy from Kyushu won.

Phil Laudenschlager: "We learned quite a bit about that island from the local people. They evidently had quite a history. The warriors of the king were fighting over some woman and the battleground was that island. The other guy finally won. The one killed in the battle was more of a favorite than the other.

"Of course, when we went ashore we were the laughing stock of the town. 'Ha, ha. YOU guys got that ship up there.'"

Few American ships make Moji a port of call. As a result the people the crew ran into ashore were less mercenary than in ports that normally dealt with the American dollar.

Phil Laudenschlager: "That was the thing about Moji. The people were much more congenial. Not so commercial. They weren't pressing after you all the time for your business."

The crew had all admired a new Japanese tug they saw working in the harbor. It had the latest type of propulsion, vertical propeller blades.

John Mena: "I remember looking over at Moji on a windy day. A Liberty ship had let go from a buoy and the wind caught it. It didn't have enough speed or power to control itself and it got blown down on the dock where the tug was. You could see its prop going around fanning the breeze. It cut a hole in just about every small craft that was alongside, including that fancy tug with the vertical blades. It sunk right there at the dock. The ship finally cleared the pier and went out and anchored."

John Mena: "They had the [U.S.] Navy come out and try to get us off. First we lightened the ship a bit. Took some cargo off into barges, then took the barges over to Moji. They brought out a Navy tug and put on a tow line. They started pulling at slack water. The tide changed. They didn't even budge us. The tug started moving upstream, the tide was dragging him down. Then he was abeam and then he was going down the stream. He was caught between the tide and the tow line. He couldn't go any further and he started heeling over. He got his overboard discharge under the water and his engines conked out. They had to cut the towline. Then they lightened the ship some more. It was almost five days for them to get us off. They had almost all the cargo out."

Phil Laudenschlager: "They had to offload a whole lot of this stuff and put it on lighters and barges. It wasn't until they actually got a full sized seagoing tug that they finally pulled us off.

"Fortunately it was a sandy bottom. They sent some divers down to check it out after they took it off and decided it didn't do any major damage . . . put a few ripples in it but that was it. Then they had to reload all the stuff off the lighters."

When the ship sailed from Moji on December 19, most of the crew hoped they wouldn't see it again. At least in Pusan the ship was just another freighter rather than the center of attention.

John Mena: "In Pusan they were all hungry. People were stealing bread out of the kitchen. We were told, 'don't let these guys sleep in the holds because they build fires.'

"At the end of a cargo watch you go along checking things. I saw a guy's arm sticking out between a pile of lumber and I said, 'Hey you. Get out of there.'

"About fifteen guys came out of the cargo hold."

On another occasion, "I looked over the fantail. There were two guys with their fannies hanging over the pierside taking care of business. One guy started falling back. He reached out to his friend to keep himself from falling over. They both fell in the drink and one of them drowned.

"One of the deckhands on the ship gave the guard at the gate my name as being his, and told them he was the third mate.

They caught him down on the black market with this ham that belonged to the ship, trying to sell it. So an MP came aboard and tried to throw me in jail because I had walked off the ship with a ham."

Sailing from Pusan on Christmas Day, the ship went to Kunsan.

John Mena: "We went into Kunsan, Korea and the tide range in Korea is fantastic. All this was new to me. I was a fresh cut third mate. We had an army sergeant for a pilot. We went up this damn river into the anchorage area. There was a little Japanese coastal freighter in there, right in the middle of the anchorage. And this pilot took the ship right on up, placed the bow right over the bow of the little coastal freighter and dropped the hook. It bounced off the bow of the coastal freighter. And he said, 'Get that damn thing out of here.' He made him move it.

"We were running into a high tide and they brought the barges alongside. The barges were riding to a hawser that was taut because the tide was running. I looked over the side about the time the tide changed and I noticed there was a Korean guy sitting on a bitt leaning back on the lines, dozing. There was a small boat alongside with a guy in it with a scull. The tide changed so fast the dang line went slack and this guy fell in the water. I guess none of them know how to swim. The current was running so fast, and the other fella on the boat took off after him sculling that boat. I don't know if he ever got him.

"When that tide finished running there was nothing but mud where we were sitting all the way out to the beach."

As sailing time approached it was necessary to round up the crew ashore.

John Mena: "Coming back to the ship in a liberty launch and the operator locked himself in the cabin with a drunk sailor. I guess he didn't want everybody walking in and out. The drunk sailor wanted to take over the wheel. They were fighting in the cabin and the damn boat was running without directions. It was running right to the side of the ship. He had the window open and somebody got his hand in there and turned that wheel so we missed the side of the ship. Talk about drunken sailors. I don't know how we survived."

Sailing from Kunsan on December 30, the ship went to Sasebo.

John Mena: "We spent a lot of time in Sasebo. Spent New Year's night, 1952 in Sasebo. The old man didn't want the whistle blown during New Year's night. The radio operator got up in the stack where the cord [to the whistle] was. He started blowing the whistle. The old man was calling the engineers, 'You better fix that damn whistle.'"

From Sasebo the *Lane Victory* went to Naha, Okinawa.

Phil Laudenschlager: "You didn't see him (Olson) very often. He'd come down to eat and that was about it. That used to bother the hell out of Tom (second mate) and I, too, really. On the trip going down between Sasebo and Okinawa we ran into some fog and, Holy Jesus, you couldn't see anything. And, of course, we didn't have any radar. I called him up and told him, 'The damn fog, we oughta start blowing the whistle.'

"And 'Ah no, no, no. It keeps me avake.'

"So we survived it somehow. Of course, fortunately, most of those trips the route that we took was dictated. It was usually an out-of-the-way route. It wasn't in the sea lanes so you had at least some security that way.

"After we left Sasebo, which was right after the first of the year, we went down to Okinawa and loaded up a bunch of stuff they had down there. That was an interesting little trip because Okinawa was pretty much totally run by the Army. And in fact we went down there, we were light. We were light and another typhoon was going through so we had to anchor out on the lee side of the island before we could go into the port the next day. Buckner Bay was where we went in. We were out there overnight before we could get in and then we must have been four days at least in Okinawa.

"That was one of the places where Ellis [the chief Mate] was out at the army bases buying all the jewelry he could find. He was an interesting old guy. He was married and he had a penchant, an attraction for buying all this jewelry for his wife. He was always buying rings and diamonds and stuff. He must have had ten thousand dollars worth of jewelry when we got back."

One of the worst sailors in the crew was Torres. "He just went out and got drunk. He got drunk at every port he went to. He'd go crazy you know. He was beating up on some MP's and stuff . . . some bar and they threw him in jail. I don't think the captain went to get him out, I think the purser had to go get him out. I think they waited until the ship was going to sail. Then the captain fined him."

John Mena: "[Olson] used to go ashore and buy army skivvies."

Phil Laudenschlager: "He'd come down to the wardroom to get something to eat, middle of the night, in his skivvies, in his army, olive drab skivvies. He always had a toothpick in his mouth. He was a huge lumbering guy. He must have been six foot-three or so. He must have weighed 250 pounds, most all of it was muscle."

Olson had a sense of humor that came out in strange ways.

John Mena: "He thought he could take lines of sight in a fog so thick you couldn't see the end of your nose. He'd say, 'See that island, Mister Mate?'

"I said, 'No, Sir.'

"He said, 'Well, I can't make you see it, but, doggone it, *I* can.'

"He'd take a sight on the damn thing and then he'd go in and lay it down on the chart. And he'd put it right about where he wanted it and he'd draw this big dark line down there. He'd have me go read the taffrail log while he was doing this 'cause he trusted implicitly on the taffrail log. He'd always adjust it so that it would give him the speed he wanted. He'd get the dead reckoning fix."

Phil Laudenschlager: "We had to have that running. That was the only thing he'd believe. He'd go out and read that . . .

He had somebody go out there and rig that thing and . . . I think the second mate had to go read it. I never had to go read it. As far as I can recall, he was the only one that ever went out and read it. He'd come back and make some more marks on the chart, piss off the second mate."

John Mena: "That sucker always got it to where he was going. It was really the second mate that was getting him there."

Phil Laudenschlager: "He had no sympathy for either John or I, 'Young kids.'

"He'd come out at every noon and the second mate was out taking his latitude and the captain was right behind him taking his. Check on him. And he used to hate that. Oh, he'd get so mad. The second mate. 'What the hell am I doing this for if he's going to do it.'

"He'd go in there and he'd get his pencil and he'd make these scribbly great heavy lines across the chart. The second mate would go, he was very neat and precise and lettered everything carefully and the captain would come in there and draw the damn lines on there and mess it all up. He couldn't erase it because they were too heavy."

John Mena: "After Pusan, we shuttled between mainly Japan and war ports, like Okinawa and Kunsan and those places, picking up busted-up tanks and military material. So we shuttled around for six months or so and then came back to the United States."

One of Capt. Olson's chief complaints was about having to give the sailors shots for venereal disease. John Mena once heard him say: "All these guys do is go ashore and they never take care of themselves and they come back and they want me to give them a shot."

Phil Laudenschlager: "It was the purser that was supposed to handle the medicine chest there and the captain was complaining 'cause he was using up too much stuff. Too much medicine. He was really in everything, cutting corners. He even looked at you kind of funny if you asked for a second helping at a meal."

The final trip into Yokohama stayed in Phil Laudenschlager's memory because of the unusual cargo they carried. 'We brought back a big forty-five foot crash boat across the deck, across the top of the hatch. When we got up to Yokohama they had to float out this huge, huge floating crane to get it off. I know we had to wait to get that crane to get the boat off and that was a couple of days. It was bigger than our gear could handle, we had about thirty tons I guess."

Again it was a case of hurry up and wait. While at anchor waiting for a berth, some of the officers got mischievous. Phil Laudenschlager: "We were under radio silence. We were sitting in Tokyo Bay at anchor waiting. They had this Armed Services Radio broadcast that we were listening to and they wanted requests. So we talked the radio operator into going up and breaking radio silence and put in a request for Marinus Olson. So he did it and sure enough half an hour later on the air, 'The crew of the *Lane Victory* wants to wish Marinus Olson a happy birthday from them.'

"That was pretty funny. We thought that was a big kick. I don't think Marinus even heard it."

After unloading they were again told to wait for further orders. But eventually that, too, ended.

"That was the end of that. We waited there for a couple of days to get something else and they decided to send us on back. So we ballasted down and it was snowing, I remember it was snowing in Yokohama."

The *Lane Victory* sailed from Yokohama in early February, 1952.

Phil Laudenschlager: "We always had that reconstituted milk which wasn't that great. Whenever we got into a port the steward would go out and get some pretty good food and we'd have food for a while. He was pretty good about having something when you get up at night to go on watch. There was something there. Chief electrician, he made coffee. He made the best damn coffee. Percolator. And he'd be up there all times of day and night."

But John Mena considered the ship an unhappy ship. mostly due to the attitude of the chief mate.

"The first mate was one of those no overtime guys. One night the block on the heavy lift broke loose. It hadn't been secured properly. The ship was rolling in a heavy sea and the block was swinging from one side of the ship to the other as the ship rolled. I called the old man and he said, 'Get ahold of the mate and have him break the gang out and secure that block.'

"So the mate went down to break out the gang. The gang said, 'Sorry, we don't want the overtime.'

"They were pulling that kind of stuff. The mate wouldn't give them overtime when they needed it. The ship looked like a rust bucket.

"So he took me, I was the mate on watch, left the helmsman up there by himself. I went down with the standby and the mate, who was an older man, and we tried to snub down that block. We did. We damned near killed ourselves, throwing a line around it to snub it down."

Phil Laudenschlager: "The chief mate, Ellis, he'd tell the bosun what he wanted done and then he'd disappear. Never see him. And then nothing would happen, the crew wouldn't do any thing that he really wanted them to. They didn't want to be bothered. It was just lack of respect. They knew he didn't know anything. I don't even know that he was particularly competent in the first place. Nice guy. Sit and talk to you for hours. But. . . ."

John Mena: "It was an unhappy ship and that's why most of the people got off when they returned to Portland. The mate stayed on, the old man stayed on. They got almost an entirely new crew."

Phil Laudenschlager: "It was unhappy in the sense that there were things that the crew was concerned about. But they were pleased on that trip back to Portland because they were going to end the voyage. So they were all looking forward to getting off, that was for sure."

John Mena: "We got to Portland, Oregon, and most of the crew got off because she was going into the yard, we thought. And they turned her around and put her on a grain run to India."

The deck officers on Voyage 11 of the Lane Victory. *From left to right, Junior Third Mate John Mena, Third Mate Phil Laudenschlager, Second Mate James L. Singleton, Chief Mate Frank R. Ellis and Captain Marinus Olson. Courtesy John Mena.*

Phil Laudenschlager: "When we left the ship in Portland they were getting ready to repaint it. They terminated all the charter contracts, 'cause they were painting over all the APL stuff. I can't remember the name of the agency. But I guess it was the Navy Sea Transport. NSA. It may have been MSTS at that time. Anyway, they took over and that's when Stilleke got on. As far as I knew the APL charter had ended and what may have happened, they may have entered into a different kind of a charter where all they did was provide the crew."

Voyage 11 terminated in Portland, Oregon on February 19, 1952. The ship would load grain on her next voyage but this time the destination was not in the Far East. She was bound for England.

10

ATLANTIC SHUTTLE

O nce again the *Lane Victory* would sail the Atlantic waters. Taken off government charter, American President Lines was allowed to continue operating her on a time charter basis.

Commencing one minute after midnight on February 23, 1952, voyage 12 began in Portland, Oregon.

James Stilleke was a classmate of John Mena and Phil Laudenschlager. An engineer, he was flown from San Francisco to Portland to catch the ship. His classmates left one day and he joined the next. Almost literally passing in the night, they didn't know until years later how close they came to sailing together on the same ship.

His official discharge shows James Stilleke as joining the ship on February 22.

"I took that job because it was going someplace that looked interesting, that was the fun of it. There was no sense in going on the damn Filipino run all the time.

"When I went to the union hall it was on the board in San Francisco. They usually said where you were going to go and it said United Kingdom. I said, 'Damn, that sounds interesting. I wouldn't mind going over there.'

"So I ran downstairs and called the office and got a hold of the port engineer over there and I says, 'Where the hell is that thing going?'

"He says, 'England, Ireland, or Scotland.'

"I says, 'Well, hell, I never been there, I'll give it a shot.'

"So I threw my card in and got the job.

"They flew us from San Francisco. That was an interesting ride. We got on the airplane, an old DC-something with propellers, at San Francisco airport. We come out of there and banked and God Damn our port engine was fartin' and snarlin' and flames was coming out of it. So they set down in Oakland and we stayed three or four hours while they were changing spark plugs and doing this, that and the other thing. They finally got it running right and we went on in to Portland. We were supposed to be in Portland that afternoon early enough to clear the union hall and get the ship. We got in late enough that night that we had to get a hotel room and stay overnight and go to the union hall the next day and get cleared and get that ship. Of course that was an omen we were going to have bad trouble but it certainly wasn't, cause we had no trouble a'tall."

"I was the junior third engineer. They did change charters and we had three voyage numbers. We had a company number and there was one Maritime Commission number and something else. But the company always has a voyage number, still APL. Chartered and sub-chartered and this kind of damn foolishness. I don't remember the particulars of that. The mates might a known better, because they kept more track than the black gang. We just went along wherever they went. We took A full load of wheat."

Sailing from Portland on March 1, the *Lane* made the long haul down the Columbia River.

James Stilleke: "I like that Columbia River. That's kind of pretty. I came up on deck for a little while coming down the river. That's a pretty ride down there, very nice. It was a good time."

From the Columbia River Bar the course was south along the Oregon and California coasts to Wilmington, for bunker fuel.

When a ship carries general or break-bulk cargo overloading is not a problem. The cargoes carried are relatively lightweight or stowed in such a way that some carrying space goes unused. In such a case a complete load of cargo can be taken, all the fuel tanks filled, yet the vessel won't be down to her Plimsol marks. Bulk ores or grain, however, are different. Grain, such as wheat, sifts through hatchboards, flows behind sweatbattens, fills every nook and cranny. Because the grain pays the way, steamship companies naturally want to carry as much as possible while still keeping on board enough fuel with a twenty-five percent safety margin to reach the next major port. This must be accomplished in such a way that the ship isn't loaded below her marks. A vessel loaded below her marks would not be allowed to sail if caught or would be fined if discovered later.

Considered by many the worst piece of ocean in the world, the Atlantic is so rough that ships' Plimsol marks carry a special designation for traveling that sea in the winter. In other words, a ship cannot be loaded as far down when crossing the North Atlantic in the winter as it can at any other time or in any other ocean. Because she would be crossing the Atlantic in winter, the *Lane Victory* carried even less cargo than she might otherwise.

One way to maximize the amount of grain that can be carried is to refuel several times along the way. Fuel wasn't a major expense at the time and the price was fairly constant in the world markets. So the *Lane Victory* stopped at Wilmington for fuel on the 4th of March and sailed the same day.

Continuing south she arrived at the Panama Canal on the 13th of March. James Stilleke thoroughly enjoyed the canal transit.

"That was a hell of a kick. Spend the whole damn time in the engine room on the throttle but once you're off, heck yeah, go through. Almost every time in those days it was in the day time. I been through it a time or two before. This time we just went through it and didn't come back. I enjoyed that, the mechanics of getting it through there, raising all the water and all this kind of thing. It was real fun.

"Sometimes it got a little hot in the engine room. But other than that, why, it was nice."

When the canal was first opened in 1914 teams of mules were used to pull ships through the locks and hold them in position. In time these beasts of burden were replaced with steam and then diesel locomotives. But the name stuck. The engines that pull the ships through the canal today are still called "mules."

James Stilleke: "Mules, there would be four, two on the bow and two on the stern. Keep us straight. I don't think the stern ones did as much steering. I think the forward ones kept it lined up, did the pulling, and these other ones just lined you up to go on through so you didn't hit something.

"Eight to twelve hours. There was two sets of locks, Miraflores and Pedro Miguel, and through Gaillard Cut, and Gatun Lake and the locks on the other side. There was three down over there. That was a fascinating ride to me, because you'd see a damn palm tree growing and it didn't look like the plot of dirt it was coming out of was any bigger than this table. Just in the middle of that thing."

The fresh water in Gatun Lake is considered a bonus for canal transit. The engineers always fill up the fresh water tanks, "and mates gave it full washdown. Everything got washed down going through the canal.

"That was a kind of a fun trip. I went through there when I was on the Cal Maritime School Ship. I made a trip through and back . . ."

After refueling once more, the ship sailed from Cristobal for England and the crew settled in for the run across the Atlantic. The days passed easily with the unbroken routine of watch-standing and meals serving as the only markers of time.   The crew enjoyed the serenity.

James Stillike: "Yeah, 'Shorty Dominguez,' the chief engineer.   They always called him Shorty, not to his face, but he was just a little guy.   And he was always . . . I don't know what he was designing.   It seems to me that he was working on something that would supplement or help a Butterworth machine, which is for cleaning fuel tanks and the tanks on tankers.   He would sleep till noon every day.   When the whistle blew he'd get up, have lunch, make out his noon report, and then he'd be around in the afternoon.   Then after supper he would go down in the engine room and he would work on the lathe.   He was always grinding, turning this or turning that or something else.   It was always a little project he had.   He would work every night 'til midnight or one or two o'clock in the morning.   He just didn't get up very early."

The wheat was booked for Liverpool.   The ship arrived on March 27.

James Stilleke remembered it as, "A big dirty city.   We laid out about a day-and-a-half.   We laid outside the harbor after we got arrival because it was so damned foggy we couldn't do nothing.   When we did start in, they got a set of locks in there at the Liverpool harbor.   The mates really loved that because after we got in and tied up to the dock the only time they had to move the lines was when the cargo come out.   They weren't out there fighting lines when the tide changed.   And so they had no tide.   It was kind of a crazy set up.   It was pretty neat, yeah.

"J. Arthur Rank's flour mill is where we were at, unloading wheat, nine or ten days.   We were in there something like that.   They loaded us pretty quick in Portland because they just dumped the [railroad] cars over and we were gone.

"They didn't treat us too bad.   I didn't have too much to do being junior third.   I had the four-to-midnight watch and there wasn't much I could do because they closed the damn pubs at ten o'clock.   One night the third and I swapped off and I worked all that one night and he worked all night the next night so I could go ashore. But I didn't get around too much and it was a big, big city. And I never was much on big cities.

"The little bit I ate there, I wasn't impressed. I didn't get sick, but I wasn't impressed."

The next cargo waited on the East Coast of the United States. The *Lane* departed Liverpool, empty, on April 4.

Voyage 12 ended in Philadelphia ten days later on April 14. Voyage 13 began the following day with the first of a load of army trucks. At the same time the entire unlicensed crew left the ship.

James Stilleke: "The deal was in those days, that when we got to the East Coast all of the unlicensed crew got off to get their transportation money. And if they stayed they didn't get their transportation money which was $185 in those days back to San Francisco. So they all bailed off. The engineers, we could stay as long as we wanted. So all the second crew we got was all East Coasters. That was a horse of another color too.

"We was in Philadelphia and they [the cooks] tried to make chop suey or chow mein and that didn't work so good. It was just bad, bad, bad . . . We were used to this [West] coast. When I was on the *Philippine Bear* we had some Chinese cooks. They grew their own bean sprouts right on the ship and everything so when they made chow mein or chop suey or whatever, boy, it was good. But those East Coast people, different breed, yeah."

Sailing from Philadelphia for Germany on the 17th of April, he discovered that "East Coasters" were different in other ways. "Being junior third, I had to go on watch at ten minutes to eight. So I was always in the messroom quick in the morning. And the first morning, or maybe the first two mornings, I ordered ham and eggs over easy and some potatoes and toast, coffee. I did that about two or three mornings in a row and after that I didn't get chance to order. I'd come in and sit down and they'd hand me my breakfast. Had to change my mind the night before. But other than that it wasn't too bad."

"I think the West Coast black gang was better. There was that one guy, came from south Philadelphia. He had a wife and four kids and when we went on that trip to Bremerhaven we were only gone about twenty-five days. And that son-of-a-bitch made the trip without leaving his wife an allotment. He says, 'She's got enough money, she runs out, she'll get some from her mother.'

"He was slightly different and I decided right then that East Coast people were different than West Coast people."

The cargo was scheduled for Bremerhaven where the ship arrived on the 27th of April.

James Stilleke: "We took a load of Army trucks from there to Bremerhaven. We loaded them, that didn't take any time at all. We were only there about three days, unloading, two days. It was no time at all. We got in there in the evening, they started the next morning. They just unloaded us and then we came back empty. We just hauled ass back.

"Bremerhaven, that was just the opposite of the English. The English shut everything down at the gin mills at seven to nine or whatever it was. The Germans don't have any locks on the doors. So if you want to go ashore . . . We tied up after midnight and the guys were going over the side, going there and getting drunk and everything else. And seems like the third didn't show up, didn't get back so I wound up standing his watch. I had my four-to-midnight and his midnight-to-eight. He come back. I think he give me twenty dollars for working eight hours. In those days twenty dollars was a lot of money. I just said thank you and put it in my pocket. I got over there one evening.

"We weren't there long enough to go anyplace, we just stayed around. The people that we met . . . Well if you go in a bar they're always friendly. The dock workers or the stevedores that we did talk to, nobody was unfriendly to us."

From Bremerhaven the *Lane Victory* went straight back to Philadelphia, sailing from Germany on the 29th of April.

James Stilleke remembered Capt. Marinus Olson well: "He was, Jesus Christ, he was seventy-five then I guess. He was an old timer, yeah. He got some trouble with the sailors. They did something and he logged a couple of them. And then they played sick and got their time back. 'You get me, I'll get you. But I can't make my watch . . .'

"So they got their time back."

The North Atlantic did not belie its fearsome reputation. James Stilleke: "We busted a bilge keel, on the starboard side at the front, forward of the engine room. Just from pounding. It made the goddamndest racket. Every time you'd go down below in the forward end of the engine room on the starboard side, whang, whang, whang, whang. So we finally decided what it was, the mates and the chief engineer and so forth. Then when we went back in to Philly they sent some divers over the side. They just took a torch and cut it off and let it drop and I guess it's still down in the harbor.

"As far as engine problems or ship problems, it was pretty uneventful. That bilge keel was probably the most serious thing we ever had. We didn't have any bad problems on there at all. It was a good running ship. You'd get down there and keep an eye on things and everything went fine. It was a good runner."

A long voyage lets the crew get to know each others foibles and quirks.

James Stillike: "Joe Clark. I remember his name. Clark was a great big black-haired guy. He'd tell the port engineer, 'I won't do anything any time that I won't do in front of your face.'

"So when we get to the other end of the line, he wouldn't go ashore. In a foreign port, he'd stay aboard. If you needed him he was clean and sober. If he was going to get drunk, he was going to get drunk right at the port in the United States where the port engineers could see him and everything. He said, 'No, look, that's my deal, I take care of it on the other end, you guys are here, you take care of it.'

"But he was a good engineer and he was a good guy."

Philadelphia was one of the few large East Coast cities James had ever been to: "It was all right. What the hell did they used to call it, City of Brotherly Love and something else very unkind to them? But they had some bar laws back there, it was kind of hard to get a drink when they closed. But I saw my first big league baseball game back there, the Phillies. We stayed there, eight or nine days one time, I think. I got out and looked around and walked around . . . big country boy in the big city . . . so it was kind of fun.

"The second trip in there, my dad was working for Safeway, a truck division of Safeway Storage out of Oakland. He went back into Washington, D.C., for some reason, for them. My mother was with him and they drove to Philly and I met my mother and dad. And so we went to Bookbinder's. It's quite a famous old restaurant down towards the lower end of Philly down there and had a big dinner and everything and must have cost us five bucks."

Once the cargo was ready to load, little time was lost. Voyage 13 ended on May 15 and voyage 14 started on the 16th.

"They just loaded us up in jig time. We waited for a place to load. The minute they loaded us we were down there and we were gone."

Departing on the 18th of May there was a problem with overloading.

James Stilleke: "We took a load of coal briquettes out of Philadelphia to Trieste. We were over the marks when we cleared Cape May for the simple reason that the mates screwed up. They rolled the railcars up and I'm going to say eight inch, I don't know what it was but it was a big water line that they run over the gondolas and wet the coal briquettes down so they didn't have as much dust. And they'd roll them over. Roll the whole gondola over. They had a chute like thing, we loaded in just a matter of eighteen or twenty hours. Like loading a tanker. They loaded us real quick. Well the mate forgot to calculate in that damn water and so when we got ready to sail we were about six or eight inches over the Plimsol marks. We slowed down coming down the river so that when we cleared Cape May it was a little dark. They couldn't see we were over."

James was always fascinated by his fellow crewmembers. "There was one guy that was an oiler on there . . . he got drafted in the Army and then he did things to get himself an undesirable discharge, deliberately. And this was his first trip back, I think, after he got the dishonorable discharge. I think he was on the four-to-eight watch. But he was a good oiler. He worked, no monkey business at all. He was good."

Gibraltar was a fueling stop for the ship. The *Lane* arrived, fueled and sailed on May 28.

James Stilleke: "We stopped in Gibraltar. Just to get oil, because we were so low. We were so loaded that they cut us down on oil. We were too deep in the water. We could have carried more oil, but we wouldn't, legally we couldn't."

Piracy is not a thing of the past. The Philippines, Korea, Malaysia, and Gibraltar during the 1950s were known for their pirates. Natives board the ship by climbing up the anchor chain or with grappling hooks. Immediately they grab anything they can — dunnage, mooring lines, cargo — and throw it over the side. Whatever floats, even scraps of wood, can be sold ashore.

"Some of those people came out in Gibraltar and tried to come aboard, some of the bumboats. They're throwing stuff over the side and the mate wound up with the sailors out there and they had the fire hoses all going. We started fire pumps in the engine room and they were blowing the fire hoses . . . We hadn't cleared customs and they didn't want anybody off the ship or anybody on the ship.

"We were just there six or eight hours, loaded the oil and we were gone."

As on every ocean voyage the crew got to know each other very well. Confined in a small area, their idiosyncrasies came out.

James Stilleke: "Jerry Dougherty. Yeah, he would only sail third and he would only sail on Victorys."

"One of the sailors got a dose of clap. On a lot of ships the purser was the pharmacist, and on there Olson was, and he's about to give the guy a dose of penicillin. He's got his britches dropped and got him bent over and he's got everything out ready to go and he's not sure. He stops to read the book before he gives him the shot."

Sailing through the Mediterranean, the ship turned north through the Adriatic Sea to Trieste where it arrived on the 2nd of June.

James Stilleke: "Trieste. Right at the top of the Adriatic Sea. They said it was supposed to be a free state at that time. We were in Trieste for eight or nine days. 'Cause they hand shoveled that sucker off. They shoveled those coal briquettes out with shovels and big baskets. Picked them out, strictly hand work.

"I thought it was a real pretty town. I went one day and rode a tram thing, went up the side of a hill, kind of like San Francisco in a way. And got way up top of this hill. There was some real nice fancy houses up there and you could look back over the whole harbor and everything.

"I was always kind of shy about eating ashore in those places and I didn't do much of it. The purser and one of the mates went in to one of the, they said, finer restaurants in Trieste, and hell their bellies were in turmoil for about three days. It might have been something they drank rather than ate. You never know. So I usually came back to the ship and ate rather than eating in those places.

"It was beautiful in there, flowers were blooming. The other thing, too, is that the women bring their lunches to the stevedores, and they'd have a big feed out there on the dock at lunch time up on deck. They had pots that set in one another and stack three or four of them together and carry them. But it was a pretty town and I suppose if I was going to go visit one I'd kind of like to go back and take a look at it."

Empty again, the ship sailed on the 9th of June, cleared Gibraltar on the 14th and headed for New York City.

Ships are rumor factories, especially as the end of a voyage draws near. Where will she go next trip? How long will she be in port? Where will she load the cargo?

James Stilleke: "The rumor was different. Ten days before you got back in to the coast, why the stories run rampant, as to what you were going to do. Nobody knew. I think somebody was sitting up there dreaming them up. But it wasn't just on that ship, on other ones, too."

The *Lane Victory* arrived in New York on the 23rd of June. It was a special occasion that James Stilleke always remembered. "The one highlight, maybe it means nothing to you or me either, but I thought was a highlight. When we came back in to New York, the last trip, the third trip I made on there, we came in the same morning that the *United States* came in on her delivery voyage. We got to see her coming up the channel . . . fireboats . . . beautiful sight. Hell of a view. I was on deck. I got to see some of that. We weren't terribly close, but we could see it and it was a pretty sight. The story went around then that the night before she slowed down because they had four tin cans [Navy destroyers] coming up from Newport with her as an escort and she walked off and left them. She was pretty fast. She left them tin cans and then she slowed before they came in and they picked her up."

Although he regretted leaving the ship, James Stilleke wanted new experiences and adventures. He returned to the West Coast.

"The big city of New York. Yep. Bought a brand new 1952 Chevrolet and drove across country. That was in June."

"And me like a damn dummy, I got off of that [*Lane Victory*] and got on the *Sea Serpent* for PFE [Pacific Far East Lines] on this [West] coast. It was a Sun-Doxford five cylinder opposed piston. If you want a workhouse, a bunch of iron, that was it . . . I had a lot of fun on her and we got ten percent more money, so I stayed on there for about fifteen months, but it was nothing like running one of these hot water deals [steam turbine]."

"I got on the *Sea Serpent* and then got literally drafted off of that into the Navy. And the Navy was wondering why I was so goddamned bitter when I got there. This guy said something to me and I said 'You know, I was making better than $1,000 a month and now I'm making $250 a month, you guess why I'm bitter.'

"I was used to making these nice little runs and you'd get home and get to say, 'Hello, how are you,' once in awhile."

The *Lane Victory*, meanwhile, made another run to Bremerhaven. Departing on her fifteenth voyage on June 24, she sailed from New York empty. Loading cargo in Bremerhaven she sailed on July 10 and returned to New York. There the voyage ended on the twentieth and Capt. Marinus Olson left the sea. John Mena: "When he retired I understand he went to the Sausalito old sailor's home. He had to turn over all his funds. He had money in Denmark or Norway or wherever he was from that he couldn't touch unless he spent it over there. He couldn't take it out of the country. Then he had plenty of bucks here."

From August 2 to 15, 1952 the *Lane* was deactivated, then placed in the Hudson River Reserve Fleet. It was a short stay. She was called up again the following year.

Voyage 16 in the ship's career began April 10, 1953 at Leonardo, New Jersey. The cargo was ammunition. On April 16th the first load was aboard and as the fifty-ton mark was reached the 10% bonus started.

Sailing on April 22, the *Lane Victory* arrived at Balboa on April 30. After stopping in San Pedro on May 8 for fuel, she sailed for the Far East. Her first port of call was Yokosuka, Japan followed by Inchon, Korea, where the ammunition was discharged.

After an uneventful crossing, the ship returned to San Francisco, where the voyage ended on July 10, 1953.

Voyage 17 started on July 11. After the usual loading of general military cargo at Oakland, the ship sailed on July 17.

Arriving in Yokohama, Japan, the *Lane's* new naster, Capt. Keymer, was faced with a problem that defied resolution.

It began with one of the sailors who simply refused to work. For several days he started arguments and fights with other crewmembers. Finally, when ordered to turn to with the rest of the crew, he stayed in his room. The captain had him jailed by the military police. He was logged one days' pay as a penalty after spending nine days in military prison.

At the time there was a U.S. Coast Guard office in Yokohama. The sailor was so difficult the captain insisted that they do something about him. Capt. Keymer was hoping they would pull the man off the ship and send him home. The Coast Guard conducted a hearing and decided on a warning. Instructing the sailor that he must conduct himself in an orderly fashion and cause no more disturbances, the Coast Guard returned him to duty.

A few days later, in Sasebo, the same seaman was found in a beaten condition at the launch area. He had a bottle of phenobarbital in one of his pockets. Taken to the Navy hospital for treatment, he was released within a few hours. The master reported the incident to the Coast Guard at Yokohama pending further action.

The following day the *Lane Victory* returned to Tokyo Bay, docking at Yokosuka. There the same sailor was found passed out ashore. Put into the hospital and listed as a user of narcotics, he was again found in a beaten condition. The master asked the Navy doctor to send the man back to States as soon as possible and the incident was reported to the Coast Guard.

On September 29, the ship was still in Tokyo Bay, now at Yokohama. The same sailor was found beating his head against the bulkhead. Again phenobarbital was found in his possession. The captain called the Military Police aboard and had the man removed to the hospital. This time he sent the sailor's gear with him. He had no intention of getting him back.

It's not easy to remove an American seaman from a ship in a foreign port. Legally the steamship company is responsible for a crewman's wages and subsistence until he returns to the port at which he signed on the vessel. If a crewmember leaves a ship in Yokohama, the steamship company is responsible for flying him back to the United States. If the crewmember, as in this case, can't be immediately flown out, the company is responsible for his wages, room and board, until he can be flown out. The only exceptions are when the American Consul can be prevailed upon to act as shipping commissioner and sign the sailor off at a foreign port. Capt. Keymer tried to get the consul in Yokohama to do this. The consul wouldn't have any part of it. Reviewing the matter he listened to the captain's complaints and saw the results of the Coast Guard hearing (a verbal admonishment), but refused to sign the man's articles unless the master agreed to full wages and transportation to the States. The captain declined. When the ship sailed, on October 2, 1953 the seaman remained as a hospital case at Yokohama.

The final voyage of the Korean War years terminated on October 15, 1953 in San Francisco. After a two week deactivation period, the *Lane Victory* arrived at the Suisun Bay Reserve Fleet for lay-up on October 30, 1953. It would be thirteen years before she saw action again. But, as always, she would be ready to do her duty and do it well.

11

THE THIRD WAR

Once again the war clouds gathered. It was 1965. The Vietnam sealift was growing and the Navy's Military Sealift Command needed more ships. The Maritime Administration in Washington, D.C., sent the order to stand by. A teletype came through to the Pacific Coast District of MARAD [Maritime Administration] in San Francisco to break out ten Victorys. Eventually the number would rise to sixty-one on the West Coast alone, with MARAD shepherding a total fleet of 172 ships. Approximately one-third of the war cargo sea-lifted to Vietnam was carried by this fleet of 172 Victory ships. Six thousand American merchant seamen would be involved in the effort. The *Lane Victory*, idle for twelve years, was one of the ships called back to duty.

Reserve Fleet ships are moored side by side, bow to stern, so that each row of ships is held in place by anchors in two directions. Located in the middle of a row of ships, the *Lane*

Victory first had to be moved to the outer end of the row. Because each ship has both anchors out this move was made by MARAD tugs. Commercial tugs refuse to work around so many anchor chains due to the possibility of damage to their propellers. When the ship was in place, a call was made to MARAD San Francisco. They, in turn, notified the ship's agent, Pacific Coast Transport Company (PCTC), who would husband the ship throughout the Vietnam conflict.

On Saturday August 20, 1966 at 1040 a small "riding" crew boarded the ship from the tug *Sea King*. Capt. J. W. Allbright of PCTC boarded at 1100 and took delivery of the ship from G.D. Phoebus, Superintendent of the Reserve Fleet.

John "Swede" Jansson was one of the engineers in the riding crew. In his melodious Swedish accent he described the occasion. "Ve recommissioned her in '66. They took her out of Suisun Bay and ve took her down there to Richmond. Capt. Allbright vas the Port Captain. PCTC. He become a pilot later on in San Pedro. Yust Capt. Allbright, his boy and Yorge Hatchley. He vas de port engineer."

With Capt. Urnser piloting, the tug *Trojan* alongside, and the tug *Valiant* assisting on the port quarter, the ship was ready to go. The last line connecting the *Lane* to the Reserve Fleet and a dozen years of idleness was thrown off at 1120. Carefully, the pilot turned the vessel, guided her through the fleet, down the channel and backed her through the Southern Pacific railroad bridge. It was a delicate operation requiring great skill. The tide was ebbing, making the ship difficult to control. Clearing the bridge at 1144 the ship was towed through Carquinez Straits to the eastern shore of San Francisco Bay. There she was carefully maneuvered into graving dock no. 1 of Willamette Iron and Steel Shipyard, Richmond, California. By 2130 that evening, the dock was dry and the vessel secure on the blocks.

John Jansson: "Took her in drydock there. I vas over dere tree, four days I tink."

When a ship is deactivated, all the underwater external openings to the sea are blanked off with steel plates. The ship must be drydocked to remove the plates. Any heavy gear such as winches and lifeboats stowed inside the ship is taken out and relocated to its original position. The propeller shaft is removed and gauged and any necessary underwater repairs are tended to.

On August 26 the ship was refloated. At 0855 a shifting crew boarded with the pilot, Capt. Jack Frost. At 0922 the tug *Sea Rover* was fast on the starboard quarter, the tug *Sea Queen* fast on the port quarter. Clearing basin no. 1 she was towed out Richmond channel at 0927. A few hours later she was all fast portside to pier 66 in San Francisco. This was the operating pier and repair facility for the AAA shipyard.

John Jansson: "Then we vent over to San Francisco, Triple A, and ve started up dere. Capt. Allbright vas the port captain, Yorge Hatchley vas the port Engineer, Red Smith, he vas a MARAD man."

"When ve got shore steam on it, me and Clyde ve tested the vhistle, see it vork. Ve blow the vistle, the shore steam. And she vorked. Right avay. Ve got shore steam, whoooooooo."

"Ve stayed there for quite a few days in dat yard. There ve renew all the water vall tubes. Ve renew all the water valls, clean all the consol oils out. The shipsyard did dat. And ve steamed her up. Ve took her out there, ve gave her full bore and den crash. She run. Whatever ve gave her she took. She vas up to twenty-four nozzles on the crash run. Ve open her vide open and ve gave her full ahead and full astern. And she stopped. It was going astern and MARAD said dat's better than average. And dat's hell of a strain on the engine. Full bore and full astern. Ve took her out an she took it. She vas the best Victory I had."

Having passed the operating test, there remained the cargo gear and auxiliary systems to prepare. What on other ships would have been difficult somehow was easy on the *Lane*.

"Everything function on the ship. Ve didn't have no problem wid vinches. Dey were vorking perfect. The only problem vid the winches ve have vhen dey started up dey have consol oil in. Dey vere smoking a little bit, but dere vas no burning. De winches vere vorking, you know. Longshoremen,

I think they said burning vinches, I said, 'Don't vorry about it, they yust the consol oil.'

"They clean them in the yard but they didn't do so good . . . you know a hundred percent. So they coming fumes and everything out of the vinches.

"And, oh yeah, they had to clean shit out o' the deep tanks aft. I guess the cleaning crew had left a few rags in. And ve got there and ve couldn't pump ballast. Vell, ve got the rags all right. Ve open the deep tanks. Fuel oil. Fuel oil aft, you know. And dey clean dem down dere in this yard and dey left the rags and dey come in the line. Vell, ve got them out. You take the bonnet off. Reach down there, pull the rag out, den pump some more.

"The evaporator vas good on there too. There vas a high pressure evaporator. And that's vun of the few evaporators of that kind, I didn't have no problem vid. Never had a vater problem."

On September 29, another milestone in activation was reached. The Coast Guard tested and approved the steam smothering system. This is the primary firefighting equipment on a ship of this type.

It had been more than a month, a much longer time than it took to reactivate for Korea. Engineer Jansson recalled: "Vell, the biggest problem vas, they didn't have too many yardworkers. They're hard to get. Especially boilermakers. It vas normal [to take that long] ya."

With most activation work complete, the ship shifted on Oct. 1 to pier 54 in San Francisco. This was a fitting out berth, a place to take on the crew, fuel and stores for the coming voyage and to prepare for the final activation tests.

"Swede" Jansson: "I know she vas APL in the Korean War because dey still had that down in the engine room, the eagle. It vas yust painted on the after end on the turbine level, the operation level."

On October 2nd, the ship was ready for fuel oil. Engineer Jansson was proud of how quickly the fueling went.

"Ve took on bunkers, me and Clyde Taft and vhat's his name. Nobody believe ve could take on board it so fast. Ya, I remember that very well."

There was a four-hour dock trial, with the engine going ahead and astern at twenty rpm. Then came stores and emergency and lifesaving equipment.

John Jansson: "Ve vent in dere and took all de supplies an stuffs on board. After the shipsyard was finished. 'Cause they didn't take no stores before."

As the new crew came aboard and became acclimated to the ship, crew problems developed. From the deck log:

October 5, 1966. 0110 Purser, Mr. Allen Todd arrived at foot of gangway in Yellow Cab, 1965 or 1966 Ford. Mr. Todd got out of the cab and had a discussion with the cab driver, apparently regarding the fare. On observing Mr. Todd it was obvious to the gangway watch, Mr. W. E. Rolfe, American Patrol badge #208 that Mr. Todd had been in some sort of accident and yelled for the nightmate to come to the gangway. When Mr. Todd boarded the vessel it was noted: 1, that his scalp had approximately a 1 1/2 inch long cut, 2, his arms chest and face were covered with blood, 3, his jacket was missing, 4 left hip pants pocket tore down to back of knee. Mr. Todd advised nightmate that he had been struck from behind and he was missing money, paper, and keys. He requested that his room be opened somehow as he wanted to lie down. Mr. Todd sat down in the fireman and oilers cabin just off the gangway while the nightmate tried to find some way to open Mr. Todd's room. During this time it was decided by the nightmate that the police should be called and Mr. Todd taken to the emergency hospital. On returning by the nightmate to the quarterdeck, Mr. Rolfe was requested to call the police. Mr. Rolfe answered that Mr. Todd had just called the police. 0120 Police officers M. Mullane and E. Fowlie arrived in car #281. After some discussion with nightmate and police Mr. Todd agreed to go with police to Harbor emergency hospital where doctors could look him over and stitch his head. At 0215 police returned with Mr. Todd at which time he was put in second mate's cabin and Capt. E. McMichael notified. The police advised the night mate that the doctor had examined Mr. Todd, stitched his scalp and released him with the recommendation that Mr. Todd have his chest x-rayed later this morning. The police further advised that Mr. Todd told them that he was missing $80 of his own money and $480 of the vessel's. Additionally the police officers will send the Master care of PCTC two copies of their report and robbery detail officer will be aboard later today to question Mr. Todd.

The final sea trials and acceptance took place on October 6. Similar to the sea trials for delivery of a new ship, this included running the ship in circles in San Francisco Bay to test and adjust compasses at various courses, adjusting the RDF [Radio Direction Finder], and testing the anchors. The final phase was a twenty-four hour endurance test that started at midnight. Beginning at 80 rpm the ship went out past the Farallon Islands, steered various courses and periodically increased by ten rpms until maximum speed was reached. At 2400 October 7, 1966 reactivation was complete. The *Lane Victory* was ready to do her part in the war in Vietnam.

Thomas J. Patterson was Chief of Ship Operations for the Pacific Coast District of MARAD at the time.

"Capt. Edward A. MacMichael, Pennsylvania School Ship '36, World War II master and Navy CO, and my mentor, former boss and predecessor came by the office and said, 'Tom, how about giving me one of the Victorys?'

"I told him the *Lane Victory* was being activated and that I would call the general agent to see if they had assigned a master.

"'We would be pleased to have Capt. MacMichael,' said John Albright, GAA Coordinator and Port Capt. of PCTC. With Ed's vast knowledge and experience both with U.S. Lines and with Maritime Administration in Washington, and in the Pacific Coast District, *SS Lane Victory* quickly became the 'Flag Ship' of the GAA's and the ship to beat."

John Jansson: "I remember Capt. MacMichael. He vas a yentleman's yentleman, you know. Oh, he vas a sailor. Yah, he vas very fine man, McMichael. I vish he still vas alive. Ya, he vas captain on the [nuclear ship] *Savannah*."

At 0001 October 8, 1966 voyage #NSA 7- PCTC #1, U.S. Department of Commerce, Maritime Administration commenced. It was the eighteenth voyage in the ship's career. At 0840 the ship passed under the Golden Gate Bridge from sea trials, and returned to Pier 54. There were still a few small items to pick up.

"Swede" Jansson: "Then we vent to Redwood City and ve loaded napalm bombs."

Arriving at Redwood City Monday October 10, the ship started working cargo

Capt. Edward A. MacMichael, taken at the Concord Naval Weapons Station in February of 1967. Photo by RADM T.J. Patterson.

immediately. Taking on a full load of fire bombs and bomb fins in all hatches, she shifted from one berth to another as each incoming load became available. Even as cargo was being worked, last minute repairs were completed in the engine room.

The vessel shifted to the San Francisco Bay explosives anchorage on October 14 to top off with a few tons of munitions, then sailed on October 15 for the Far East.

During rough weather on the way across some of the deck cargo broke loose.

From Capt. MacMichael's letter to Pacific Coast Transport Company:

It was evident that the ship was stiff and indeed had an excessive metacentric height when we stopped to drop the pilot at San

Francisco Light Ship. Snap-rolling was experienced. With the Farallon Islands well astern it was noticed that the swell, while predominantly from the north, also ranged from northwest, through north, to northeast. Various courses were tried to ease the ship throughout the night with reasonable success, with the roll controlled to about 10 degrees plus or minus. In effect, we were tacking north and south of the base course of 238 degrees.

At about 0620 hours a heavy swell from a northwesterly direction caused the ship to roll approximately 25 degrees to port and snap back to about 20 degrees to starboard in approximately four seconds. Splintering noises were heard on the foredeck and the lookout, then stationed on the bridge, was sent forward to investigate, it being evident that something had carried away.

It developed the deck cargo, on deck adjacent to #2 Hatch, had shifted. The Deck crew was immediately called and told to stand by to secure the cargo. This cargo consisted of 192 napalm bombs tiered three-high from port to starboard, and was shored into three lots as follows:

> Port side #2 Hatch, on deck---57 crates
> #2 Hatch, square on deck------78 crates
> Stbd side #2 Hatch, on deck---57 crates.

Weight of the individual crates and contents is 1,060 lb. They are constructed of typical citrus fruit crating. The cargo was shored in four directions with 4 x 4s and 2 x 12 string pieces, then lashed with 3/4" wire and turnbuckles. Quality of the shoring material was a poor grade of ungraded resawed lumber, full of knots, checks and soft spots.

Apparently the shoring on the port side of the bulwark rail carried away when the ship rolled to port, and the port side lot shifted outboard about 20 inches, pulling the shoring adrift between the port side and the hatch square, and the starboard side lots. When the ship rolled to starboard all rigid support was weakened and the hatch square cargo shifted about two feet to starboard, and the deck cargo starboard shifted outboard against the bulwark, and all three lots were working back and forth in their lashings.

At 0625 hauled south to 225 degrees gyro and sent Chief Officer C.A. Carlson, along with Boatswain N. D. Luster and Carpenter Carl Payden to survey the situation. At 0715 hauled south to 180 degrees to put predominant northerly swell directly astern.

After establishing set of whistle signals for Deck crew to work with (i.e., 1 blast-go forward, 2 blasts-take cover, 3 blasts-come midship) and posting a man-overboard lookout on the bridge wing, commenced securing cargo at 0718.

This activity continued throughout the day until 1830, when it was deemed prudent to set a course of 290 degrees to head for the next route check point. Standing orders were issued for Deck Watch officers to haul off as required to ease the ship in event of excessive rolling.

Appropriate messages were sent to COMSTSPAC and that command was kept appraised of the situation until base course was resumed to the next route check point.

Deck cargo was finally secured on 17 October at 1700 hours. Reason for the rather lengthy activity was dictated when it was discovered that two bomb crates in the middle and bottom tiers outboard, on the starboard side, had been crushed and one bomb was bent and dented, but not punctured. This necessitated relieving stress on all three tiers to prevent further damage, and doubling up on all shoring where possible.

The undersigned would be remiss if in this report no mention were made of the behavior of the unlicensed deck crew. Under the circumstances, their work was outstanding in all respects. By their aggressive support, a bad situation was prevented from further deterioration and was corrected in a timely and efficient manner. The services of Boatswain Marvin Luster, Carpenter Carl Payden and Able Seaman Myron Johnson were particularly noteworthy.

> Respectfully,
> E. A. MacMichael
> Master
> *S.S. Lane Victory*

The problems weren't over. A few days later the cargo began leaking onto the deck.

John Jansson: "Ve had leaking napalm. Ve didn't have any problem vid that. Fact, ve didn't spend no attention to it. When ve vas in Redwood City, loaded, the fire department come aboard. You can even light a match on top of it, it von't burn, you know. There's a yelly in the bomb and it come in the atmosphere and it don't explode. I understand it crystallize itself. It's hard. They're not considered a explosive because you got ammunition bonus . . . napalm is not under that. Not napalm bombs. Ve didn't get it. They yust loaded the crates, big vuns, long vuns, I don't know how many feet long dat vas."

Admiral Tom Patterson: "On one voyage to Southeast Asia with a deck load of Napalm bombs, the ship encountered hot weather. The Napalm expanded and leaked out on deck. Messages to MARAD and the Navy requested instructions. A final message from *Lane Victory* ended with N.S.O.L. The Military Sealift Command in Oakland called and wanted to know what N.S.O.L. meant. I said, 'No Strain On the Lane.'"

Arriving in Subic Bay on November 3 the *Lane Victory* discharged a few tons, then shifted to an anchorage on November 5. It was another case of "hurry up and wait."

The anchorage at Subic Bay is large but well-protected by tall, rounded hills whose jungle covering is lost to the eye of the seaman because of distance. Depending on how many ships are in the harbor, the ride ashore by Navy landing craft would take anywhere from half an hour to an hour or more. There one walks from the boat landing, through the clean, well-maintained base, across a bridge to the town of Olongopo — Sin City. Here seaman found every form of service and entertainment imaginable, from barber shops, restaurant and souvenir stores to bars, brothels and floor shows.

John Jansson: "Ve vent to Subic Bay, ve drop anchor, laying out of us, there vas quite a few grey vuns out there you know.[1] Laying for anchor."

---

[1] During the Vietnam conflict, ships chartered to the government were painted grey.

While still at anchor on November 19 the ship received word that typhoon Nancy was tearing her way across the South China Sea. It didn't hit Subic Bay but two days later the edge of the storm went through with winds southerly at force 5 (17-21 knots) and the barometer at 29.58. The sea state was recorded as "moderately rough," the sky, "cloudy overcast." It wasn't severe enough for the ship to leave the anchorage.

Meanwhile the crew got to know each other. By a quirk of fate many of those on board were from the "old country."

John "Swede" Jansson: "Quite a few Svedes on there. The radio operator vas Nelson, second electrician vas a Svede, his name vas Blumqvist, Carlson, vas an oiler, he's another Svede. And there vas Yergenson, the carpenter vas Yohnson, Leroy Yohnson, and there vas an AB named Myrn Yohnson. Robertson vas a third mate. Clyde Taft vas second on there, second assistant. Orville Lyttle, he vas the third assistant. And chief electrician, Gross, Lewis Gross. Ya, vas quite a few sqvareheads on dere."

"The only tragedy ve had vas that fireman got a heart attack. Ve saved his life. And the chief mate, ve give him oxygen, took an oxygen bottle up and ve give him oxygen from a regular oxygen bottle, burning stuff, ya. Vell we save his life. Then the Navy come and took him, take him ashore. He didn't die. I vent up and visit him in the hospital."

The deck log for this incident: "2055 Dec. 8, 1966 Ira P. Sears, Oiler reported difficulty in breathing and pain, 2105 contacted US Navy. Contact with USS *Coral Sea* and instructions given master by medical officer 2135 Subic Bay Naval Station. Sent by boat to Naval hospital."

Idle time bothers everyone. After weeks at anchorage even the mates on watch were bored. The deck log for one period read, "11/28/66 still at stupid anchorage."

John Jansson: "Subic Bay, ya. I remember dat because the damn agent boat come out, ve're loaded up vid San Miguel beer. The captain turn his head. He valked off the bridge ving. They only cost tree dollars a case. We ver laying for anchor there long time. Yeah, San Miguel beer, tree dollars a case. The ship chandler come aboard. Yust to order it."

Some people got lazy.

John Jansson: "Vun time the chief cook vas boiling the steaks before frying them. And the damn crew raised hell, so Capt. McMichael vent down and he says 'You spoiled the steaks.'

"So he vas saying 'You gotta pay for the damn things.'

"Dat vas one thing."

As always, the pleasures offered ashore were compelling. Sometimes too much so. Having beer on board could be winked at if kept under control, but hard liquor was another matter.

"Vell, der was no drinking on the ship. I think I vas short a couple o' engineers for three or four days. But, vhat the hell, them Victory kind o' run by'm selves, you know.

"----, he used to come up and make a draw vhen I didn't see him. And he did the same ting in Nha Be. I think the son-of-a-guns, he come aboard and vent up and get some money and den he took off again. Ya, he used to go ashore and stay."

"Carlson, Chief Mate Carlson, he vas a really good old seaman, you know. They had hang the flag upside down one time. That mean distress. Yee vhiz, the flag is upside down. I guess the guys had too much beer. Because back aft they had a big box, and they had line it vid sawdust. Vhat they take aboard vhere everybody keep the beers nice and cold, you know. And I guess bosun vas the bartender. I'm almost sure of that. He vas the bartender. But Carlson comes, 'Hey, Yesus, the flag is upsidedown.' That vas funny."

More than a month after arriving at Subic Bay, the *Lane Victory* finally received orders to sail. From the deck log: "0945 December 12 anchor aweigh and sailed for Cam Ranh Bay. Arrived December 14."

Unfortunately, no one at Cam Ranh Bay knew the ship was coming nor did they want it there.

Again from the deck log: "5 minutes after dropping anchor in Cam Ranh Bay received orders to sail for Qui Nhon. Departed 1236, arrived 2245 December 14, 1966. Let go anchor 2330. 2333 Finished With Engines (FWE)."

It seems that the authorities at Qui Nhon were as nonplussed as those at Cam Ranh Bay.

According to the deck log: "December 15, 0752 received orders to proceed to Cape St. Jacques. December 15, departed Qui Nhon 1142. Arrived Cape St. Jacques 0736 December 16. Anchored 0855."

It was almost the same thing again. "Scheduled to go up river on December 17. 1350 orders canceled. December 18, weighed anchor and went up river to Nha Be."

The Saigon River is picturesque. It winds, snakelike, across a wide jungle delta. Vessels coming down river look like land ships cutting across the lush green rice paddies and mangroves. The river could also be dangerous. Ships must slow down to negotiate hairpin turns. Several ships suffered rocket attacks going up river. At Nha Be the river widens and in the middle of it were several partially sunken ships pointed up or down stream. Traffic passed on one side or the other. War raged for so long in this country that no one remembered how the ships got there.

John Jansson: "I vas in the engine room. Ve had der armed guard. Ve had dem vid the rocket launches and stuff. 'Course friend o' mine was skipper on the vun that blow up. They got a mine. That vas a Victory. His name vas Carlson. Capt. Carlson. It happen up the river from Cape St. Jacques. The pilot froze. Capt. Carlson, how I know him very vell, he vas a Svede, you know, Carlson vas a Svede. So he run her up on the bank, there. She vasn't sunk. But the ship before vere loaded wid ammunition and dey vent ahead. Vhen come Nha Be der, ve had a ship too vas sunk but dat vas a Norwegian company. You know, and old steamers, you know the China steamers out there [sunk in the middle of the river]."

Nha Be is downstream from Saigon. The jungles that lie between it and the capital make it a dangerous trip by land.

John Jansson: "Nha Be vas very dangerous. I vent up to Saigon because I had something to do up dere. There vas a Coast Guard station dere you know. United States Coast Guard. And I rode a pick-up truck up there. And ve don't have right side and left side . . . full bore down the middle. Is very dangerous from Nha Be. The guy was first kinda pissed off at me an he say, 'Vhy you gotta go to Saigon?'

"'I hab business up der.'

"Vat I was gonna do, I got orders to go up get a few bottles of vhiskey. At vas ship's business. So he say 'You vanna get up to Saigon, take a goddamn Caltex truck.'

"'The Caltex trucks,' he say, 'They don't shoot them. They shoot at this kind.'

"See, the oil companies they paid money for the Viet-Cong to leave them alone. Not to bother dem."

With all the napalm finally off, the sailing board was posted on December 22, for San Francisco.

Sailing on December 23, the ship safely entered the South China Sea only to have generator trouble. Christmas Eve found the ship without electrical power — both the gyrocompass and the radar were inoperable. Repairing the generator required spare parts that weren't on board. On Christmas Day the ship made an unscheduled stop at Subic Bay for repairs.

Parts for the generator were ordered from the States. This meant another wait. Waiting meant more idle time. Idle time caused another crew problem.

On December 27, the chief mate was told by the chief steward that one of the messmen was violent and dangerous. Investigating, the mate found himself and one of the sailors, a deck maintenance man, under attack. The messman was put in handcuffs and he immediately calmed down. Thinking the difficulty was over, the cuffs were removed. Lashing out again, the messman went after the second cook. The cuffs were put back on. The deck log states, "Cuffs put on by order of master for his personal safety."

The following day the messman was sent ashore in a liberty boat escorted by a sailor and the purser.

The generator parts arrived on January 4. The generator was fixed and the sailing board finally posted for departure on January 6, destination: San Francisco.

But there were further delays making the repairs. It was two days later, at 0924 January 8, that the *Lane Victory* finally departed Subic Bay.

John Jansson: "Ve had a yenerator and ve repaired that yenerator. That vas electrical trouble. There vas no mechanical trouble in the yenerator. So ve took the yenerator itself, the electrical end and then the shipsyard . . . the Navy repaired it and took that salt vater test you know."

Once the ship was underway, the return voyage was uneventful. On January 26 at 1312 she arrived at the San Francisco pilot station. Her first voyage to Vietnam ended at midnight that night. She was tied to San Francisco's pier 54.

John "Swede" Jansson: "I get off in San Francisco. They transferred me to a C-vun named *Cape Elizabeth*. I always liked the Victorys better. In fact, dey is the best ship you have up in the yard. A Victory ship can vork. You can steam vidout electricity. The *Lane Victory*, she vas yust like a new ship. You could do anything vid her. She vas steaming all over and good, very good. You know, they never had no problem vid that ship, she was a good running boat. *Lane Victory* vas in my book . . . I had quite a few Victorys, I had about ten of them, maybe I had more, ten I had . . . Anyway *Lane Victory*, she vas a vork horse."

"Ve had like a family on that ship. It vas a hundred percent SUP [Sailor's Union of the Pacific] crew and they vas a really good crew, you know. Had good electricians and good oilers. The crew vas top, top notch crew. Mates, engineers, everybody."

After being idle for a few days, the ship began taking bunkers for her next voyage.

A freighter such as the *Lane Victory* is versatile. Where she carried napalm and munitions on the previous voyage, she would carry general cargo — PX stores in military jargon — on this one. Shifting to the Alameda Reefer docks on February 3rd, she began loading. After a few hours she was moved to Oakland

Army Terminal for the remainder of her Bay Area cargo. PX stores and vehicles were the main commodities.

On February 7 the sailing board was posted for departure the following day. As was typical in war time, no one was sure exactly where she was headed. The destination chalked on the board was "San Diego or Port Hueneme."

Sailing at midnight, February 8 she arrived in San Diego the following morning.

After briefly loading in San Diego, her next loading port was Port Hueneme, where she arrived on the 10th and took on board general cargo. Most of it was in boxes or crates but some was in small containers called vans or mil-vans.

On February 13, the *Lane* pointed her bow westward, destination Bangkok, Thailand.

The voyage across was uneventful with the ship arriving at the mouth of the Chao Phayra River on March 9.

On the 11th there was a power failure but it was quickly repaired. The ship was beginning to show signs of age.

Once more it was a case of hurry up and wait. On March 12 the anchor was raised as the pilot came on board and the ship went up river to anchor across from the port. After another six days the ship shifted to a berth and finally started working cargo.

Despite the exotic surroundings, one of the ABs was depressed. Perhaps he received bad news from home when the ship arrived. As occasionally happens in seafaring he decided to end it all. The entry in the deck log explains what happened:

Monday, March 27, 1967. On about 0830 while I was on the stem of the ship watching as a vessel astern was departing, there being about 40 feet astern of the ships, some of the native guards reported a sailor had jumped down the port side into the river. After talking to the guards it appeared that a crewmember had jumped overboard. The Master was called who took charge. About 0850 the harbor police was called. (signed) William S. ----- 2nd mate.

p.s. Man later identified as Healy, Able seaman. Appropriate authorities notified. (Signed) MacMichael.

The master's financial records for the voyage show that it cost $5 to have Healy's body removed from the river.

Trying to sail on March 31, the ship developed condenser problems and had to anchor while repairs were completed. She departed the following day and arrived at Manila on April 5.

Wars are never operated with economy in mind. Normally, a ship won't call at a port unless several hundred tons of cargo are involved. Operating costs are too great to make a call for less. In wartime, however, if a ship is nearby it is used to get cargo from one place to another despite the costs.

Nine tons of cargo loaded at Bangkok were discharged and twenty-six tons loaded for Okinawa, with an additional two tons for Yokohama.

On April 6 the *Lane* sailed for Taiwan. She arrived in Kaoshung on the 8th and anchored. The first cargo came aboard on April 10.

While the ship was at anchor a condition 2 warning about typhoon Violet was issued. At first the weather wasn't bad. The wind was northwesterly at force 3-4 with the barometer at 29.68. Cargo operations were quickly finished, the hatches closed and the ship made ready for sea. She sailed directly into the full force of the storm.

From the deck log:

"Wed. April 12,
  1520 slow down to 80 rpm.
  1540 slow down to 75, due to vessel pounding.
  1600 vessel pitching and rolling heavily, partly cloudy. Short deep swell, rough sea. Wind NxE force 7-8, 29.91, waves NNE 6-8 feet swell NNE 14-16 feet.

Fortunately the storm passed over quickly. By the following day the weather entries were: "Thu. April 13, 1250 reduced speed 65 rpm. 1200 wind dir 150 force 3, 30.07, waves 3-4 feet, swell 8-10 feet."

In many countries of the world American cigarettes are used to ease the entry of a ship into port. What in the United States might be considered bribery is thought of in most foreign cultures as the common way of doing business. When an American ship arrives in a foreign port, it is expected that cigarettes will be given to boarding officials. Should this not occur, the ship will find itself delayed for days, if not weeks, before being allowed to load or discharge its cargo. Capt. MacMichael's report for the voyage up to this point is revealing.

Accountability Report
Cigarette and Tobacco from Slop Chest to Foreign Port Officials

Date	Port	Gratuity Items	Port Officials
3/12/67	Bangkok	8 Ctns cigarettes	
Arrival		1/4 lb. can tobacco	Immigration
in		4 ctns cigarettes	Customs-Forms, etc.
Port		2 ctns cigarettes	Customs-seal slop chest.
Area		8 ctns cigarettes	Customs-40 man srch pty.
		1 ctn cigarettes	Pilot
3/17/67	"	6 ctns cigarettes	4 Customs officials to open Slop Chest for issuing cigarettes to crew.
		1 ctn cigarettes	1 Customs official assigned to ship.
3/18/67	"	2 ctns cigarettes	Harbor Master
		6 cans tobacco	Customs to open slop chest for issuing cigarettes to unlicensed crew.
3/24/67	"	2 ctns cigarettes	Customs-slop chest
		1 can tobacco	sales to all crew.

Total: 34 ctns cigarettes 8 tins tobacco.

4/5/67	Manila	2 ctns cigarettes	Quarantine
		2 ctns cigarettes	Immigration
		1 ctn cigarettes	Customs

Total: 5 ctns cigarettes

4/6/67	Bataan	2 ctns cigarettes	Customs
		2 ctns cigarettes	Immigration

Total: 4 ctns cigarettes

4/8/67	Kaohsiung	3 ctns cigarettes	Quarantine
		1 ctn cigarettes	Pilot

4/9/67	"	4 ctns cigarettes	Immigration & Security Police
		4 ctns cigarettes	Customs
		1 ctn cigarettes	Immigration guard on ship
4/12/67	"	6 ctns cigarettes	Immigration, Military Police and Chief Foreign Police due to early departure before usual hours of officials.
		1 ctn cigarettes	Pilot

Total: 20 ctns cigarettes

Arriving off Naha, Okinawa on April 14 the ship anchored offshore awaiting a berth. One opened up two days later. After discharging her cargo, she sailed on April 17 for Yokohama. Entering Tokyo Bay on the 20th the *Lane* anchored briefly then on April 21 shifted to North Pier, the traditional military cargo pier in Yokohama. There she discharged the small amount of cargo loaded in previous ports and took on a load of p.o.v.'s (privately owned vehicles) for the States.

Leaving the Far East on April 23 the *Lane Victory* had a peaceful Pacific crossing, arriving in Oakland on May 5.

Voyage 2 for PCTC ended at 2400 May 5 with the ship shifting to Stockton, California. There, voyage 3 commenced at Berth 2. Capt. McMichael was relieved by Edward D. Wentworth as master.

Stan Coppel of Atlas Steamship Company (general agents): "He (Wentworth) seemed like a nice fella, but he was a tanker skipper. They're a different breed."

Morgan Vail sailed with Capt. Wentworth a few months later on the *Pacific Victory*.

". . . this was back in '67. We went to Saigon. He was a first class tankerman and he was a first class ship handler. He was a graduate of California Maritime Academy, and he'd been with Pacific Coast Transport for quite a number of years. He was one of their senior masters."

The next two weeks were spent loading at various berths in the San Francisco Bay area: May 12, Berth #4 Oakland; May 15, Berth #2 Stockton; May 17, Oakland Army Docks.

Bill Cunningham joined the ship in San Francisco as third mate. He recalled at "the last minute we were required to go to a South San Francisco shipyard for emergency engine room repairs. That *was* an experience. The pilot, Capt. Wentworth and I were on the bridge. The inside pier space allotted was very little beyond the beam of *Lane Victory*. Several ship lengths away from projected pier moorings the pilot called for port and starboard anchors out to water depth plus about fifty feet. No tugs now. 'Full ahead,' orders the pilot. He had to repeat the order twice for me to push the telegraph to 'full ahead' as I looked to Capt. Wentworth for counter orders! The ship settled to a calm, straight course, very slow speed. Eventually 'half ahead' carried the ship safely and comfortably to the allotted tight space as though in supernatural hands. That pilot knew his bay bottom and his job! I'll never forget his confidence and bearing. Nor will I ever forget Capt. Wentworth's concentration and concern while sensing his split second thinking."

Departing San Francisco on May 19 the vessel sailed for Long Beach, arriving at Los Angeles Berth 51 on May 20. After a brief idle period while cargoes were assembled, she shifted on May 22 to pier B, Berth 18, Long Beach and commenced loading. There the crew signed foreign articles for the coming voyage to the Far East.

From Capt. Wentworth's voyage letter to Pacific Coast Transport: "May 25 Depart Long Beach. At Long Beach the usual confusion. We had no manifest or stowage plans on departure." Confusion was a typical state of affairs at this early stage in the Vietnam conflict.

"Fair winds and smooth seas for most of the trans-Pacific passages. Two days of heavy weather approaching the coast of Japan."

The weather slowed the ship down. Her average speed to Yokohama was 14.13 knots. She was capable of sustaining 15.5 knots.

"June 10, 1967 arrived Yokohama, took on bunkers, supplies and immediately posted board for Manila. Teddy L.

Kinder off due to injury. Sailed for Manila, arrived June 16, 1967."

Most steamship companies don't have offices in the ports their ships travel to. They rely on a shipping agent to handle the vessel's affairs for them. A shipping agent has offices in all the major ports in a given geographic area. Atlas maintained offices on the West Coast of the United States. Jardine Matheson at this time was in Hong Kong, Bangkok, Singapore and other ports. Evergreen operated out of Taiwan and serviced Saigon, Okinawa, Hong Kong, Yokohama and other ports. Once a ship crosses a certain line of demarcation, whether it be the International Dateline or enters the South China Sea, a particular shipping agent takes over all responsibility for husbanding that ship. Arranging for berthing, stevedores, fuel, stores, crew changes and other necessities, the agent ensures the efficient operation of the ship in foreign waters.

At this time the most efficient means of communication was the radio-telegraph. Each agent signed his telegrams with a one word signature. It was far cheaper, when sending telegrams to thirty or forty ships five or six times a day, to sign the message "Sugarcraft" rather than, for example, "The Far Eastern Management and Trading Company of Taiwan." The following radiogram from the ship's Far East agent is remarkable for packing so much information in so few words.

"MASTER LANE VICTORY KECW MANILA
ETA NOTED
VIEW DAY PIRACY
SUGGEST ARRIVE DAYLIGHT
GUIDANCE
STATUS STANDBY
ACKNOWLEDGE

SUGARCRAFT"

It is addressed to the master of the ship with the vessel's call sign and current port listed. Next, the estimated time of arrival is acknowledged. Because of frequently occurring piracy in Manila harbor, the agent suggests the captain adjust the ship's speed so that it arrive at daylight to minimize the chance of piracy. The master is informed that he is on a "standby" status. In other words anchor and await further orders. In still other words, hurry up and wait. Finally, the agent asks the captain to acknowledge receiving the message and signs it with the codeword "Sugarcraft" so that the captain will recognize the message as coming from the ship's authorized agent for this area.

On June 16 the ship arrived at Manila and anchored to await orders. Piracy didn't occur on this voyage but it typically took the form of natives coming aboard a ship at anchor and throwing anything over the side that wasn't nailed down. On other ships this has included mooring lines, dunnage, cargo, tools and brass fittings.

Departing Manila on June 23, the ship sailed for Qui Nhon. On the 24th she entered the war bonus zone and arrived at that harbor on June 25.

It was almost a repeat of an earlier voyage. The military authorities didn't know what cargo the ship was carrying. Neither did the master.

"The army came aboard and asked what our cargo was. It was embarrassing to tell them we didn't know what cargo was loaded last at Long Beach." [Wentworth voyage letter.]

Apparently they decided the only way to find out was to start discharging. This they did on June 29, working at anchor and setting the cargo into barges to be taken ashore.

The following day a cargo plan materialized and the military decided they wanted what the ship had. Shifting it to a pier they began discharging in earnest. The cargo plan showed: housewares, oil, fat, powdered milk, canned fruit, canned juice, canned vegetables, condiments, sugar, batteries, general cargo, plywood, furniture, furnishings and paper. The canned juice included pineapple juice, Pepsi-Cola and Coca-Cola.

Third mate Cunningham remembered the stevedores were Korean. They quickly discovered the ship had an ice-maker on board. "Twas surprising how much the *Lane Victory* ice cube-making facility helped Korean morale."

On Independence Day 1967 the ship completed discharging and shifted from the dock to anchorage to prepare for sea.

At 0930 the morning of July 5, the *Lane Victory* sailed from Qui Nhon to Subic bay, crossing out of the bonus area that same day. Enroute she was rerouted to Manila.

Arriving at Manila on July 7 cargo operations started immediately with vehicles being loaded in hatches 1 and 3.

"Two hours before sailing from Manila I received orders to delay sailing and off-loaded an automobile that was put aboard by mistake. Per usual, four cars had to be moved to get at the one to be off-loaded." [Wentworth voyage letter.]

On July 8 the ship departed for Oakland.

"Fair winds and smooth seas for most of the Trans-Pacific passages. Average speed 15.2 knots." [Wentworth voyage letter.] Arriving in San Francisco on July 25th at 1730, the ship was two days ahead of schedule.

Thomas Nation, third mate on the twelve-to-four watch recalled, "When we got to San Francisco the chief mate was applauded for having such a clean, fresh painted and well-maintained ship."

One reason seamen were so eager to sail during the Vietnam era was the money.

Morgan Vail: "Early in the war the one thing that made it worthwhile for some of these seamen to accept such a job was that they got a war bonus. A hundred percent, plus ten percent for ammunition, plus they got a lot of overtime if they wanted to work. They had an open book and early on you could work every day. If you were on the four-to-eight watch you could work six hours overtime Monday through Friday and get overtime on Saturday and Sunday plus get docking and undocking and this and that. They made a lot of money if they chose to."

Unionism created some unusual differences in the way ships were manned. In general, most ships got their deck officers from the Masters Mates and Pilots Union, their engineers from the Marine Engineers Benevolent Association and the radio operator from either the Radio Officers Union or the American Radio Operator's Association. If a ship was operated by an East Coast company, the unlicensed crew came from the National Maritime Union. Gulf Coast ships were crewed by the Seafarer's International Union. But West Coast ships got their sailors from the Sailor's Union of the Pacific, their unlicensed engine crew from the Marine Firemen, Oilers and Watertenders, their steward's department from the Marine Cooks and Stewards, and a Purser from the Marine Staff Officer's Association. Because West Coast ships had seven unions to contend with, and each jealously guarded their positions on board ship, they carried larger crews.

Stan Coppel: "Gulf Coast ships ran with a crew of 42 (SIU) and West Coast ships carried 52. It was a difference of $1,000 a day in wages. Once a Gulf ship came in with 44 men in the crew. I asked them if they wanted me to get more men. 'Hell no. Take two off,' they said."

Other Victory ships active at the time were: *Winthrop Victory, Bowdoin Victory, Hunter Victory, Queens Victory, Nashua Victory, Hope Victory, Lindenwood Victory, Creighton Victory, Grove City Victory, Mayfield Victory, Brazil Victory.*

The SUP shipped 928 jobs during the month of July, 1967.

After discharging the vehicles at Pier 5, Naval Supply Center, Oakland the *Lane* shifted to Pier 64, in San Francisco where the voyage terminated 2400 August 2.

Capt. Wentworth couldn't resist bragging about the voyage. He ended his voyage letter to the company by saying, "A very good crew this trip. They put out good professional work as you will see when you come aboard. I had several compliments on the crew's behavior and the condition of the ship from shoreside personnel."

The *Lane Victory* was popular with the Sailor's Union of the Pacific (SUP). From the August 11, 1967 edition of the

"West Coast Sailors," the Patrolmen's reports state, "Pacific Coast Transport: *Lane Victory* — Together with Charlie Russo, paid this ship off in all three departments. Came in clean without a single beef. It was a pleasure to pay her off." This came from a page with forty-three other vessels, most of which had some type of union problem.

The master circled the comment in the paper and left it in his desk. It was found there in September of 1990.

12

Just One Voyage
After Another

By the late '60s, the war in Vietnam was taking an ever
greater toll on the United States. A grim mood gripped
the nation as it struggled through a conflict that it could
not win. The first months of stepped up American involvement
were marked by fits and starts. After so many years of inactivity
the war machine had trouble getting into gear. There were
weeks on end of idle time and "hurry up and wait." The *Lane
Victory* reflected the national mood as she plodded across the
ocean from one port to another — loading here, discharging
there. At times it was like a bus run, monotonous and
uninteresting. Once in gear, however, the machinery ran with
determination, purpose and efficiency. The voyages during the
"middle years" of the Vietnam war would pass like boxcars at
a railroad crossing — rapid, repetitive and uneventful.

Voyage 4 for Pacific Coast Transport Company, No. 10
under the National Shipping Authority, began August 3, 1967 at
AAA shipyard in San Francisco. It was normal for government-

owned ships such as the *Lane Victory* to spend a few days at the
end of each voyage undergoing repairs. Commercially-owned
ships in such circumstances wouldn't waste the time; repairs
could be made while the cargo was loaded.

The *Lane's* next cargo waited in the Pacific Northwest.
Sailing for Coos Bay, Oregon, she arrived there August 4.

On August 9 the sailing board was posted for departure
the following day, destination Newport, on the central coast of
Oregon. The ship sailed on time, but couldn't get in because of
thick fog. Anchoring at 1900, August 10th, she waited three
days for the weather to clear. Finally able to go alongside on
August 15, she loaded briefly then sailed for Westport, Oregon.
August 17 found the ship shifting to Longview, Washington on
the Columbia River. On August 18 she sailed for Seattle arriving
there the following day. At Pier 91, berth A, she loaded crated
goods, plywood and creosoted pilings. On August 21 the ship
shifted to the West Waterway Mill Dock in Seattle and on August
24 shifted to Pier 91 berth M. Departure from the West Coast
of the United States was August 25 with Yokosuka, Japan being
her next intended port.

Then, in mid-Pacific, Capt. Wentworth received orders
to proceed directly to Vung Tau.

Arriving at 1930 September 16 the *Lane Victory* recorded
a passage of 21 days 7 hours and a speed of 14.04 knots.

On September 17 she was taken alongside the pier at
Vung Tau. This was a new development for there was no pier
at Vung Tau (Cape St. Jacques) until the U.S. military installed
one in the late '60s. It enabled an easy source of supplies to the
lower Saigon River Delta area.

Unlike World War II, the war in Vietnam was basically
a ground war. The Viet-Cong had no Navy or Air Force to
speak of. The effect on merchant ships was to eliminate the
threat of torpedoes or aerial bombing. The only real threat to
merchant ships and crews came when the ships were within
reach of the Viet-Cong army, primarily, in the harbors and up
the rivers.

The threat of attack from the river banks became serious enough that the Maritime Administration issued warning instructions to their GAA vessels.

INSTRUCTION TO MASTERS AND CHIEF ENGINEERS OF VC2 SHIPS
DEFENSIVE MEASURES RECOMMENDED FOR TRANSIT OF SAIGON RIVER

Prior to and during transit of the Saigon River, defensive measures designed to minimize the effect of possible enemy action should be placed in effect on all ships. Such measures should include, but are not limited to, the following:

DECK DEPARTMENT
A. Prior to Transit
   1. Conduct emergency steering drills
   2. Brief crew on general precaution measures to be taken by all hands:
     a. Install anti-grenade screens in all portholes. Secure dead lights if available.
     b. Issue protective equipment (helmets and flack jackets) to those crew members required on deck. All other members to remain in their rooms or messrooms.
     c. Secure all weather deck doors. Joiner type doors to be left on ajar hooks.
     d. Ventilation system to cargo spaces to be secured when nature of cargo permits.
     e. Both anchors ready to "let go."
     f. Pressure on fire mains and weather deck hoses strung out and charged.
     g. Towing wires rigged fore and aft in a manner that will allow tugs or other vessels to take ship under tow without assistance from ship's crew.
     h. Pyrotechnics as required to be at the ready in bridge area.

i. Radio Operator on watch in radio room guarding Voice
Radio 2716 KCS and/or CW (4150 KC) per MSTS
communications instruction Annex "Charlie."

B. During Transit
Provide licensed deck officer in steering engine room and one
able bodied seaman.

ENGINE DEPARTMENT:
A. Prior to transit
1. Only necessary personnel in engine room on watch.
2. Shaft alley quick-acting water-tight door secured.
3. Both boilers and generators on the line.
4. Both power feeders to steering gear energized.
5. All deep tank internal isolating valves secured.
6. Fore and aft peak tanks secured at tanks.
7. Pressure on fire mains and all fire-fighting equipment ready
for immediate use.
8. All fuel oil, bilge, ballast manifold valves secured except
one fuel oil settler suction.
9. Standby fuel oil service pump warmed-up and ready for
instant change-over.
10. All unnecessary machinery, i.e., centrifuge, evaporators,
fuel oil, transfer pumps, etc. secured.
11. Main and auxiliary air ejectors, circulating pumps,
condensate pumps, lube oil pumps operating. Bilge and
ballast pumps warmed up and ready for use.
12. Both fuel oil settlers topped and 100 degree F. Temperature
maintained. Distilled water tank filled. Standby lube oil
gravity tank topped off.
13. Emergency diesel generator fuel tank topped off and diesel
generator running with electrician standing by in emergency
generator room.
14. Steam smothering system activated to distribution manifold
with man in attendance. All valves clearly labeled.
B. During Transit
Chief Engineer or First Engineer on duty with Watch
Engineer in Engine Room.

GENERAL:

Plans for administering first-aid in case of injury to personnel should
be formulated, medical supplies and first-aid items should be readily
available, and contingency plans prepared in advance.

After discharging for several days, the ship shifted on
September 24 to Saigon where she tied up to the Newport Army
dock.

Completing her discharge on September 30 she
immediately began loading retrograde cargo. It was a repeat of
her duty in previous wars. The cargo consisted of damaged
scoop loaders, bulldozers, steam rollers, and several hundred
conexes (small containers) of empty artillery shells. Scheduled
for the U.S., the cargo would be rebuilt (rearmed, in the case of
the shells) and used again.

On October 6, 1967 one of the ABs was logged for being
absent for six days and was fined four days pay for each day
absent. This was a stiff fine but missing work for an entire week
is serious.

On October 7th the vessel shifted back to Vung-Tau and
took aboard a passenger, Capt. Maynard. D. Pollad, of the 44th
Medical Brigade. Reporting aboard on October 8, he was booked
for passage to the first Pacific Coast port. He was due in the
United States by October 30 and there was no military
transportation available. He would disembark in Oakland.

Sailing on October 8, the ship once more pointed her
bow toward what the military termed CONUS (COntinental
UNited States): destination Oakland.

Merchant seamen are always inoculated against the
diseases common to the ports they visit. Every American seaman
carries a shot record and shots are methodically given as part of
the process of signing on the ships' articles. One is not allowed
to sign on unless one passes a physical and receives the shots.
Typically a sailor is vaccinated for smallpox, typhoid, typhus

and cholera. If the ship travels to certain parts of the world he will receive a yellow fever shot. Vietnam was unusual because it added another shot to the list — bubonic plague. Plague is carried by fleas which live on rats. It became part of the homeward bound routine on ships returning from Vietnam to set traps and check for rats.

From the deck log: "Oct. 14, 1967 0930, 24-54 N. Lat. 136-16 E. Long. Inspected all holds. Caught one rat in #4 Lower Hold. No evidence of sores on the nose or tail of the rat. No evidence of any rodents in the rest of the hatches."

Because of such vigilance, there were no known cases of plague brought into the United States on merchant ships during the Vietnam conflict.

The ship's store or "slop chest" on a freighter doesn't carry much. "Slop" comes from a Dutch word referring to sailor's clothing. In the early days of sailing ships a chest of such garments was usually kept on board to sell to the crew as needed. On modern ships, cigarettes and soft drinks are the biggest sellers.

This late in the *Lane Victory*'s voyage the only cigarettes remaining were probably the brands that nobody wanted such as Newport, Old Gold or Herbert Tarryton. The most popular were Pall Mall, Winston, Salem, Camel and Lucky Strike. These could be traded ashore in foreign ports for other commodities: food, souvenirs and even the favors of women. By law the ship is allowed to charge no more than 10% profit on all slop chest items. Prices on this voyage were:

> Reg. cig., $1.25/carton
> King size 1.35/carton
> Benson & Hedges 1.50/carton
> Almond Roca $2
> Chewing gum .90/box
> Life Savers .65/box
> Mixed nuts .65/can

peanuts .45/can
7-up 2.80/case
Assorted sodas, $2.65/case
Pepsi or diet-cola 2.70/case
Aqua Velva .65
Old Spice 1.25
Toothpaste .60/tube.

Arriving at the San Francisco Light Vessel on October 27, the ship later tied up to Oakland Army Dock berth #8 and began discharging.

On October 29 she shifted to Willamette drydock in Richmond for routine drydocking. Voyage 4 ended there at midnight October 31.

In keeping with tradition, Voyage 5 for PCTC began one minute after midnight on November 1 at Willamette Shipyard dock 3. The ship shifted the same day to NSC (Naval Supply Center) Berth D in Oakland.

The *Lane Victory*'s cargo this voyage was miscellaneous general cargo, pov's and milvans. But rather than returning to Vietnam, she was scheduled for an "island run" to supply military bases in the Pacific. It was a voyage reminiscent of some of the ship's World War II trips.

On November 5 she sailed for Pearl Harbor where she arrived on November 11, then shifted to Honolulu.

What does the average seaman carry with him on an oceangoing voyage? The chief cook missed the ship when it sailed from San Francisco to Pearl harbor. His personal effects were gathered, inventoried and sent ashore to be shipped back to the mainland. They consisted of:

1 - Ctn. Cigarettes
2 - Wallets containing papers (2)
3 - 1 pr. work Shoes
4 - 2 Dolls
5 - 2 Pocket Knives

6 - 2 Alarm Clocks
7 - 1 Ukelele
8 - Assorted Shaving gear
9 - 1 Pr. Chop Sticks
10 - 1 Kodak camera
11 - 4 shirts
12 - 3 Pants
13 - 1 Shorts
14 - 21 "T" shirts
15 - Socks and Underwear
16 - 11 Pr Socks
17 - 1 Pr. Glasses (reading)
18 - 1 Sea Bag
19 - 2 Suit Cases
20 - 1 Work Jacket

November 12 found the vessel returning to West Lock Ammo Dock at Pearl Harbor. She departed that evening for Kwajalein.

Arriving at Kwajalein on November 18 two days were spent discharging. She sailed November 20 for Guam.

Apra harbor, Guam, was entered on November 25 where the remainder of the cargo was discharged in three days, some cargo backloaded, and the ship returned to the United States West Coast. It was probably a great disappointment to those who signed on anticipating a Vietnam war bonus.

The first American port of call was San Diego where cargo was discharged on December 15. Following a short hop up the coast to Long Beach to discharge a few more tons the ship headed once more to San Francisco.

On December 17 the ship arrived in Oakland, discharged the few remaining tons of cargo at NSC berth 1 and shifted to pier 46 in San Francisco. Voyage 5 ended there on December 20.

On Voyage 6 which commenced December 21 the *Lane Victory* would again carry ammunition. Shifting to Port Chicago on December 24 the first order of business was to sheath the inside of all the cargo hatches with lumber. Only the finest grade of wood is used, without knots, cracks or distortions. The interior of each hatch is floored and walled off so that the cargo is loaded inside what amounts to a large wooden box. This box acts as insulation for the ammunition and makes it easier to stow. In addition, there is no danger of friction causing heat, sparks or fire as there is no danger of bombs or containers rubbing against the ship's metal frames and plating.

This was the only Christmas the *Lane Victory* spent in the United States during her active career.

By 1967 public opinion against the war in Vietnam was growing. Some gathered to peacefully voice their opposition. Others were loud, abusive. Still other anti-war feelings came out in strange ways.

From the deck log for December 28, 1967:

0050 received anonymous phone call that a bomb is aboard and set to go off at 0200. Port security notified.

0125 on orders from CDO (Command Duty Officer) all hands ordered off vessel with the exception of the engine room watch. 0240 upon request Chief Mate return to vessel. Bomb demolition and guard searching vessel.

0410 search of vessel complete, all in apparent good order.

0700 Crew is allowed to return aboard.

On January 3, 1968 the ship departed San Francisco, bound for Subic Bay and further orders.

After a quiet crossing she arrived on January 22. Capt. Wentworth received orders to immediately sail for Sattahip, Thailand. Departing at 1830 the same day the ship made her way across the South China Sea arriving at Sattahip on January 26.

The cargo came out quickly and by February 1 the ship was outbound for San Francisco. On the 3rd orders were received to divert to Bataan, in the north part of Manila Bay. Arriving on February 5 the ship took on fuel and prepared to wait. Further orders came immediately: continue on to San Francisco.

San Francisco was reached on February 21, with the ship tying up to Oakland Army Base Pier 7 West and the voyage ending on February 23.

The next load of cargo was ready and came aboard quickly. Voyage 7 for Pacific Coast Transport Company began February 24 and the *Lane* departed on the 28th at two in the morning bound for Manila.

Then, on March 14, as she neared the Philippines, orders were received to proceed directly to Saigon. March 20, found the ship anchoring at Vung Tau.

The wait was a mere three days. On March 23 the ship proceeded upriver to Saigon, tying up to Newport Army Dock No. 4 K.

The cargo came off as quickly as it was put on board. After only six days, the ship departed Saigon.

On April 2, she arrived at Naha, Okinawa and anchored awaiting a berth. Shifting to the pier on April 6 the ship loaded retrograde cargo [damaged vehicles] and sailed on April 11.

The return voyage brought calm weather and fair seas. The ship arrived at the San Francisco Light Vessel on April 25, with the voyage ending at midnight that day at Pier G in the Naval Supply Center.

Voyage 8 for PCTC and 14 for NSA began April 26.

After discharging the cargo the ship shifted to Pier 64 San Francisco for voyage repairs.

On April 30, while breakfast was being prepared, a fire broke out in the galley range. It was quickly put out with portable carbon dioxide bottles. The cause was found to be grease in the range's drip pans. Five fifteen-pound bottles of CO_2 were used to extinguish the fire.

With no major harm caused by the fire, the ship shifted to Berth 3, Pier 3 at Port Chicago and took on a full cargo of ammunition.

This time there were no bomb threats. The sailing on May 8 was routine. The destination was Subic Bay for further orders.

As in Voyage 7, the *Lane Victory* was again diverted — this time to Guam. On this occasion it wasn't the military that was responsible, but the *Lane* herself. There were problems with the boilers caused by too much salinity.

From a letter to PCTC's Port Engineer:

On May 25 the salinity in the boilers was getting beyond control. Had a slight leak in the main condenser so decided to put sawdust in the system. The ship has no sawdust injector so have to stop and drain the condenser to put the sawdust in. Was unable to secure the saltwater. The way the main low sea suction valve was screwed down it was apparent that this was off the valve stem. The captain was notified and I recommended that the ship divert to the nearest port for repairs to the valve. The nearest was Guam. A radiogram was sent there requesting divers and machinists on arrival for this work.

The vessel arrived in Guam, Sunday, a.m. May 26. The agent informed us that the navy only does work and furnished men when there is no commercial outfit to do the work. The divers that were used, Campbell is the name, are commercial. The navy furnished machinists. The divers had never done a job like this before. Remember we had this same sort of job on the "Filmore." I suggested that the divers use heavy canvas but he told me that wasn't sufficient that he was going to do the work. So I figured he knew. Anyway he came aboard Sunday at 1230, sent his diver down and removed the bilge screen, not asking the size or data about the work to be done. Campbell did come to see me saying it didn't look like the right screen to him. This was on Sunday with the navy machinist standing by. Then the divers said they wouldn't do anything until 0900 Monday as they had to buy some plywood and some foam rubber and the stores didn't open until 0800 Monday.

Monday at 1000 they came back with plywood and foam rubber, the machinist standing by. They tried four times to seal off the water with plywood with no success. So in the afternoon I suggested that navy divers be used as they weren't making any headway. So at that they went ashore and got some canvas, the flow of water was stopped, the valve opened, the disc was removed from the valve bonnet. It was standing in an upright position at the side of the valve. The guide stem was lying in the screen and we couldn't get that out. The valve bonnet was secured back in place with the valve stem hole plugged and the disc and stem taken to the navy shop for repairs. The area in way of the stem holding nut recess on the disc was wasted away. That had to be removed and a new piece put in place. A new holding nut was made for the stem and this is locked in place with a lock screw. A new guide stem was machined and welded in place. The machining and all was very good.

Apparently the trouble with these valves comes from the guide stem unscrewing and allowing the valve disc to wander any such way in the valve body till it becomes loose. The valve was reassembled aboard, inspected by ABS representative E.E. Springer and Commander Pruitt, U.S. Coast Guard. The valve was installed and tested OK at 0130 5/29. Mr. Springer made an entry in the vessel's logbook. Will forward the certificate to the Wilmington office through the agent.

We then filled the main condenser and the ship's crew tested it for leaks. One leaky tube was found and plugged. Divers wasted or caused to be wasted approximately 24 to 36 hours. Total port time for Guam was 75.5 hours allowing one hour in and one hour out.

Hoping this meets with your approval,

(Signed) P. S. Morgan
Chief Engineer

Departing Guam on May 29, the ship reached Subic Bay on June 2. The days of long waits at anchor were over. Only two days later the vessel sailed for Cam Ranh Bay arriving there on June 6.

There was a one week delay awaiting ships already discharging. Then on June 13 she went alongside and commenced discharging.

The *Lane Victory* had the reputation of being the best-kept ship of all those taken out of the Reserve Fleet. In the mail received at Cam Ranh Bay was a letter from Pacific Coast Transport Company praising the master and crew for the condition of the ship.

Dear Captain Murray:

By the enclosed copy of a portion of the physical inspection report you can feel justly proud of the appearance of your vessel. The officers and crew are to be commended for their visible efforts in accomplishing and maintaining a superior rated vessel. Again congratulations, thanks for a job well done and best sailing to you, your officers and crew.

(signed) Monty W. Klepper
Port Captain

The enclosure reads:

SS Lane Victory, General remarks section: The *Lane Victory* was inspected while at loading berth at the Naval Weapons Station, Concord, California. It is becoming increasingly more difficult to write a survey on this ship without becoming repetitious. The ship continues to be a superior ship. The spaces which are in other than in GOOD or EXCELLENT condition are harder than ever to find. Since the last inspection requested improvements and condition were noted in but not limited to the following areas. Insurance wire has been slushed and the reel was covered. The shelves in the steward's dry store room have been cleaned and painted. The bridge deck has been coated under the gratings and the drains cleared in the gun tubs on this deck. The blackout switches on the watertight doors in the poop house have been tied up out of the way. The ship has now acquired the proper crystals for the radiotelephone. In addition several of the crews rooms have been painted and work has commenced upon upgrading the poop house, especially the deck heads.

There is little else that can be said about this ship that has not been said in previous inspections. To say that a ship looks like the *Lane Victory* continues to be a short hand method of saying that a ship looks like an excellent ship.

Sailing on June 21, the *Lane Victory* once more headed for San Francisco. As she neared California, on July 4 she received diversion orders to Newport, Oregon.

On July 7 there was trouble with the master gyrocompass. The ship steered by magnetic compass until repairs were made. On July 8 orders were again received to divert, this time to Raymond, on Washington State's south coast. Arriving on July 9, the voyage ended the following day at the Raymond pier.

Voyage 9 began on July 11 with the ship sailing from Raymond to the Puget Sound. There she loaded treated lumber at a series of ports: Tacoma, July 11; Pier 91, Seattle, July 15; Everett, July 17.

Mark Owens, fresh out of California Maritime Academy, caught the ship just as it sailed from Everett. "When I graduated, we completed our ceremony, my mother drove me to the Oakland Airport, I flew to Seattle, the agent met me at the airport, we went down to the ship, the shipping commissioner was standing there on the dock. I signed on. I left my bag in my stateroom, went back aft, let go and then I went up on the bridge and stood a watch.

"I ended up clearing Cape Flattery by myself. Wentworth never came up. He might have been looking out the porthole down below or something but he never came . . . he wasn't on the bridge."

In one of the few voyages not to load in California, the ship sailed on July 21 directly for Qui Nhon.

At first Capt. Wentworth showed an interest in the new third mate.

Mark Owens: "When I reported aboard, I didn't have a sextant. Capt. Wentworth came down and was talking to me about it later on. And he suggested that I use his. He had a very nice wartime Plath, swastikas stamped all over it. I thought that was just very, very nice of him to be that concerned about me."

As the voyage progressed it became clear that the rest of the deck officers had other things on their minds.

Mark Owens: "I was the only officer that I know of not involved right then in the middle of a nasty divorce. They were all fairly unhappy. Wentworth, Clayburn and Moldrup were running a real tight race to see who was the most bitter about their circumstances."

The purser was a help to the new third mate in adjusting to his environment: "This purser, O'Hara, told me that he'd gone to sea an awful lot and then let his deck license lapse and become a purser. He was in his late sixties. I think he probably was in square riggers at one time. I don't remember too much about him except that he was kind and nice. I probably learned a great deal about how to get around the ship and get by, by talking to him."

On some voyages the crew just doesn't get along. No one knows how it starts or why, but soon there are disagreements, arguments and intrigues. On this voyage grudges that began on earlier voyages came to a head, often in peculiar ways. Mark Owens: "There was a black engineer and everybody was riding him pretty hard. When they loaded the cargo we had mostly beer down below and creosoted lumber on deck. The ship was full, if it wasn't down to its marks besides, it was certainly full. And they had taken several pallets of beer and put it in the lazarette and they were all merrily drinking.

"One night at sea, I was looking over the after rail and I saw this guy climb out of the one of the ventilators with a case of beer. I told the chief mate that maybe he'd want to put a padlock on . . . Now, inside the masthouses is a little manhole that goes down over the hatch. You couldn't get in the door to the hatch so this guy had gone down through the ventilator and then down through that manhole. I told him maybe he ought to put a padlock on that, on the manhole. He told the crew that I was writing letters to CID [Criminal Investigation Division of the Navy] about stealing beer. Of course all these guys thought that I was writing about the several pallets they had in the lazarette. And in fact somebody was and I found out later it was this black engineer that now was trying to even the score for some of the dirty tricks they played on him.

"There's a laundry, port side down below the main deck. I was down there washing my clothes one day and a delegation of the sailors came and told me they were going to put a head on me if I said anything more about this beer. I was holding them off in the passageway with a hatch batten.

"I couldn't figure out what to do about that, so later on I made a real obvious theft of a case of beer and they never bothered me again. I just made sure they saw me take the case.

"That trouble came from the chief mate telling the delegate that I was the one that was writing the letters.

"These guys were really very unhappy. When I was there I didn't realize it. I was having a hard time with a lot of it, a lot of these nuances that I just didn't pick up on."

As the ship neared the Far East she again had boiler problems. On August 4, 1968 the Chief Engineer reported that repairs to port boiler couldn't be accomplished with ship's personnel. A Casrep (Casualty Report) radio message was sent to COMSTSFE (Commanding Officer Military Sealift Transport Service Far East).

On August 6 orders were received to divert to Manila for boiler repairs.

While approaching the anchorage the ship touched bottom in Manila harbor.

Mark Owens: "We went aground in Manila. Not a big deal as groundings go. We only realized we were aground when the ship stopped moving. There wasn't a lurch or anything we just went up into the mud. But Ed (Capt. Wentworth) was very concerned about it. I didn't realize at the time but they were all worried about whoever this mysterious person was that was writing the letters about the beer. And they were afraid they would write another one about the grounding. That was just about the time that everybody realized that somebody had written to the CID about this beer. He was real upset at first to find out who was writing the letters. 'Damn well better not say anything about the grounding.'"

Although there was no obvious damage and soundings indicated no leaks, a survey was required.

From the deck log:

> 1845 August 16. Surveyed vessel while afloat at anchorage South Harbor Manila P.I. In consequence of a reported grounding on August 12, 1968 and found tight at this time. The undersigned considers this vessel seaworthy and recommends she be retained as classed with the bureau.
>
> (Signed) Donald Z. King.

Mark Owens: "We went to the Philippines the first time in my life. I went ashore and went into a gin mill at the head of the dock. Bought out one of the girls and took her home. And it was the chief mate's girlfriend. He never forgave me. Of all the bars and all the girls in the Philippines, I happened to find his."

Sailing from Manila on August 17, the ship arrived at Qui Nhon on August 19.

Qui Nhon is an attractive harbor. Mark Owens recalled fondly, "Qui Nhon I rather enjoyed. It was a pretty place. They had a river port there. The offshore side was a very mountainous narrow peninsula and then the dock was on the inshore side of the river. And it was flat after that."

Occasionally new third mates learn hard lessons about unionism. Mark Owens recalled that he "had the crew all walk off the deck on me one time when we were in port doing cargo ops. I needed some cluster lights. So I had the bosun bring them up on deck for me. I didn't have a good place to put them until the longshoremen were ready to rig them. There was an emergency generator room on the deck there. 'Well, just put them in there.'

"He says, 'You sure you want me to put them in there?'

"'Yeah, put them in there.'

"'OK.'

"So he sets them down in there and then the whole crew walked off the ship because that was an engineering space. Deck crew walked off because they were working in an engine space. And the engine crew walked off because they had deck people working in an engine space. They just made a lot of noise and went back to work a little later. It was just an infighting kind of thing . . . Put in overtime for it by the way."

Mark Owens tried his best to treat the longshoremen with respect. "Qui Nhon they had Korean longshoremen. They were pretty decent guys. I ended up going to town and drinking with some of them. Good time. So later on I was having coffee in the saloon with the stevedore boss and the captain and chief mate threw us out. He didn't want any Koreans inside the house.

"He (the chief mate) used to give the longshoremen such a bad time. It's amazing when you think about it. The mate's job is to get the cargo done and he'd go out and harangue these guys and get them all wound up."

Vietnam was dangerous, even for merchant seamen. Mark Owens: "I went ashore with the radio operator. We'd gone to some little place and we were coming back, walking around town, and the VC started shooting the place up. Some GIs picked us up in a jeep and they were going to drive us back to the base. We passed a kind of a roadblock and there's a couple of guys behind this barricade shooting. They said, 'Wait here, we better help these guys out.'

"They jumped out of the jeep and they go over there and shoot three or four shots. Meanwhile we're sitting up high in this jeep watching this. Then they come back to the jeep and drive us away.

"Later I went to get my hair cut. I went to a Vietnamese barber. He cut my hair so I looked like a six-foot Vietnamese. Right while he was doing it the place came under attack again and he jumped so I had this big bald spot on my head. Then he pulled down this bamboo curtain on the front of his shop, like that's going to keep the bullets out. But after a while he got too nervous and he let me out the back of his shop and down a bunch of alleys and then he pointed me toward a safe direction and he went somewhere else. But he was a decent fellow. These alleys were so narrow that anybody could drop a rock on us. He just wanted to get out of the fighting.

"This one night the VCs were on the mountain side of the river shooting across and our guys were shooting this way and some helicopter came overhead and was shooting at them. I was sleeping up on the flying bridge and all these [shell] casings came down on me. I didn't know which way to jump when all this stuff started happening. I had to get out of there."

Discharging the last of her cargo, the *Lane Victory* then sailed on August 26 for Buckner Bay, Okinawa. She arrived there on August 30.

Mark Owens: "It was an anchorage and it was right up in a corner. There was rocks on three sides, more or less.

"I thought we were dragging one night. But they made a big number explaining to me, 'The hook's here and the chain's here and the ship's here,' and this kind of thing.

"I remember that lecture pretty clearly."

Late summer and early fall is typhoon season in the Eastern Pacific. On Monday, September 2, at 1200 the sailing board was posted to read "no more shore leave due to the proximity of Typhoon Wendy."

At the time the wind force was 4-5 with the barometer at 29.65 and falling. The seas were northeast at a height of four feet with the swell north-northeast at a height of eight feet. The weather quickly deteriorated. By the following day the wind was force 9, the barometer 29.18 with ten-foot waves from the west and thirty-foot swells from the northwest.

On September 4, the *Lane Victory* weighed anchor for sea to avoid the typhoon. The day started with a force 7 wind, eight-foot seas and fifteen- to twenty-foot swells.

Mark Owens: "There was another American ship anchored in Buckner Bay too. He asked us, 'Which way are you going to go?'

"The captain told him, 'I'm headed south.'

"The other guy says, 'Well, I'm going to go north.'

"We went south and got clobbered.

"I was reading my copy of Conrad's book *Typhoon* right in the middle of this thing. The wind was blowing real hard.

"You know, 'I'm going to go out and experience this.'

"I walked out on the weather bridge wing and I'm hanging on to the stanchion and it's blowing pretty hard. I walked back in the wheelhouse and out on the lee wing and I looked down a deck or two below on the house there and there's this big fat greasy AB sitting in an aluminum lawn chair reading a pornographic magazine. So much for the typhoon. Just below the bridge, the longshoremen had spilled a box of nails. Those nails stayed there the whole typhoon. Kind of taught me not to worry about things so much."

"When we went south we went the wrong way and we danced around the dangerous semi-circle of that thing two or three days before we got back up there."

Rather than returning to Buckner Bay on the east side of the island, the ship was directed to anchor off Naha, on the west side to await a berth.

On September 6 she went alongside Pier 4, Naha and loaded cargo for San Francisco.

Mark Owens: "Took a lot of retrograde stuff. In those days the retrograde wasn't too clean. Had the occasional body parts . . . this was still '68 . . . they were taking the stuff, the burnt up equipment right out of the field and sending it to Naha and they'd sprinkle this powder and stuff around. They picked up all the obvious things but they told us not to mess with it because it was contaminated. It had all this stuff in it. Some of it you could smell two or three days later. It came very quickly from Vietnam to Naha to the ship. I heard later they changed their procedures so that by the time the civilians got it there wasn't any real evidence left."

The first purchase a new third mate makes when he has saved some money is a sextant. Mark Owens was no exception: "I bought a Japanese sextant in Okinawa, a Tamaya. Everyone . . . all those deck officers, the captain and chief mate particularly, despised orientals. I didn't quite have enough money for the sextant. I had to come back and get a draw. He [Wentworth] didn't want to give me the money because I shouldn't buy a 'gook' sextant. They were our enemies during the war. I should buy a good Plath [made by Germans who were also our enemies during the war]."

Departing September 11 the ship had a difficult return voyage. The following log entry was typical: "Sunday, September 15, 2000. Very rough seas, SExE'ly sea and heavy swell. Taking water over bow and on foredeck. Vessel pitching and rolling heavily at times."

As the ship neared the West Coast, Mark Owens was startled to have Capt. Wentworth burst in to his room one night. "We had this radar, it's one of the earliest models to come out on merchant ships. But it did have a switch from relative bearings to true bearings. I had it on true one night and this Neils Moldrup was the second mate. He was a first class character in his own right. He generally relieved the watch by sweeping everything off the chart table and telling me to get out of there. So later on he noticed that the radar picture wasn't right. I usually set things back to the way I found them, but I forgot that night. So he called the captain. The captain came up to look at the radar. He flipped that switch and when he did it shorted out an old capacitor someplace in the radar and there was a huge pop and a flash of light and the thing was dead. So he came down to my fo'c's'le. I'd already been asleep a couple of hours. He kicked the door in and told me I blew up his radar and I was fired.

"Later on he indicated that I wasn't really fired. Just angry. I got a real kick out of noticing that my old room is still missing a kick panel. There's a fan in that door now where the kick panel is supposed to be."

CANAL ZONE GOVERNMENT

CANAL ZONE

Port of Cristobal

CLEARANCE

This is to certify to all whom it may concern:

That E.D. Wentworth

Master or Commander of the USA SS LANE VICTORY

burden 5193 net

tons or thereabouts navigated with a crew consisting of (45)

crew members and no passengers bound for SOUTHPORT NC

has here entered and cleared his vessel according to law.

Given under my hand and seal this

12th day of October

nineteen hundred and sixty-eight

Every ship transiting the Panama Canal must pay fees based on her Panama Canal tonnage (a volumetric measurement) and receive a clearance. This is the Lane Victory*'s clearance for her voyage to Sunnypoint, North Carolina. Courtesy the* Lane Victory.

By the end of the voyage Mark Owens was anxious to get off. "You get so you just don't talk. And that's the way it was. I just didn't talk to anybody. And you don't say anything to the people on watch with you."

Reaching the San Francisco Light Vessel on September 26 the *Lane* went to Oakland, Naval Supply Center Berth A and terminated her voyage there the following day.

Voyage 10 commenced September 28, 1968 with the ship shifting to Pier 64, the AAA repair dock at San Francisco. Four days were spent completing voyage repairs then on October 2 she sailed. She was to carry ammunition again, but not from Port Chicago. Her next load waited in Sunnypoint, North Carolina.

Sailing in ballast, the vessel arrived at the Canal Zone on October 11.

What should have been a routine transit suddenly became nerve-wracking. While approaching the first lock at the Panama Canal the rudder stuck at ten degrees to port.

Like the bomb threat at Port Chicago in an earlier voyage, it was believed to be a deliberate act. The Chief Engineer described the incident in a letter to PCTC's Port Engineer:

> At approximately 1000 hours Saturday 12, October 1968 while approaching the entrance to PEDRO MIGUEL Locks in the Panama Canal, Capt. Wentworth called the Engine Room and notified me that the Rudder Indicator was stopped at 10 degrees Left Rudder, and that neither the Ship or the Indicator were responding to the wheel.
>
> I immediately left the Engine Room and went to the Steering Engine Room. Upon investigation I found that the #1 Toggle Pin Connecting the linkage between the TELEMOTOR and the STARBOARD PUMP was not in place. I took # 2 Toggle Pin from the Port Steering Engine and inserted it into the Starboard Linkage and notified Capt. Wentworth.
>
> After testing the Steering Gear to the satisfaction of the Captain and the Pilot I looked about the STEERING ENGINE ROOM

further. I found #1 Toggle Pin approximately four (4) feet from the linkage under the STEERING ENGINE Mechanism. This pin in no way could remove itself from the linkage due to the Toggle at its end.

I then placed the Chief Electrician on watch at the Steering Engine Room and he remained there for the remainder of the Canal Transit. The pin found on deck was placed in the linkage to the Port Pump and the Steering Engine was back in full operation.

We feel that we know who is responsible for this act of sabotage, but lacking definite proof we must of necessity refrain from using names.

I sincerely hope that this will explain satisfactorily the failure of the Steering Engine during the Canal Transit of 12, October 68.

/s/ respectfully   R.R. Burnham

Ch/Engineer

Had the steering gear problem occurred a few moments later the ship might have collided with the gates at the end of the lock, blocking traffic for days to come. Fortunately, the problem was cleared and the ship went through the lock, departing Colon the same day.

Arriving at Cape Fear at the mouth of the Cape Fear River on October 17th, the ship went up river and docked at Sunnypoint.

The Vietnam sealift greatly increased the number of active ships in the U.S. Merchant Marine. With the increase in ships came more jobs, so many, in fact, that there weren't enough people to fill them. There were occasions when ships waited at anchor, loaded, until a minimum crew was found. In some cases, registered aliens were allowed to ship on American-flag ships to meet the shortage. Someone in the crew complained to local authorities about all the registered aliens on the *Lane Victory* and the fact that they were illegally landing in the United States. The purser, Mr. O'Hara, acting for the captain, called the Coast Guard to straighten the matter out.

From the deck log for October 18:

1015 purser Mr. O'Hara called the Coast Guard Captain of the Port office and spoke to Mr. Simpson who stated that as long as registered aliens were cleared by the Coast Guard to sign on government owned vessel they were cleared to go ashore. Mr. O'Hara then called the Port Security Officer and reported same to the desk Sergeant and the men were OK'd to have liberty. Department heads were notified by Mr. O'Hara. Mr. Norman Guy of the U. S. Immigration Office, Wilmington, phoned the ship and cleared the registered aliens signed on the vessel.

With a full load of ammunition, the ship departed Cape Fear on October 29.

Arriving in Cristobal on the 3rd of November, the ship transited the canal safely, but had engine problems as soon as it reached Balboa. The MARAD representative came aboard and wouldn't let the ship sail until repairs were made. This delighted the crew, for the ship anchored and sea watches were broken until repairs could be completed. They anticipated several days ashore savoring the delights of Panama.

With repairs completed, the MARAD representative, Mr. Howard, came aboard. He insisted on taking the *Lane* out for a trial run. This was done and everyone agreed the ship was operating properly and could continue her voyage. She departed Balboa on the 8th of November.

On November 22 the vessel was stopped at sea to clean the main condenser.

On November 27, the Chief Engineer reported he suspected a hull fracture at #1 double bottom port side. After pumping on that tank for two hours he found the liquid level in the sounding pipe unchanged. It would have to wait until a diver could be hired to examine the hull. "Touching bottom" at Manila had come back to haunt them.

The first death on board the *Lane Victory* occurred on December 2, 1968. From the deck log:

0005 Lat. 16-05 N., Long. 149-00 E. Mr. Robertson, AB 8-12 watch called Mr. O'Hara and stated that Mr. Robinson AB 12-4 watch was on starboard side of boat deck gasping for breath. Mr. Brugman, third mate 8-12 watch was also present.

At 0010 Mr. Robinson gasping and seeming unable to breath. Mr. O'Hara had Mr. Robertson get the oxygen equipment from the bridge. Attempt to get oxygen into Mr. Robinson was unsuccessful. Tried mouth to mouth respiration and artificial respiration.

At 0015 hours Mr. Robinson stiffened and Mr. Brugman third mate, Mr. Robertson AB and Mr. O'Hara, purser could not affect any pulse or heartbeat or feel any sign of breath.

At 0029 hours Capt. Wentworth was notified and called Mr. Retzer chief mate. Assembled at cot on boat deck were Capt. Wentworth, Chief Mate Retzer, Third Mate Brugman, Robertson AB, Monahana, bosun, and Mr. O'Hara. It was noted that Robinson had voided himself at this time. Capt. Wentworth asked each person if in his opinion Mr. Robertson was dead. All agreed that this was the case. Capt. then called out the radio operator Mr. Horton and notified Capt. Thomas of the casualty.

At 0136 hours Mr. Robinson checked again and showed no sign of life. Search for pulse, heartbeat by Capt. Wentworth, Mr. Retzer and Mr. O'Hara. None could be detected.

0250 hours Capt. Wentworth and Mr. O'Hara again checked Robinson for heartbeat and pulse. There were none.

0325 hours, Mr. Brugman third mate made mirror test of Robinson's nostrils there was no glass smudge. This was done to confirm earlier findings.

0335 hours covered body with sheet and placed cot with body alongside bulwark on boat deck as it is cool there.

At sundown on the same day, in Latitude 15°-25' N., Longitude 145° E., the vessel was stopped. As Mr. Robinson's body, wrapped in canvas, slid off a board into the sea, the ship's whistle blew a mournful farewell. The following entry was made in the deck log: "Darwin R. Robinson, AB who lived on the sea, died at sea, was committed to the sea."

The ship arrived on December 7 at Subic Bay, anchored for three days and sailed for Vung Tau.

Arriving in Vung Tau on December 12, the *Lane* anchored once more. Several of the crew had missed the ship in Subic Bay and were brought on board by the ship's agent on December 14.

On December 16 the anchor was raised and the ship shifted to Cat Lai. Located part way up the river, this was a seaplane base left over from the French occupation of Indo-China. It was the main ammunition port for that part of Vietnam.

Completing her discharge the ship sailed on December 21 for Korea.

Arriving at Suyong, Korea near Pusan, the vessel anchored off the Choryong lighthouse on December 28 and shifted to the dock that same day.

A diver was hired to investigate the tank that couldn't be pumped down earlier in the voyage. He found a fracture six inches long in a weld on one of the hull plates. A second diver was hired and he confirmed the finding.

The American Bureau of Shipping surveyor who inspected the ship recorded the following entry in the deck log:

> The undersigned examined the vessel under flooded condition in #1 port double bottom tank. Diver checked underwater body in way of tank and reported that the seam weld between K and A strakes excessively corroded and fractured approximately 6 inches long about 3 feet aft of the collision bulkhead. No any other significant damage was noted. In the opinion of the undersigned this vessel is in a seaworthy condition at this time relative to this survey and fit to proceed to the USA for drydocking under light conditions.
>
> (signed) Shi Boom Shin.

On New Year's Day, 1969 the ship shifted to Pusan, backloaded a few tons of cargo and sailed on January 2 for San Francisco.

The weather on the return trip was abominable. The *Lane* sailed from Pusan straight into a force 7 wind, ten-foot waves, and twenty-five foot swells. Her deck log entries for the period show gale force winds and twenty-foot swells almost all the way across the Pacific.

Wet and waterlogged, the ship arrived in Long Beach on January 19, seventeen days out from Pusan. Quickly discharging what little cargo she had, Voyage 10 ended the following day.

The crew was laid off and the ship put in an idle status for a few days. She was drydocked and the damaged hull repaired.

There would be more voyages. But at this stage in the war a sense of futility set in. The cracks in the national foundation grew larger. Anti-war public opinion grew more vocal each day. A mood of anger and hostility accompanied the swelling demand to get out of Vietnam.

13

THE LAST VICTORY

The bus runs continued and with them the grim mood engendered by the non-ending war. After almost a month of waiting, Voyage 11 started February 19, 1969 at Berth 171 in Wilmington, California.

A crew was signed on for a coastwise voyage and fuel and supplies taken on board. On February 24 the *Lane Victory* shifted to Berth 18 Pier B, Long Beach and took on her first load of cargo.

From Long Beach she went to San Diego, recording 16.2 knots for the run; she was still capable of a good burst of speed when needed.

Arriving in San Diego on the 26th, she loaded briefly then sailed the following day for Oakland. It was while traveling up the California coast that the second death occurred aboard when the chief electrician suddenly collapsed and died.

From the deck log for February 28:

0724 W. L. McCrary, Asst. Electrician reported to Ch. Eng. that W. A. Mack, Ch. Elect. had apparently collapsed in the shower and the door was locked from the inside. At the same time H. L. Ocosta reported to Mr. O'Hara, the purser, that Mack was in the shower. After checking the door both Mr. O'Hara and the chief engineer reported to the Captain. Mr. Nevins and the First Assistant remained at the shower door trying various keys to gain entry. The vent screens had to be removed and the door unlocked from the inside. Shower water was running and after it was turned off Mr. O'Hara Purser-Pharmacist checked pulse and tested to see if there was any sign of life, but *rigor mortis* had already set in. Captain was notified, permission was given to remove the body from the shower. It was placed on a cot and covered. McCrary, Assistant Electrician stated that at 2330 hours, Mack told him that he was going to take a shower. At 0720 hours when the breakfast call was given, Mack's bed had not been slept in and he checked the shower and saw that Mack had collapsed.

When the ship arrived in Oakland on February 28 a U.S. Army ambulance removed Mr. Mack's body.

Loading penicillin and goods such as beer, coca-cola, egg nog, Bartlett pears, shrimp and apple juice, the ship sailed for Pearl Harbor on March 3.

At Berth 40-A some of the cargo was discharged and the ship sailed for Qui Nhon on March 11 where she arrived fifteen days later.

With all the canned goods off, the *Lane* then began the usual backloading run through the ports of the Far East. Departing Qui Nhon on April 3 she reached Poro Point in the Philippines two days later. On April 6 she made a short run to Bataan for fuel and further orders. Departing Bataan on April 10 she arrived at Subic Bay the same day.

Departing Subic Bay on April 11, the vessel went to Okinawa where she arrived on the 13th. After backloading she departed Naha on April 19 for Inchon, Korea where she arrived on April 21 sustaining an average speed of 15.8 knots. She was prevented from immediately entering the harbor by a thick fog that persisted for hours. From Inchon on April 28 she went to Yokosuka where she again had to wait several hours for the fog to lift. It was May 2nd before she could enter the harbor.

Departing May 4 for Oakland, the *Lane Victory* had an uneventful crossing and arrived at the San Francisco Light Vessel on May 18, tying up to Pier 6W at the Oakland Army Terminal. After discharging her cargo she shifted to Pier 44 in San Francisco on May 19 where the voyage ended at midnight.

During this voyage she carried a total of 7748 tons of cargo and traveled 16,350 miles at sea and 255 miles in harbors and rivers (called inside steaming). The voyage consisted of 89 days, 23 hours of which 44 days were spent under way, 42 days at piers and docks, and 2 days in inside steaming.[1] Her total average speed for the voyage was 15.7 knots. She burned 200 to 290 bbls of fuel per day for an average of 1 bbl. per .7 nautical mile.

Beginning Voyage 12 of the Vietnam era, the *Lane* spent several days undergoing repairs, then, on May 25, shifted to Port Chicago for a full load of ammunition.

These were the days when anti-war demonstrators used private yachts to block the passage of ships leaving the ammunition piers. To prevent such an action from developing into a major incident, the Coast Guard intervened. On June 1 when the ship departed Port Chicago she was escorted by the cutters *Point Winslow* and *Point Chico* from Port Chicago to San Francisco Bay. Leaving her escort at the Golden Gate Bridge, the *Lane Victory* plowed once more into the Pacific swells, Vietnam bound.

The crossing was not easy. On June 7 the wind was at a force of 5-6 with 5 foot waves and 8-12 foot swells. Just after dinner the shoring on part of the deck cargo carried away. Located on the starboard side of the after deck abeam of #4 hatch, it

---

[1] Although the voyage started and ended at midnight, it was one hour short of 90 days because the West Coast went to Daylight Savings Time while the *Lane Victory* was at sea.

created a dangerous situation. The cargo was bombs. Without shoring to hold them in place, they could easily roll into the bulwarks and explode. Slowing the ship down, Capt. Wentworth turned with her stern to the sea to make for an easier ride. The bosun, carpenter and daymen began rebuilding the supports holding the bombs. Fortunately, the cargo stayed in place. By 8 p.m. everything was in order and the ship resumed her course.

On Sunday, June 22, the vessel arrived at Cam Ranh Bay.

Apparently the Chief Mate and Second Mate weren't getting along. On July 5 the Second Mate made the following entry in the log. "2343 Chief Mate R. 0. Reinhart informed me that as soon as I reached San Pedro. [Signed] Frank Miller 2nd Mate."

Whatever the Chief Mate informed the Second Mate of or that he could or couldn't do, was left out. Whether the entry was made in anger or intoxication is not known.

On July 7 the *Lane* departed Cam Ranh Bay, arrived at Vung Tau the following day and immediately went up river to Cat Lai and unloaded.

Sailing from Cat Lai on July 11, there was a brief stop of one day at Manila and then the ship headed toward the United States West Coast.

Arriving on July 30 in Puget Sound, the *Lane Victory* tied up to Pier 91 Berths A & B where she discharged her cargo and ended the voyage on July 31.

Voyage 13 began on August 1. On August 3 the ship shifted to Bangor, on the Hood Canal. Bangor was the ammunition facility for the Pacific Northwest at the time. Later it became a missile-loading area for Polaris submarines.

Morgan Vail, who signed on this voyage as Chief Mate, said Bangor was the beginning of the worst nine months he ever experienced.

"I went on articles in Bangor, Washington on August 1, 1969 in the capacity of Chief Mate and E. D. Wentworth was master. We went to Bangor, which was a munitions facility similar to Port Chicago and we loaded a full cargo of bombs, bound for Vietnam.

"The ship was a veteran ship that had been sailing to Vietnam for about three years. It had a hodgepodge crew because they were having trouble getting qualified crew. There was an anti-war movement going on and some of the seamen were definitely of that camp.

"As I recall they had another ship already waiting to come in and take our berth. They'd send you out to anchor to secure for sea. They didn't want you sailing at night or they didn't want you sailing under unsecured conditions so maybe it'd be the next day before you sailed.

"The bosun nearly missed the vessel. He wasn't back at eight o'clock when he was supposed to. He came back more like noon."

Capt. Wentworth had changed since Morgan Vail last sailed with him. His divorce had affected him badly and he was drinking heavily.

Frank Filas, an AB (Able-Bodied seaman) on the same voyage recalled: "Yeah, he had a drinking problem."

Morgan Vail: ". . . during this time, well, Wentworth was quite an exceptional man I'd have to say. And his wife was quite exceptional. They had one daughter. His wife opened a dress shop for ladies, evening gowns and party dresses, in the waiting area of the *Princess Louise* where people who were waiting for tables in the restaurant upstairs had to wait and kill some time and browse.[2] And everybody said, 'What a foolish idea.'

"But it was a barn-burner because they had all these affluent patrons who had time on their hands. The women were well-heeled and the men had the checkbooks to pay for it. Wentworth used to complain that he had to go to sea all year just

---

[2] Originally a Pacific Northwest passenger steamer, the *Princess Louise* was converted to a floating restaurant and moored in Los Angeles Harbor. Her popularity waned with the coming of the *Queen Mary*. She mysteriously sank at her berth one evening while undergoing repairs.

to pay taxes on his wife's business. That was his way of looking at things.

"So sometime after . . . You know, he's gone an awful lot of the time. Either some time during that time or shortly thereafter they were divorced. And I guess to him, this was quite a setback."

Departing the Hood Canal on August 13, the *Lane Victory* sailed for the Far East. After a smooth crossing she reached Subic Bay, "for orders" on September 1.

The orders were quick in coming. She sailed the following day for Danang.

The war was not going well. Maintaining security in harbors was more and more difficult. Many ports, particularly Danang, started the practice of having ships go to sea at night and return in the day. In this way they weren't vulnerable to attack.

When the *Lane* reached Danang at 1330 the afternoon of September 3 she was ordered to stay at sea and come in the next day. She continued this practice of steaming at night and anchoring in the daytime until September 9 when cargo operations began.

On September 19 the sailing board was posted to sail for Sasebo. Departing on the 21st the ship arrived in Sasebo September 26, discharged some retrograde cargo and departed October 2nd for San Francisco.

Part way across, the ship received orders to alter course because of typhoon Grace. Reducing speed, the captain also changed course to ride out the storm. At the time the swell was fifteen feet high, the wind at a force of 5-6, and the waves had five foot peaks. The barometer was 29.85.

Successfully evading the storm, the ship received orders to divert to Long Beach.

Morgan Vail: "We got over there, discharged the vessel and then basically made a round trip. We came right back. We left in early August and we got back to Los Angeles on October 20th."

Actually the ship arrived at Pier 225 in Long Beach on October 19th and the voyage ended on the 20th. Voyage 14 began the next day.

There were shifts from one pier to another in Long Beach as the *Lane Victory* loaded her next cargo for Vietnam. Morgan Vail. "We took a whole shipload of napalm to Saigon in those big wing tanks that the planes dropped napalm with. We shifted to Long Beach and loaded napalm and a day later, they signed articles. It didn't take long to load napalm. Within three or four days they were ready to go to sea.

"I clearly remember loading napalm because I remember the shoddy job the longshoremen did of securing the cargo. They figured they could cover up the hatch while I was at my meal and get away. I made them come back and uncover it and re-shore, because they basically had done very little."

Signing foreign articles on October 28, the ship then shifted to anchorage on the 31st to load detonators. She sailed that evening.

Most seamen are philosophical about the dangers involved in carrying ammunition. AB Frank Filas tried to put his feelings into words. "Well, yeah, you kinda think you know, one little hit there, you're gone, you know, final. Sure, it's natural, I guess. They say that that thing will not explode like a lot of people think it will. I dunno how true that is either. I sailed a lot. Things like that . . . You know, a lot of people are scared of flying and all that. I said well, heck, flying, if you go, you go, you know . . ."

Crossing the International Dateline on November 9, the ship entered the Straits of Luzon on November 19 arriving at Danang on the 21st.

Morgan Vail: "If a ship had explosives on board, they went out for night steaming. They didn't want the vessel in the harbor or at the dock or even where it was in danger . . . a rocket attack or 'sappers' that might come alongside and try to blow a hole in the hull or something. It was common practice that when you had munitions on board, you went and did night steaming outside the harbor. They wouldn't let us come in because we got there so late. We must have come in the next day."

Completing her Danang cargo discharge, the ship sailed for Vung Tau, arriving there on November 26. The following day she weighed anchor and went up the Saigon River.

Morgan Vail: "Going up the Saigon River in daylight they used to give us flak jackets . . . considerable military escort . . . and ordered everybody to stay inside the house. I think they even had steel helmets for the men on the bridge. They had a Vietnamese pilot. They said just don't go sunning yourself on the open deck in case there's a sniper out there or something. We got up to Saigon without incident.

"We still had napalm on board. We didn't discharge the entire load in Danang."

"As the voyage progressed various crew members got off and the ship ended up being shorthanded. Replacements were very, very, hard to get out in the Far East. We would come in to Saigon for example shorthanded . . . and they knew it. At that time there were many Americans, who were not military personnel, in Vietnamese jails for drug offenses. When these people had served their term they were put in the custody of the U.S. Embassy who was responsible for getting them back to the United States. They didn't want them loose in Vietnam or committing more drug offenses out there. So the U.S. Embassy didn't want to shell out thousands of dollars for trans-Pacific airline tickets. The easiest way was to sign them on an undermanned vessel as a workaway. So we were getting these workaways who were not seamen, who were either criminals or drug addicts or unqualified people. And on the ship they weren't doing their job. They were potentially creating problems among other members of the crew who were doing their jobs."

The *Lane* docked at Newport, on the Saigon River, that same afternoon.

One of the tactics the enemy used against ships was to have someone plant plastic explosives in a vulnerable area on the ship such as the propeller, rudder or sea water intake. On November 28 this reality of the war was brought close. Guards spotted a Viet-Cong swimmer under the docks near the ship. He was killed immediately.

Discharging all her napalm, the ship left Newport on November 29, but not without incident. Perhaps the shooting of the Viet-Cong swimmer brought the reality of war closer to the crew. They refused to stay on deck stowing the lines, as the ship proceeded downriver to the sea.

Chief Mate Vail wrote up the incident, sending it to PCTC's offices in San Pedro.

Dear Captain Klepper:

Captain Wentworth has directed that I report to you about an incident which occurred aboard this vessel earlier today. This involved a refusal by the unlicensed members of the Deck Department to obey a lawful order of a superior officer, and was also a violation of section 6, Orders and Rules, of the S.U.P collective bargaining agreement.

The vessel had been berthed at Newport docks, Saigon and had orders to sail at 0630 today. The Master relayed orders to me to have the sailors stow the mooring lines below decks before proceeding to sea. The reason for this was that heavy weather and gale force winds were reported outside of Vung Tau, and that for the safety of the ship, her equipment and personnel, it was essential to get the mooring lines off deck before proceeding to sea.

All lines were aboard, and the vessel was clear of the pier at approximately 0650 at which time I gave orders to ---- to stow all mooring lines below before knocking the men off for breakfast. This he refused to do. Next ---- approached me and stated that the men would not obey my orders unless they were put in writing and signed by the captain.

I asked ---- why he was refusing orders, and he stated that the men considered it unsafe to be working on deck in the river alongside the docks at Saigon. At this time the vessel was underway towards Vung Tau, but the Master and the Pilot did not consider it necessary to clear the decks of personnel in a secured area, until reaching Nha Be which was approximately one hour and a half distant. This would still provide plenty of time to get all lines below and the men off deck by 0800, in time to have breakfast.

At this time ---- who had knocked off from his assigned station at the stern without orders, approached me on the bow in a very belligerent manner and proceeded to indulge in considerable backtalk about refusal to work on deck in an unsafe area, and threatening to "call the Coast Guard" if he had to stow the lines below. I might add that at this time the ship was situated near downtown Saigon, during daylight, in the same place these very same men had been clustering on the open deck, of their own choosing, taking pictures and conversing, during the ship's approach to the docks two days earlier. Now, when work was expected of them it was suddenly unsafe."

I repeated my orders to ---- and explained that they still stood. I told him the captain was very occupied on the bridge and too busy to issue written orders at this time. Next ---- demanded that I write and sign written orders directing the men to stow the lines below. I had orders to standby the anchors while transiting Saigon port, and was in no position to do this under the circumstances. The sailors were milling around, doing nothing. ---- still refused to carry out my orders.

At this point an impasse was reached, and I ordered ---- to send the men to breakfast at 0700, and that I would inform ---- the Master after I had orders to secure on the bow.

It is getting to the point where the seamen think they can decide themselves what work they will do, when they want to do it, and decide which orders they will obey and which they will not. This is clearly a violation of their own contract. Section 6 states "If a crewman believes that a direct order of a superior officer is inconsistent with this agreement, he shall nevertheless comply with the order, but upon request made to his department head he shall receive written confirmation of such order from the superior officer giving such order."

In this instance the order to stow lines was not, "inconsistent with this agreement." It is part of the normal duties and work expected of members of the deck department. Technically speaking, they had no cause to demand orders in writing in this incident, and no reason to refuse "lawful orders of superior officers", which had in this case, emanated from the Master.

Very truly yours,
Morgan W. Vail II
Chief Mate

The weather predictions were accurate. Reaching Vung Tau and the open sea, the *Lane Victory* found herself bucking winds of 50 to 60 knots.

On December 1 orders were changed to head to San Francisco instead of Subic Bay.

On December 6 another change in orders came through. Yokosuka would be the next port of call. The voyage was far from over.

Frank Filas: ". . . up in Japan, that was when we were shuttling between Vietnam and Yokohama. We were spending three weeks in port . . . with fifty hours or so at sea in between the two places."

On December 9 the ship tied up to a buoy at Yokosuka in Tokyo Bay. Loading a full cargo of PX stores, she sailed from Japan the day after Christmas.

One of the unforgettable episodes of the Vietnam era was the tragedy of the *SS Badger State*. Loaded with ammunition which shifted in bad weather near Wake Island, the ship sank with only twelve survivors. Merchant seamen throughout the world were stunned.

Morgan Vail remembered she was "another U.S. Flag merchant ship that had loaded at Bangor and whose cargo had shifted. Apparently the *Badger State* had loaded its previous voyage to this at Bangor, had problems, then the *Lane Victory* came in, loaded at Bangor, went out, then the *Badger State* came in and had fatal problems.

"It was a primary topic of conversation aboard the *Lane Victory* at this time. We were glued to the radio and newspapers because these were fellow seamen."

On December 31 boiler trouble developed. The *Lane* had to go in to Subic Bay on one boiler. Four days were spent on repairs and she sailed on January 5th.

Returning to Danang on January 7 the ship was once again subjected to anchoring and working cargo in the day, then steaming offshore at night. This was especially trying on the crew because they had to secure the hatches and booms for sea every night, something they normally did only on the final departure from a port.

Frank Filas: "Oh. I knew we had a bunch of beer because we were getting some of that ourselves. And, well it was military cargo. PX supplies and stuff like that . . . and what other military cargo might be trucks and stuff, you know."

Sailing from Danang on January 9 the ship went to Qui Nhon, anchoring there the same day. There was no shore liberty, the town was off limits.

The United Seaman's Service is a church-based organization which operates clubs for seafarers throughout the world. They are supposed to be places where a merchant seaman can relax, enjoy American food such as hamburgers and hot dogs, and avoid being hustled by the natives. Unfortunately, they are often dreary, colorless establishments devoid of personality. Their only saving graces are that they're open when other places are off limits and the prices are fair. In Vietnam there were clubs in Cam Ranh Bay and in Qui Nhon. During this stay in Qui Nhon the club was open but the town was considered too dangerous for Americans.

On January 15 several of the *Lane Victory*'s crew went ashore to the seaman's club only to have the weather turn so rough they couldn't get back to the ship. It was January 17 before they returned.

Sailing from Qui Nhon on January 25, the ship returned to Danang, arriving the following day after again spending the night at sea.

Empty once more, the ship sailed January 28 from Danang.

Chief Mate Morgan Vail had difficulties with the way the captain ran the ship: "Wentworth would not intervene. He would not assert authority. He would not take disciplinary action. He just basically went to his room, closed the door and took to the bottle. It was fortunate if he was well enough to get the ship out of port. Once we were out of port he went back to his room and closed the door and you didn't see him for days. "Among the deck officers he was known as 'Whiskey Ed.' That was his nickname."

Frank Filas remembered Capt. Wentworth more fondly. 'Well, he was a good captain. He was good in giving us a draw, stuff like that. If he didn't handle it, O'Hara [the purser] handled it. He loved his 'heave ahead' I mean, but he always done his duty. He was always on the ball doing his job. And he never neglected his duties, I can say that for him."

Nevertheless, the *Lane Victory* was a happy ship. Frank Filas: "Well you know we had a wonderful crew on there . . . had a good gang on there. She was a happy ship. Yeah, like I say, we were spending more port time than we had sea time. Oh, yeah, yeah. All the crew. And we weren't even in a hurry to go home. Some guys get homesick, want to go home after a trip or two over there, but no, we wanted to stay out there. We're having a ball and making a good buck."

On January 31 the ship arrived at Kaoshiung, Taiwan for a load of reconditioned trucks.

Morgan Vail: "It was the first time I ever went to Taiwan. Now Kaoshiung was the main seaport on the west coast of Taiwan and it wasn't that far from Vietnam, for that matter. They left Danang on the 28th and arrived less than seventy-two hours later at Kaoshiung.

"The reason for going to Kaoshiung in the first place, there were two principal products that were being loaded there. The first being reconditioned U.S. Army trucks. They were trucks that had been beat up in the war zone that needed major repairs — broken axles and things like that — that were taken out by outgoing vessels and dropped in Kaoshiung and then reconditioned by Chinese workmen and then painted up and put back together again. Then they were brought back to Vietnam, in this case by the *Lane Victory*. The other thing that they frequently loaded there was the cement. Of course they were doing a lot of building airstrips and streets and this and that and buildings. Most of ships at that time went into Kaoshiung to load cement."

"The Taiwanese were also very strict about currency control at that time because the U.S. dollar was a hard currency and the Taiwan dollar was a weak currency. All the Chinese were anxious to get the U.S. dollars on the black market. The rate of exchange between the black market and the real market was quite a disparity. They didn't want to have the market being flooded by greenbacks from U.S. seamen. They would not let the master give out a draw in U.S. dollars which caused great consternation among the crew. So the master had to contact the agent. The agent came up with the solution that although they wouldn't give a draw in greenbacks, the agent would make arrangements so the crew could get a draw in U.S. travellers checks. Some of the seamen were a little bit suspicious because they weren't accustomed to getting draws in travellers' checks, but if they wanted any money at all it was going to be that or nothing."

The draw is given out by the purser or master. In this case, purser O'Hara gave out the advances. Frank Filas: "Well, he was a character, we used to say. Anyway, if there was a mistake on anything it was always more for the company, than it was for the crew. That part I do remember. That's the problem we used to have with O'Hara. But other than that he was all right, too. Couldn't very well knock anyone down on that ship. We did get along and the work was being done in all departments."

On February 5 the *Lane* sailed from Kaoshiung without some of the crew. One of the sailors was in the hospital with a twisted knee. One of the engineers didn't come back at sailing time. Frank Filas simply came back too late.

Frank Filas: "Well I had a little of it (a drinking problem) myself. I missed the ship, you know. I still have my discharge and I missed it in Kaoshiung . . . February 4, 1970 and I caught it . . . I don't drink anymore. I can't hack it. I was drunk on the beach but I caught the ship again in Saigon."

"I can tell you that was a funny incident. I was trying to catch it with a little dinghy, had the kid in there rowing away, you know, and the ship was getting further and further away. Anybody on the stern would a seen me they would of hollered over, thrown a ladder over the side. And I would've got aboard you know."

Morgan Vail: "The ship was short-handed, undermanned. It was hard to get replacement people. So when they loaded the trucks in Kaoshiung we sailed from Taiwan and went back to Vung-Tao and went back up the river to Saigon . . . this is in February of 1970."

Arriving at Vung Tau on February 8, the *Lane Victory* was at anchor for four days, then went up river to Newport.

Saigon was a popular port for most seamen. The rate of exchange was favorable and the Vietnamese women, dressed in their flowing native costume were delicate, exotic and friendly. Frank Filas remembered it fondly. "Oh yeah, we had some favorite places there. If we ran out of draw money we'd always get it up from mama-san. Yeah, we had some times over there. That's for sure. We kinda called it our home port, you know . . . we spent so much time over there, called it our home port. Anybody wanted port time, we were getting so much port time if you wanted sea time you couldn't do it on there. Ran you dry on your draw list."

While tied to the dock at Newport, the ship came close to burning up its main engine.

Morgan Vail: "I guess we deckies don't have an understanding of what goes on in the lower reaches of the engine room at night in the middle of a foreign port. But this happened at one of those times. We were tied at Newport, Saigon, working cargo. I was off duty and asleep. It was at two in the morning. I was suddenly awakened by the Chief Engineer. He was really agitated and urgent. He said, 'Hurry up, I need you right away, we're about to lose the plant.'

"What apparently happened, there's some sort of an underwater intake for cooling purposes in the engine room beneath the water level . . . and because these berths in Newport had pretty much vertical up and down solid fronts, concrete, without pilings to fender the vessel off, the intake had come up flush with the pier. The engineer on watch reported to the chief, 'We're losing something, and if we don't get the ship off the dock so that the water can get into the intake we'll lose the whole thing.'

"I didn't even have time to put on my shoes. I slipped on a pair of pants and a pair of slippers and went running down to the main deck to see what seamen were around and what could be done. What they determined was we needed a combination of stevedore's forklifts and wooden four-by-fours or larger pieces of wood to fend the vessel off the pier. The stevedores would push [the ship] with their forklifts and then we'd push the four-by-fours down between the hull and the dock. If we got enough of these and got far enough off the pier . . . it was really one of these things that they said, 'We don't have any time to lose, we can't play around.'

"I managed to round up maybe three or four seamen and one of the third mates. We had to go running back to the fantail, find this wood, run up the deck and, somehow, we managed to save the ship. But it was the last minute."

On February 15 the ship sailed from Saigon, dropped the pilot and headed for open sea.

Morgan Vail: "We left Saigon empty and headed toward Sasebo, Japan and arrived on the twenty-first and didn't leave until the second of the following month. We were loading munitions again.

"There had been more than one attack on U.S. munitions stores in South Vietnam by the Viet-Cong and they blew up a substantial quantity of munitions, not the entire stockpile, but what was left was in questionable condition. They were taking munitions back to Japan and then sending them to South Vietnam once they had been reprocessed."

More than a week in Sasebo unloading ammunition created too much idle time and as ever, idle time became a problem for everyone.

Morgan Vail: "I clearly remember it because it was a long night. One of the officers came on board in the wee hours of the morning quite intoxicated, quite belligerent, raising a ruckus . . . going around banging on other people's doors at two in the morning, waking them up and causing a disturbance. He even banged on the captain's door. So that obviously woke Capt. Wentworth up. Capt. Wentworth told him to go to his room. The guy wouldn't go to his room. He was still up and creating quite a disturbance.

"Wentworth was quite pragmatic. This was the only time I can remember when the captain put a deck officer in irons. It happened on the *Lane Victory*. It happened. Believe me, I saw it. I was there.

"Wentworth went into his room, I believe he probably had the handcuffs in his safe. And on a Victory, as you probably recall, the master's office opens into an athwartship passageway. On the aft end of the athwartship passageway is the license rack for the deck officers. So this one particular officer just wouldn't settle down and would not comply with the master's orders. He slapped the handcuffs on one of his wrists and slapped the other cuff to the handrail beneath the license frame and went back in his room and shut his door and left the guy there handcuffed to the handrail with one hand free.

"So the guy is flailing about and calling for help. Wentworth is not going to respond and next thing I know I hear crashing glass. I thought, Oh, no! Wentworth, of course, couldn't ignore it either. He could hear it, too. In his flailing around and banging on the bulkhead, trying to get free and get attention or sympathy or whatever, he managed to completely break the glasses that the licenses were held behind. It wasn't plastic, it was glass. The kind of glass that cuts the wrist. It was bleeding. So it had to be bandaged. The bleeding had to be stopped. And that was done.

"Obviously, you couldn't leave the guy dangling in the passageway in those conditions. So the orders from Wentworth were take him to his room and put him in his bunk and stay there all night. He was afraid that the guy in his thrashing about would tear the bandages off, restart the bleeding and might bleed to death. So I had a very, very, very long night baby-sitting this man in his room. Fortunately, once he got there he just kind of went to sleep.

"Wentworth did not log the man. He may have privately admonished the man, saying, 'If this happens again . . .' that sort of thing.

"He didn't order me to do anything. He just expected me to be up at eight o'clock the next morning fresh, ready to put in another day's work."

Sailing from Sasebo on March 2, the *Lane Victory* arrived at Danang four days later.

On March 10 the ship shifted to the docks and started backloading.

Morgan Vail: "What they were backloading was cargo that was to be carried to Vung Tau and then to Newport. Here was another one of those incidents that kind of gives you a picture of what conditions were like on the vessel at that time and why for me it was the worst voyage. What we loaded at Danang, believe it or not, was beer. We were going to carry to Saigon. There was some soft drinks but mainly beer. Of course, the crew clearly knew there was beer in the holds.

"Once we got underway, Capt. Wentworth confronted me privately and said, 'I want you to go down and take the locks off the door to the escape trunk of number five hold so the crew can go in and help themselves.'

"Now the crew was already under great stress, you know, being in the war zone and having been out for so long. Some of these people had made the previous voyage like I had and been on that ship for nine months or longer. And here you go on a coastwise voyage that lasts less than a day in a war zone and under those conditions, you know, what do you do?

"You're given an order that you consider to be unlawful. You know that if you don't do something that the conditions are going to get worse. You're not going to have a competent helmsman or you're not going to have a competent lookout or you're not going to have competent seamen to tie the ship up once you get to Newport or who knows what?

"I didn't want to deliberately disobey the master's orders. On the other hand, I knew what I felt to be an unlawful order. So my response was, 'Captain, if you'll put that in writing I'll do it.

"He just turned his back and walked away. He knew that if he put it in writing he would be found at fault. He never retaliated. He just dropped the issue like a hot potato."

Capt. Wentworth was near the end of his tether at this point.

Morgan Vail: "He was trembling constantly whenever he was out of his cabin, which was seldom. This was near the end. And he knew the end was coming 'cause he knew we were going back to California and were going to go into lay-up.

"I suspect that his motivation to give me such a command was he wanted to satisfy the crew or reward the crew so they would continue working for him so that the ship could continue sailing so it wouldn't be laid up."

Dropping anchor at Vung Tau early in the morning of March 15 the ship started up river at 0730 the same day, arriving in Newport at 1200.

One of the better sailors was an ordinary seaman named Patrick. Chief Mate Vail was impressed with his work. "Pat was the Yul Brynner. He was the man with the shaved head. Very handsome, very rugged. I believe he was about age forty. He originally joined the vessel as ordinary seaman. He was like a breath of fresh air. Patrick was one of the few who remained loyal, remained hard-working, remained dependable, wasn't drunk, wasn't malingering. He was a hard worker and a fine person. I had a great regard for him. Unfortunately, after the vessel got back to San Francisco in April of 1970 and he was discharged, he entered the Marine Hospital in San Francisco. He was diagnosed with a liver disease. He died shortly after."

The workaways weren't all dregs. Some, such as Hernandez, who joined the ship in Saigon, were simply victims of war.

Morgan Vail: "I remember Hernandez because he was a Honduran alien. How he got to Saigon or why he got to Saigon is beyond me. He was quite glad to be leaving Vietnam for whatever reason. He was very appreciative of finding a job that would get him back to the States. And he was a hard worker even though he was not a seaman by trade. He was willing to step in and do his share of the work. He made a lot of mistakes at first, and everybody had to keep an extra eye on him because he was not a seaman. But he somehow pulled through."

On March 20, at noon, the ship sailed from Newport, clearing the mouth of the river by 1600.

On March 27, the *Lane Victory* entered Inchon. Inchon is not a favorite port among seamen.

Frank Filas: "Oh that Inchon, that Inchon was a cold son-of-a-bitch . . . Takes forever to tie up over there too . . . the tide, I don't know how much there was over there, but I know there was a lot 'cause we was forever tying up."

Morgan Vail: "I don't remember the nature of the cargo. I believe it was other equipment to be reconditioned. We brought damaged trucks out that were going to be refurbished in Korea."

On March 28 the ship sailed from Inchon arriving in Pusan two days later. Cargo was loaded for the United States and the ship sailed on April 2.

Low morale continued. The ship was short-handed, the hours were long and the food was poor.

Morgan Vail: "Drugs were quite accessible . . . it was the peak of the drug culture in the late sixties. I uncovered a concealed drug stash that couldn't be traced to any one person but we knew it was hidden by one of the crew. It was being used.

"Another factor was the quality of the food. For example, here we're out in the Orient shuttling around for six to nine months and the initial provisions run out. We have to buy foreign provisions and they're just not up to American standards. The food went downhill and the crew morale went downhill with it. And that was another factor, low morale, extremely low morale.

I can only remember one other instance in my entire career where I think morale was lower or as low as it was on the *Lane Victory* during early 1970.

"By the end of the war, by the time the *Lane Victory* laid up, these men were so burned-out in the war effort they didn't want to work. They were given the opportunity to work overtime to do essential maintenance on the vessel. For the most part they declined."

On April 5 the ship stopped in Yokohama for refueling and resupplying.

On April 7 the *Lane Victory* departed Yokohama on her last trans-Pacific crossing.

Passing over the dateline on April 13, she arrived in San Francisco on the 20th and paid off her crew two days later. It was the thirty-first and last commercial voyage of her career.

According to Morgan Vail, the reason the *Lane Victory* continued to run while others were laid up was the captain's cunning. "That was due to Wentworth. It continued to run until the very last minute and even then it almost went out again. Wentworth had been considered the permanent master of the *Lane Victory* for quite some time — from '67 to '68 and '69. He didn't really want to relinquish his command because he knew if he did he might have a hard time getting a job in the tanker fleet. By that time about fifty percent of the time the vessel was carrying munitions. And they needed sheathing and sweat battens and special conditions on the vessel. Now, to insure the vessel continued operating, Wentworth, when we left the port, would radio the Navy or whoever was controlling his next assignment. He always used the phrase, 'sheathing and sweatbattens ninety-nine percent in place," or something to that effect.

"What commonly happened over there in the war zone was that the longshoremen, who were contract Koreans for the most part, would strip the vessel of the sheathing and sell it ashore. And we were under a great pressure to keep this from happening. Sometimes it wasn't always possible. He felt other

The last meal on board was posted on the blackboard in one of the crew messrooms. The message remained until 1989.

ships were being stripped and they wouldn't have to re-sheath his ship. That would keep him going and apparently it worked for a while. Somehow we managed to get another load when other ships were being sent back to be laid up. Finally, near the end, we knew we were going back."

A skeleton crew was left on board to deactivate the ship and take it to the Reserve Fleet.

Laying up the last Victory ship marked the end of an era. With fewer ships in operation, many steamship companies that sprang up during the Vietnam war went out of business. Pacific Coast Transport was one of them.

After a few days of preparation, the ship made the final trip to the backwaters of Suisun Bay.

Morgan Vail: "They retained me. We were in Triple-A shipyard until April 29th. Wentworth was still master so he was on the vessel. And then I rode it up to Suisun Bay. It might have laid idle at Triple-A beyond the first of May and then brought up to Suisun Bay by a riding crew of which I was chief mate for a day. I remember us getting off and being bussed back to San Francisco. And that's the last time I saw the ship."

John "Swede" Jansson: "I tink *Lane Victory* vas either the last vun or the second last vun go up in the boneyard. 'Cause I had a night yob and she vas in dere at Triple-A shipsyard. And I vas surprised, I valked on board, you know . . ."

The *Lane Victory* arrived at the Reserve Fleet on April 29, 1970.

14

THE BONEYARD

By mid-1970 the supply side of the Vietnam war was winding down. What military cargo was needed was carried by the active American merchant fleet. The *Lane Victory* and her sisters were no longer necessary. Finished with their third war, they were put back on the shelf.

Previously, ships in the Reserve Fleets were preserved by the "contact" method. Doors, winches, gears, valves, piping — everything was open to the atmosphere. Any metal surface that might rust was either painted, smeared with cosmoline, or submerged in consol oil. This took weeks of dismantling and draining. Further weeks were involved in painting and applying preservatives. When the ship was called up for service, removing the preservatives took more time than applying them. Effective but labor intensive, this type of preservation was costly.

As Victorys were laid up after Vietnam a new method was used for deactivating them. The plumbing, piping, boilers

247

The Lane Victory, *left, with several of her sisters at the Suisun Bay Reserve Fleet.*

and condensers were drained. Valves, motors and machinery in the engine room were left open. All the running rigging, lifeboats, winch motors, forced draft blowers and loose gear was stowed in number three hatch, which was then sealed. An opening was cut in the watertight bulkhead separating the engine room from that hatch at the lower 'tween deck/engine room operating level. All the doors to the midships house were sealed except for one access door. In essence the midships house, engine room and number three hatch formed a single sealed space. Installing a dehumidification machine, this entire space was kept at a relative humidity between thirty-eight and forty-two percent. The internal atmosphere was then too dry to rust, yet not so dry that paint peeled off bulkheads or electrical wiring lost the effectiveness of its insulation.

The *Lane Victory* was briefly taken out on February 1, 1971. Prepared for permanent lay-up, she returned on the seventeenth of the same month.

But the *Lane* was a special ship and she received special handling.

Admiral Tom Patterson: "The *Lane Victory* had always been given special treatment at the Suisun Fleet. She was our 'model' ship, always ready for inspection by visiting 'brass' and news media."

The ship was made a model for all laid-up ships. The insides of the engine room and midships house were painted. All of the crew bunks were given fresh linen and the beds made. The internal lighting circuits were connected to one master switch, located just inside the access door. The ship was brought to life with each visit just by throwing the switch. Looking as if only moments before the crew went on deck to work, she never failed to elicit compliments on how well ships were preserved at the Suisun Bay Reserve Fleet.

The model ship looked so good that a Hollywood film company used it in part of a movie. Admiral Patterson: "She was the star of a Hollywood thriller 'Killer Elite' directed by Sam Peckinpaw and starring James Caan. The $5,000 contributed by the movie company was sent to the Smithsonian's new Hall of American Maritime Enterprise. You could say that *Lane Victory* made her own contribution to maritime heritage."

One of the crew hired locally to run a yacht used in the film recalled, "I skippered this sail boat for them. It played some part in the film, I don't remember exactly what, but something to do with the bad guys bringing a prisoner up to the fleet to hide him.

"Anyway, every time they filmed the sailboat, I had to go below so they couldn't see me. Then when they finished, I'd come up and run the boat again.

Movie actor James Caan used the chief mate's room on the Lane Victory *while filming "Killer Elite." His name remained on the deck outside the room for years afterward.*

Director Sam Peckinpaw used the captain's office and stateroom during the filming. Note "Capt. S." on the painted line. The film crew referred to him as "Captain Sam."

"They did a lot of martial arts stuff, karate and the like. They were practicing on the deck of the ship all the time, getting ready for the final scenes.

"One day I saw James Caan in between scenes just sitting around on deck throwing a lanyard at one of the bitts. I guess his next movie was a western or something and he was practicing for it. So he lassoed this bitt every time he tried. He must've done it twenty times in a row. So Peckinpaw comes along and he says, 'I'll bet you five thousand dollars you can't do it again.'

"So Caan throws the rope and misses. 'Double or nothing,' he says.

"So he throws again and misses. And they went like that until he owed Peckinpaw fifty thousand dollars. I asked one of the film crew, I said, 'They were just kidding weren't they?'

"He says, 'Oh, no. They were dead serious.'"

For years afterward the passageway outside the Chief Mate's and Captain's cabins bore the inscriptions, "J.Caan" and "Capt. Sam" respectively. Although no one knew it at the time, this was a prelude to many years of film work for the *Lane Victory*. Eventually she would be involved in movies and television, sometimes as the centerpiece of a story, in others, disguised as a tanker, aircraft carrier or some other type of ship. It was the first step in a new and unanticipated career. But that was in the future.

For almost two decades, the *Lane Victory* sat, proof to visiting congressmen, military dignitaries and members of the press of how effective state-of-the-art ship preservation was. During that time many of her sister ships would go to the scrappers — traded out for "modern" tonnage. It seemed that would be the fate of every Victory in the fleet. But destiny had other plans for Isaac Lane's Victory. She was about to catch the eye of Joe Vernick and the U. S. Merchant Marine Veterans of World War II.

PART TWO

15

"I'M LOOKING FOR A SHIP . . ."

In 1944 Abe Rapaport was an engineer on a freighter, the *West Nilus*, berthed in England. The Naval battle that began on D-Day, June 6, 1944, was still raging. He volunteered to sail old ships across the Channel to be used as a breakwater at Normandy. Deliberately sunk for the invasion in the landing area, his vessel was one of many "block ships" used for this purpose in Operation Mulberry.

As his ship slowly sank to the bottom, Abe looked at all the activity around him. The Air Force flew overhead, the Army and Marine Corps were on the beaches, the Navy was bombarding the coast from the sea. Radios and newspapers carried story after story of the valor and sacrifice of the Armed Forces. Everyone remembers the Armed Forces, he thought, but what about the Unarmed Forces? The Navy was receiving its justly earned recognition, but what about the Merchant Marine? He realized that no one pays attention to merchant seamen. Most people don't even realize they exist. They don't know that ships of the merchant marine are the supply line for the armed forces and that critical life line is sustained by merchant seamen.

At that moment, with the Invasion of Normandy going on around him, his ship resting on the bottom of the ocean, its main deck and superstructure protruding above water, Abe Rapaport vowed to get recognition for the American merchant marine. Together with the armed forces, merchant mariners risked their lives throughout the war running the gauntlet of submarine warfare and danger from the skies to transport dangerous cargoes of explosives and ammunition, as well as equipment, medical supplies and troops to the fighting units on the front lines. Thousands of merchant seamen died serving their country, many were captured and became prisoners of war, suffering and dying in enemy prison camps. These men were war veterans as much as any man in the Navy, Army or Air Force. Abe Rapaport promised himself he would create an organization to honor the U.S. merchant marine. He would get veterans' status for merchant seamen, for the *Unarmed* Forces.

Some two and-a-half years earlier, on the other side of the world, Joe Vernick, an oiler on a merchant ship, was taken prisoner by the Japanese. He was one of 600 merchant seamen who became POWs in World War II.

Joe Vernick: "I was on the *Ruth Alexander*. We stopped at Honolulu in October of 1941 and I considered getting off there. My sister was working at Pearl Harbor and she said, 'I can get you a job in the shipyard.'

"I considered it but finally decided, 'Well, I'll just make this one trip.'

"The morning after we sailed, I noticed we were headed south rather than west. Sure enough, we started blacking out the portholes. We stopped at Suva in the Fiji Islands and from there went to Port Moresby. We could see the Australian and New Zealand troops getting ready. We knew that war was imminent. From Port Moresby we went to Borneo, Balikpappan. The night we arrived in Manila we heard that Pearl Harbor was attacked. We got in in the morning on December 8, and of course there wasn't any activity because they hadn't yet bombed Manila.

"About a week or ten days later they started bombing everything in Manila. They'd fly over and hit the airfields. If they had any bombs left after that they'd fly over Manila Bay and drop them on the ships there. The *Ruth Alexander* was there. About sixty-eight ships were sunk. All you could see was smoke stacks sticking up. Our ship was tied to the dock and they gave us orders, in case of an air raid to get off the ship. There was an air raid shelter across the street. We were tied up at what they called Pier two.

"There was a tremendous air raid. They were hitting all the warehouses and the ships. Half the crew was in the air raid shelter and when we got out the ship was gone. I learned later she went out to Corregidor. After waiting there for a while the ship made a dash for it and got hit in the China Sea where she sunk.

"So, not having a ship, American President Lines put us up in a hotel and asked us to help out. We assisted the Army running supplies in small lighters, little boats that bring the water and fuel out to Corregidor and Bataan . . . which we volunteered to do. There was a crew of five of us and five others — this was between the 15th and the end of December, 1941. We were ferrying supplies to Corregidor and Bataan. On one of these trips we brought back some of the crew of the *SS Capillo*. She was hit at Corrigidor and caught on fire.

"When we got back from this run the other crew of five was waiting. One of them was injured. They wanted to make another run. This was around December 30. And I told them, I said, 'You fellows make another trip to Corregidor and you're never going to get back.'

"The Japanese were coming in. We heard they were on the outskirts of Manila. Sure enough, those five men made the next run and got stuck out in Corregidor. They were part of the

Death March and ended up in a camp up north. Only one of them survived.

"Meanwhile, the rest of us went back to the hotel and the military people called us. Behind our hotel was a big warehouse called a bodega where they supplied the foodstuffs, liquor and clothing for all the other islands. The military authorities figured that the Japanese, in the frenzy of victory . . . We heard about the rape of Nanking. The military said, 'Let's destroy all the whiskey that's in the warehouse.'

"So we got all the sailors from the different merchant ships' crews that were in the hotel. And we had them all carrying cases of booze down the alleys and smashing them in the Pasig River. The food we gave to the Philippine people, sacks of hams and everything. I took a toothbrush and a Gillette razor. That's all I brought into the camp was just that.

"The Japanese came into the hotel, lined us all up in a semi-circle. Their soldiers were prodding us with bayonets. We're all standing with our hands up and they went down the line, 'What you? What nationality?'

"Of course there were French, British, Canadian, American, Portuguese, Mestizos, Filipinos and other nationalities. Standing next to me was a black guy who came over in 1898 for the Spanish American war and never left. The Japanese came around to each of us. They had never seen blacks. These guys were real big Japanese. They must have come from Hokkaido. They were like mountain men, like the big wrestlers. If you got tired and your arms dropped, they'd lunge at you with the bayonets.

"So it was 'American, American, French, Filipino . . .' and so on around the semi-circle.

"When they got to the black guy he said, 'I'se American.'

"They beat him up. They said, 'You not American.'

"So they came around again and he says, 'I'se American.'

"Again they hit him. They said . . . and they were rubbing his hands, they thought maybe the color would rub off. One Japanese says, 'You not American. You African.'

"So as they came around the third time, I told him, "For Christ's sakes tell them you're a fucking African. They're going to kill you!'

So finally they came around the third time, 'American', 'French . . .' and so on.

"By this time he's bleeding and he says, 'Yeah, I'se African.'

"'Ah sodeska.'

"Then they took us to a place where for about three days we didn't have any food. All kinds of people were there and they didn't know where to put us, because we were merchant marine. So they put us into Santo Tomas along with civilian men, women and children. It was a University before the war, the University of Santo Tomas which they converted to an internment camp. After about a year they moved the younger men. Of course, in those days, I was in my twenties. They moved us to another camp about sixty miles south called Los Baños. We started a new camp in that area. I spent almost two and-a-half years in that camp.

"The biggest problem was we never had enough food. Never.

"If you did anything against their rules, you were beaten up. One American went out of the camp to get some food. As he snuck back through the bushes at night they saw him and shot him. He was hit in the shoulder. When it got light they pulled him in and executed him. They were cruel. A couple of guys were shot and killed trying to escape. One guy managed to get up into the hills and got away.

"The guards took women's watches and gold and anything valuable from the internees in exchange for rice and sugar.

"After the first year the camps filled up. They brought in people from the southern islands, Mindanao, outer Cebu. They brought in ministers and priests and nuns which they separated in the camp. We had men, women and children in there by the time we were liberated.

"We had big steel pans we used to cook our gruel in and we put in vegetables or whatever else was available. The first year wasn't bad because as long as they thought they were winning the war, the Japanese were magnanimous. But as the Americans got closer, capturing island after island, the Filipinos realized the Americans were coming back. They were digging up their arms and bolos and starting guerrilla action. This created a serious disruption of our food supply in camp. Even the internee wood cutting detail, which would leave the camp with Japanese guards to fell trees for wood to cook our 'lugao' was stopped. With wood being scarce, I picked up any little piece of wood or twig and threw it under my bunk. With all of us doing that we were able to jointly cook anything edible that we got our hands on.

"So it got really tight for food. We were virtually starving. I would walk and stagger, I was blacking out. I'd get up in the middle of the night to go to the can and I'd have to blink my eyes until the blackness went away . . . from hunger . . . It was pretty bad.

"We're just starving. There's nothing to eat. I would eat grass and leaves. The banana trees were all gone. We ate the banana leaves. We chopped them up and cooked them and they took the roots out . . . anything . . . leaves, morning glory leaves. A morning glory leaf has a fuzziness on the bottom underside. I'd cook those up and eat them. They'd stick in my throat. They went down like sandpaper. I'd say to myself, 'Eat, eat you're going to die.'

"I'd eat those green things and just anything I could in order to survive.

"One guy had a pet monkey. I think he was a preacher. He kept it in between two barracks, next to a latrine. There was a space there and he kept this monkey tied up with a rope around its waist. We were about two barracks over in the last barracks. There was nothing there except two barbed wire fences and two barbed wires behind us and then the hills. And one of the guys in my barracks, by the name of Jack Holt, he was a second or third mate. He went over in the early morning and got the monkey and cut the rope. He was choking it as he ran to our barracks. I woke up at daybreak and I saw Holt chopping away and I said, 'Well, I guess Holt got lucky. Probably got himself a cat.'

"We'd try to get a cat or a dog, but when they saw us they'd run like hell. You could see their ribs sticking out under their skin, too.

"Then I saw the monkey's tail, 'That's a long tail for a cat,' I said.

"I looked at the paw and saw what looked like little fingers. He was chopping that off, chopping the tail off, chopping the head off, burying it in a hole. Then he cooked up this monkey in a one gallon can. He came up to me and said, 'Here's a spoonful.'

"'It's awful strong,' I said. 'As hungry as I am, I just can't eat that monkey.'

"So this priest was looking all over and he comes over to Holt, who was sitting next to me. He said, 'Hey, somebody stole my monkey.'

"Holt is eating it right there, eating his monkey, and says, 'What monkey?'

"A lot of pathos, a lot of people died from starvation, beri-beri and malnutrition. Older people died. Mothers and fathers gave their rations to their children and they would die, you see. We just didn't have the food.

"The most terrifying experience I ever had, I was so desperate that three of us, Jack "Slim" Von Hess from Long Island, New York, Joe Flores from Hawaii and myself decided . . . In the center of the camp was a little compound where the Japanese kept all their supplies for the 150 troops guarding us. I said, 'Lookit, we're going to die of starvation. Let's go break in. Whatever we get . . . If we get killed we get killed. We're going to die anyway.'

"So we cased the place for several nights and we watched the Japanese sentry, noticing how often he passed in front of the bodega. There was a little path coming right up to the bodega and the sentry went up that path only once every three nights. The rest of the time he walked on past. We picked a night that was drizzly and cloudy, just the weather to keep the sentries inside their boxes. Once in awhile you could see the moon and then a black cloud would go over.

"At ten o'clock the three of us headed for the bodega from the rear of the camp where our barracks was located. From that area to the back of the bodega was overgrown with waist-high weeds. Posting "Slim" as a lookout in the weeds, Joe Flores and I crept up to the back of the building and around to the path and the door.

"Joe tried picking the lock with several keys and an improvised skeleton key without any success. I was getting nervous so I said, 'Break the goddamn thing and let's get in and get out.'

"At that moment a Japanese guard walked in front of the bodega and turned onto the path leading to where we were! Had we been discovered? We were terrified.

"We crouched in the dark near the door, a few feet from the path. I could barely make out the outline of the guard, except for a split second when the moon reflected on the bayonet on his rifle. My heart was beating so hard I held my chest trying to muffle the sound of it. The guard was close enough for me to stick out my foot and trip him. If he saw me I would have gotten a bayonet right then and there. I'd have been dead. To my amazement he turned around, walked out the path and resumed his sentry post.

"By this time Joe Flores and I were wet with perspiration. Apparently Slim didn't see him because of the darkness. I said, 'Joe, let's get in there and get out right away.'

"I handed Joe a long screwdriver. He broke the lock. We went in to this bodega, and it was pitch dark. If anyone was there, it was too late. We were inside. We felt around. There was a kind of ledge and some large sacks. I said, 'What's this? Something kind of crunchy or like ball bearings or I don't know what.' Even salt would have been welcome at this point.

"I slit open the sack with a knife, and out poured big kernels of Filipino corn the size of marbles. They fell from the ledge to the floor and bounced all over the place. It was a hundred kilos, that's two hundred-twenty pounds. So we dumped out about three-fourths of it and wrapped the remainder up. We figured we had about forty to fifty pounds of corn to take back.

"Just at that time I felt something else. It didn't feel like corn. I said, 'What is it? Maybe it's salt.'

"We cut the thing open. It was sugar, brown sugar. I put my hand in up to the wrist and shoved a whole fistful into my mouth. A whole mouthful and I didn't care if they came in and killed me right then and there. I said, 'I don't care if they kill me now.'

"That was the greatest, the most glorious taste I ever had. That wonderful sugar!

"I had on a blue sweatshirt. I tore it off and tied the ends of the sleeves in knots. Then I pounded sugar in the two sleeves until they looked like two massive sausages. And I says, 'Come on Joe, let's get the hell out of here.'

"Joe said, 'Hey wait a minute. We got some Japanese cigarettes here.'

"I says, 'The hell with the cigarettes. Let's get out of here.'

"'No,' he said. 'We might be able to trade them to other internees for canned goods.'

"Some people wanted cigarettes so bad they would trade their rice for cigarettes. They smoked dried papaya and mango leaves wrapped in old Japanese newspapers, they were so desperate. So we tied the bottoms of our pants with cord and shoved packages of cigarettes down our pants.

"We then rushed out of the bodega to the rear where Slim was waiting and ran to our barracks. The barracks were divided into twelve or fourteen cubicles of about twelve by twenty feet. There were two other men in our cubicle. One of them had a big aluminum tub. We put about four inches of corn kernels at the bottom. We made a little fire alongside of our barracks and we cooked up the corn and we had this brown sugar sprinkled on top. Joe Flores grated up a coconut and squeezed it so we had real coconut milk. The corn swelled to the top of the pot when it was cooked. We sat down and ate this delicious meal of corn while perspiring with satisfaction. Oh it was the greatest . . .

"So we finished that and we buried the corn and the rest that we didn't use and covered everything up and we had a good, good meal. We spent the rest of the morning smoking "Akibono" (Rising Sun) cigarettes.

"The Japanese never said a word. They probably figured if nothing was said maybe somebody would go back there again. I'm sure anybody that would've gone back there would have been dead. They were waiting for them. But not a word was ever said and no inspection of the barracks was ever made.

"At that point I was so desperate . . . which was kind of stupid because it was just a few weeks later we were liberated, but we didn't know.

"On February 23 [1945] we were virtually starving. The Japanese called us for roll call and they were going to execute us all. They lined us all up. Two thousand of the people there they were going to execute. Somehow I think our military heard about it. The night before I said, 'This is it, we're going to die.'

"That morning about six o'clock we heard planes. I went out there and you could see eleven or twelve planes. We didn't know what they were. We'd seen a lot of Japs, but at that time we used to see American planes flying over us and bombing Manila. They were fighting for Manila which was forty or sixty miles from Los Baños. The American Navy aircraft were bombing the environs of Manila. But these planes flew over and all of a sudden little black things dropped out and I said, 'Hey, maybe they're sending some supplies to us. Maybe it's American food.'

"Sure enough, I could see the white star. All of a sudden those little black dots turned into parachutes. The next thing I knew parachute troops came down right in the middle of the camp. Guerrillas were in the back of the hills. Then from the hills . . . all timed . . . About a mile from us was the Laguna De Bay which was a big lake and Amtracks . . . amphibious tracks started coming in . . . These tanks came into the camp and there was shooting for about a good hour-and-a-half. This was right after they had this roll call where they were going to execute us all. And these tanks came in and they're shooting all over. They caught a lot of Japs. A lot of them got away. They had a tunnel underneath to get away in a ravine, but a lot of them were killed.

Taken in 1946, this photo shows Joe Vernick fully recovered from the ordeals of being a POW. Courtesy Joe Vernick.

"They piled us into these amphibious tanks and headed right back to the lake. The Japanese were shooting down on us because every fifth shot was a tracer and you could see them come right at you. And a couple of guys were very badly injured in the tanks. Eventually we got out of the range of the Japanese in the hills.

"They headed over to a place which had been a prison. The allies converted it to a rehabilitation camp like a hospital. They cooked up regular food, eggs and ham and that sort of thing. That was a terrible experience because a lot of guys died after eating that rich food. They couldn't assimilate it. I woke up in the middle of the night on these bunks, like a prison. I couldn't open my eyes and my legs were swollen. Of course, as it turned out, I had beri-beri. But my system couldn't assimilate all that good food. So when they realized what was happening, they issued an order right away — no food, you have to start with rice. Then we started with rice and worked our way up to richer food.

"After a few days they drove us to Manila and flew us to Leyte. From Leyte we went to Tacloban and they put us aboard the *Admiral Capps*. It was a Coast Guard ship and they brought us back to the States on it. Those that were very sick were immediately flown back and put in hospitals."

By the end of the war between 250,000 and 300,000 merchant mariners had served their country. More than 7,000 were killed while transporting weapons, supplies and troops across the seas. The mortality rate was second only to the Marine Corps. More than 600 merchant mariners were prisoners of war.

Abe Rapaport immediately started his new organization honoring people like Joe Vernick and other merchant marine veterans. Known as the U.S. Merchant Marine Veterans of World War II, it continued on a small scale on the East Coast after the war but died a slow death striving for recognition in the halls of the Capitol in Washington, D. C.

Then, in 1972, Abe relocated to Seal Beach, California. There he reorganized the group.

Abe Rapaport was almost fanatic about the recognition he knew merchant mariners deserved. "It's just a holy crusade as far as I'm concerned. I feel we have been forsaken by the government, kicked under the rug. The United States is the only nation that doesn't recognize its merchant mariners on an equal basis with the military during a war. We never got recognition for anything. After the war, the government gave us a few medals then cast us aside. The American public has no idea what we did."

His group wanted the same status as the other veterans of World War II — recognition, benefits like home loans and the right to be buried in a national cemetery.

They thought they had succeeded in 1977 when a law was passed, after years of lobbying, that gave veterans' status to WASPs — women pilots who ferried planes during World War II. The WASPs and thirteen other groups won veterans' status, including civilians who took part in the defense of Bataan and a unit of women telephone operators who were drafted during World War I. The merchant marine veterans were not mentioned.

Joe Vernick: "In 1982, they organized the U.S. Merchant Marine Veterans of World War II and started the newspaper called the *Anchor Light*. The first meeting was held at Dana Point. It was before my time, and this was attended by Jim Ackerman who is the admiralty attorney in Long Beach. He was one of the first ones there. There were about nine people there at that meeting and that was the real inception of the organization. That's when it actually started — in '82 with the publication of the *Anchor Light*."

Joe became a member in 1983 and was elected secretary. "I read an article in the *L.A. Times* about the U.S. Merchant Marine Veterans of World War II. With a picture of Abe Rapaport. So I called him up and found out where he lived and I went out to Seal Beach. He was holding the meetings in his home at Seal Beach. And I joined the organization. And before long I became secretary and started doing all the letter writing for him. He never cared too much about letter writing. His forte was to get on the telephone and talk for hours. But there was never a record of anything. And he didn't care about getting involved with the Army or the Navy or any of the military because, he said, 'We are civilians. Let's not get involved with them.'

"I didn't feel that that was the proper way. I figured that in order to gain stature, we'd have to get together with the Navy and the rest of the services . . . the Armed Guards and others, and I started writing letters to Admirals and one thing and another."

John Smith, the group's second Vice-President, joined at about the same time. "A friend of mine, Dick Gillelen, was vice-president with Abe at that time. He had physical disabilities but strictly old age. He lived near me then. I'd known him for years. He said, 'I want you to meet somebody you may be interested in.'

"So I got interested right away. As soon as I met Abe, he lived not too far from me in Seal Beach, he said, 'We'd like to have you join us. Here's what we propose to do.'

"I was all excited, having sailed on Liberty ships and Victory ships and seen the *Jeremiah O'Brien*."[1]

One of the earliest goals of the organization was to have a memorial to merchant seamen. Everyone agreed with the concept but deciding exactly what would make an appropriate memorial caused conflict in the fledgling group.

John Smith: "It was Abe's idea to get a Liberty ship because of the historical value. We knew more about Libertys than we knew about Victorys. We thought the Liberty would impress the public more than the Victory ship. Of course we're glad we didn't, 'cause those ships were derelicts, even though we had written about the [Liberty ship] *Protector*. The reason that we were so interested in the *Protector*, Abe had been back earlier and saw the ship.[2] The Maritime Administration said the ship was in excellent condition in all its reports. It was. The hull was excellent, the engines were excellent and everything, but it had been redesigned by the Navy so it was no good as a historical ship.

"We had a split in the organization. Many of our members split from us because they said, 'You guys are crazy, you won't ever get a ship.'

"So they started the American Merchant Marine Veterans. It was just an organization, and they said, 'We're going to build a statue. We know we can do that. You guys are never going to get a ship.'

---

[1] The *Jeremiah O'Brien* is an active Liberty ship museum in San Francisco. The only survivor of the D-Day armada she returned to Normandy in 1994 for the 50th Anniversary commemoration. *Appointment in Normandy* chronicles that voyage. *The Last Liberty* details the *O'Brien*'s history up to that point. Both books are by the author of this book, Capt. Jaffee.

[2] At the time the *Protector* was in the James River Reserve Fleet at Fort Eustis, Virginia.

"They took Abe's mailing list that he had built up through the years. They got a copy of this and they solicited all the members to join them. I got a letter and I was dumbfounded that here was this group that was separating from our group."

An added problem was Abe Rapaport's personality. Very much a "can do" type of person, he was also brusque and abrasive.

Joe Vernick: "With all due credit to him, he didn't know quite how to go about it. I found out in our trips to Washington that he antagonized members of Congress. When I used to mention the name Abe Rapaport, they'd say, 'Forget about it.'

"He really was quite abrasive with them. He was a wonderful guy. He could have been a great union leader. But in this thing here you have to be more tactful."

John Smith: "Even though Abe was abrasive — he'd tell people off — he was a do-er."

In 1985 Abe Rapaport died and Joe Vernick was elected President. National headquarters of the group moved to Long Beach. Chapters sprung up on the East Coast, in Northern California, Colorado and Hawaii. Incorporating in 1985 with 150 veteran mariners, the organization quickly grew to several thousand.

Efforts to get a Liberty ship continued. It wasn't a new idea. The *Jeremiah O'Brien*'s success as an operating museum proved that such a project could work.

The movement caught on among the upper Navy brass, coaxed by Joe Vernick's letter-writing campaign.

"I was secretary and did all the writing. Little by little we started gaining support from the Navy; from the U.S. Armed Guards, from political people, from (congressman) Glenn Anderson from Admiral Hayes in Honolulu, who I made an honorary member, and another four star admiral. We have two or three other admirals, Admiral Higginson from Long Beach who's now with the Chamber of Commerce and others. We got a lot of very good support from them. The letters indicate that. They all supported the memorial."

From Admiral Ronald J. Hays, Commander in Chief, U.S. Pacific Command on January 13, 1987:

The merchant marine and its gallant seamen were one of the keys to our success in World War II. Despite losses which at one point in the war saw our merchant ships being sunk faster than they could be replaced, despite some of the foulest weather in the world on the runs to Murmansk, despite threats from Axis submarines in every corner of the globe, our merchant marine never faltered and kept the war effort on track to victory. It is entirely fitting — and long past due — that a memorial to their courage and self-sacrifice be erected. I applaud the effort wholeheartedly.

I wish you success and assure you that we in the military fully recognize the accomplishments and vitality of the United States Merchant Marine in World War II.

And again from Admiral Hays on February 2, 1987:

I want to wish you the best of luck on your plans to take the *Protector* around to Long Beach via the Panama Canal. With that crew and the ship's ultimate purpose in mind, it should indeed be the voyage of a lifetime. Best wishes and good sailing.

Rear Admiral John Higginson, Commander Naval Surface Group, Long Beach echoed the sentiments when he wrote to Joe Vernick:

I was pleased to receive your letter proposing plans for the S.S. Protector to become a Merchant Marine memorial museum.

Please count my voice among those who fully support this worthwhile goal. Your organization's efforts will offer everyone the opportunity to pay tribute to those brave World War II Merchant Marine seagoers who paid the ultimate price for freedom's sake.

Be assured that we who wear the uniform of the U.S. Navy are proud of the special, historic relationship we share with our U.S. Merchant Marine counterparts and their fallen shipmates. To aid in the promotion of their memory is not only an honor, but a real part of our duty as well.

Best of luck in the successful outcome of this worthy endeavor.

From Admiral J.A. Lyons, Jr., Commander in Chief, United States Pacific Fleet, on March 30, 1987:

I applaud and support your organizations's efforts in saving the S.S. PROTECTOR, and your plans for overhauling the former Liberty ship into a historic "living museum". I am sure many of the men and women of our Navy/Marine Corps family would be anxious to visit such a memorial. It would be a fitting tribute to the merchant seamen who gallantly served our nation in World War II. Endeavors such as yours not only strengthen our common maritime bond, but help preserve our American Heritage and way of life.

My best wishes for making your dream a reality.

And, finally, from the Secretary of the Navy, James H. Webb, Jr. on August 7, 1987:

Your desire to immortalize the Merchant Marine's contributions to victory in World War Two, and to establish an ongoing Merchant Marine museum by preserving the Liberty ship SS. PROTECTOR, has my wholehearted support. This long overdue tribute to the Merchant Marine comes at a time when the value of the Merchant Marine to the defense of the United States is receiving new emphasis.

Through the efforts of your organization, the nation's outstanding debt to the Merchant Marine will touch America's heart and ensure that due recognition and credit is given to those merchant seamen who fought so valiantly during the war.

Best of luck in your endeavors.

Joe Vernick and John Smith went before Congress on their quest for a Liberty. "John and I spoke before Congress,

Congressman Anderson and the Maritime Affairs Committee and so on for the *Protector*."

There were only three Liberty ships left in the United States. Located at the Maritime Administration's James River Reserve Fleet, they were the *Protector,* the *Arthur M. Huddell* and the *John W. Brown.* But the *Brown* was spoken for by a Baltimore organization, the *Huddell* was tied up in the courts in crew injury litigation as well as having had all her machinery removed, and the *Protector* had been so extensively converted by the Navy it no longer resembled a Liberty.

It became increasingly apparent the *Protector* wouldn't do.

One problem was getting her to Southern California. It would be a long, expensive tow from Norfolk, through the Panama Canal to Los Angeles. Once the ship was there it would require additional expense to return her to her original merchant configuration.

Joe Vernick: "John and I and Rapaport's son went back to the James River. We looked at three ships that were there at that time. Not only was the *Protector* not a good ship for us but the hatches were sealed with steel plates because they made living quarters out of the holds . . . with steam lines and everything ripped out. It was a spy ship. Similar to the one that was blown up by Israel. Sister ship to that one. Truthfully, we never could have brought it through the Panama Canal. But Abe just wanted a ship so badly that he didn't think about the fact of what it would take and the logistics of being in the James River and the money . . .

"But actually we never could have taken possession of that ship. We never could have brought it around. When we think back we would never have a ship if we decided on that."

Another problem was asbestos. The *Protector*, because of its configuration, had large amounts of asbestos lagging in it. Due to its age, a great deal of this insulation was exposed.

Joe Vernick remembered it was completely contaminated with asbestos. "Most of the doors had asbestos signs, 'be careful, do not enter,' and there was so much asbestos you could see it in the passageways, flying around . . . we knew it was contaminated."

John Smith suggested a Victory ship. A Victory was also a World War II ship. They were the next class built after the Libertys. It would be an equally suitable memorial. And there were about eighty of them scattered among the Reserve Fleets at Beaumont, Suisun Bay and James River. A Victory ship also contains asbestos but a lot less of it. The odds were in their favor of finding a Victory in good condition.

Joe Vernick: "Luckily we heard about the *Lane Victory* through Harry Morgan and Jim Nolan. Jim talked to Tony Schiavonne in the James River and Tony said, 'What the hell do they want that ship for [*Protector*]? There's a nice ship there [at Suisun Bay], the *Lane Victory*. So we went to see the *Lane Victory* and that's how we got it."

The *Lane Victory* cast a spell on Joe Vernick. It was clean and well-lighted. It showed itself well.

Joe described his feeling when he first saw the *Lane*. "It was nostalgic after more than thirty-five years to find myself once again in the engine room of a Victory ship.

"I believe I made the last trip on the *S.S. Lakewood Victory* in 1949-50 as an engineer before it was placed in the Reserve Fleet in Suisun Bay.

"After we saw it we asked Glenn Anderson if he could make an amendment. We had to make an amendment to the Congressional bill changing the *Protector* to the *Lane Victory*."

Mr. Anderson forwarded the request to John Gaughan, Maritime Administrator. Mr. Gaughan's reply went out on October 2, 1987.

You raised the possibility of substituting the S.S.LANE VICTORY for the S.S. PROTECTOR. The reason was that the PROTECTOR contained far too much asbestos to permit it to be an acceptable economic and liability risk for a recipient organization.

Before proceeding with any such substitution, you wished some idea of the quantity and severity of the asbestos on board the LANE VICTORY.

By its very design, the LANE VICTORY does contain a much lower amount of asbestos than the PROTECTOR. The exact degree of severity of the asbestos problem on board the LANE VICTORY is not ascertainable without a detailed survey. We do not have the resources to conduct and report on such a survey. Each group (potential recipient) can perform its own survey and reach its own conclusions, and then provide specific advice to you. I think this approach is the best because it is not only the extent of the asbestos which is important; the ability and the resources of each potential recipient to deal with it are equally important factors.

In forwarding Mr. Gaughan's reply, Congressman Anderson raised another issue — one that would plague the organization in the months ahead: where to berth the ship. Abe Rapaport, Joe Vernick and John Smith had focused their efforts on achieving recognition for the Merchant Marine Veterans and finding a "symbol" for them. The question of where to berth a ship they did not yet have had not seemed an immediate problem. But they quickly realized it was a major consideration.

As Mr. Gaughan indicates in his letter, the *S.S. Lane* contains a much lower amount of asbestos than the *S.S. Protector*. However, Mr. Gaughan also indicates, and I agree with him, that you will need to conduct a detailed study to ascertain just how much asbestos is on board the *S.S.Lane*.

In addition, I would like to know how well your negotiations are going in finding a permanent berthing spot for a merchant marine memorial.

I continue to support your cause and thus will have no problem in amending H.R. 2032 by replacing the *S.S. Protector* with the *S.S. Lane*. As you well know, it is imperative that we avoid running into the same kind of problem that we ran into with the *S.S. Protector*.

Joe Vernick and John Smith returned to Suisun Bay with a group of experts on asbestos. Heading the party was Syd Carpenter, a marine contractor who had more than forty years' experience installing ship asbestos insulation on vessels in Los Angeles Harbor. In addition there were four marine engineers and one captain: Chief Engineer Harry Morgan, who was instrumental in reactivating the *Jeremiah O'Brien* and the steam tug *Hercules*, Chief Engineer John Smith who brought the *Queen Mary* from England to Long Beach, Hugh Brown, an engineer with American President Lines for forty years, and Joe Vernick. The captain was John O. Svenssen, who was licensed as both master and pilot. Taking air and particle samples throughout the ship, they sent them to an independent testing laboratory for complete analysis. They then crossed their fingers and waited. When the results of the tests came in they showed only minor asbestos particle levels, well below minimum requirements.

As to the berth, there was talk with the harbor commission about a permanent berth in Los Angles Harbor. Temporary sites in the outer harbor and a permanent berth in the Dominguez Channel were suggested. But the Harbor Commission would not make a commitment without the vessel first being assigned to the organization.

Joe Vernick and John Smith didn't realize it, but a breakthrough was at hand in the long battle to gain veterans' status for merchant mariners. On October 7, 1987, in Washington, D.C., Judge Louis Oberdorfer ordered the Pentagon to reconsider its earlier decision to deny veterans' status to the group. His order stated that their decision was "arbitrary and capricious and . . . not supported by substantial evidence." He ordered the decisions "remanded to the Secretary of the Air Force for further consideration" and further instructed them to provide him with a timetable for their deliberations.

C. E. "Gene" DeFries, president of District 1 of the Marine Engineers Beneficial Association publicly stated, "Remember, these men are not armchair Rambos who have never seen the face of war. These men were tested at sea, where they showed true courage."

More than forty years after the war ended, merchant mariners would finally receive their due.

And now they had to get the *Lane Victory*.

16

"GOOD MORNING, FELLOW SHIPOWNERS"

1988 was a banner year for the Merchant Marine Veterans of World War II. On January 19, the Secretary of the Air Force, Edward C. Aldridge, Jr., made the decision that the "American Merchant Marine in Oceangoing Service during the Period of Armed Conflict, December 7, 1941 to August 15, 1945" would be considered "active duty" under the provisions of Public Law 95-202 for the purposes of all laws administered by the Veterans Administration.

Abe Rapaport's dream, conceived on the beaches of Normandy, was a reality.

Representative Helen Bentley of Maryland, chairperson of the House Merchant Marine and Fisheries Committee, thought it was "too little, too late."

"For most seamen," she said, "veteran designation will really be minimal, perhaps nothing more than getting a flag and a headstone in a military cemetery. The seamen who are eligible for veteran benefits are now in their twilight years. We, as a nation, should have been taking care of their needs for four decades."

For the Merchant Marine Veterans, however, it was "better late than never."

Meanwhile the campaign to get the ship continued. A barrage of letters was written to Navy admirals, politicians, maritime executives, government leaders, anyone that might help with the cause. Hundreds of supporters were asked to write Congress, urging the passing of the bill giving the *Lane Victory* to the U.S. Merchant Marine Veterans of World War II.

On March 8, 1988 the House of Representatives unanimously passed H.R. 2032 authorizing the U.S. Merchant Marine Veterans of World War II to receive the *Lane Victory* for conversion to a maritime museum to serve as memorial to the merchant marine veterans of World War II.

The next level was the Senate.

Telegrams were immediately sent urging California Senators Pete Wilson and Alan Cranston to sponsor the bill.

Phase two of the letter writing campaign began. It was easier the second time around. The phrase "already unanimously approved by the House of Representatives" was a persuasive addition to letters to the Senate.

Joe Vernick: "We passed Bill 2032 in the House of Representatives unanimously and then Senators Wilson and Cranston jointly sponsored the bill in the Senate." Finally they would have their ship.

Having a ship in name is one thing. Having it in reality is quite another. The Merchant Marine Veterans of World War II knew the coming months would be difficult. They were equal to the job.

John Smith spent much of his time addressing groups in Long Beach and Los Angeles harbors. Showing slides of the *Lane Victory*, he appeared anywhere he was asked and arranged to appear in places he wasn't asked. With each showing he gained publicity for the ship and the cause. As public awareness grew, new members joined and money was added to the group's treasury.

The Veterans knew that for their project to be a success, the ship must become a living museum. Designs included a research library, a maritime history room, a combination auditorium and banquet hall and a seaman's hospitality section. At the same time, the ship had to remain "historic." It should, as nearly as possible, be returned to its World War II appearance, including guns, cannons and grey paint.

Those who weren't involved in restoration began an ongoing effort to raise funds. It would take a lot of money to berth and maintain the ship that would soon be coming.

Joe Vernick: "It passed in the Senate and on October the 18th (1988) Ronald Reagan signed the Bill conveying the *Lane Victory* to our organization."

Wording is important in legislation. The more loosely a bill is worded, the more subject it is to interpretation. The bill concerning the *Lane Victory* said it would be given to a nonprofit organization. But it did not mention the U.S. Merchant Marine Veterans of World War II by name. This oversight would cause problems in the months ahead.

But this was a minor point beside the great accomplishment — the Merchant Marine Veterans had their ship!

John Smith opened the November 1988 meeting with the triumphant greeting, "Good morning, fellow shipowners."

Meanwhile, the organization grew in size and stature. The "Victory Belles," a ladies' auxiliary group, was formed in November. It supplied much-needed support for the Veterans, in addition to pastries and coffee at the monthly meetings.

A Phoenix, Arizona chapter of the American Merchant Marine Veterans, known as the "Desert Mariners" was organized. They promised support in the future.

Discussions about berthing the ship were held in Los Angeles Mayor Bradley's office. The City of Los Angeles didn't realize how serious the Veterans were about berthing the ship at San Pedro in Los Angeles harbor. City Hall's attitude seemed to be, "Sure, the bill had passed, but they don't really have title to the ship yet. We can deal with the problem of where to put the ship later — when and if it ever becomes a reality."

The Veterans were quickly making it a reality. They began plans to tow the ship from the Reserve Fleet at Suisun Bay to Los Angeles — some 400 miles down the California coast.

The tow itself had the potential of being a major difficulty. That difficulty was financial. The vessel had to be insured for the trip. The cost of the tow was high; a commercial towing company would charge tens of thousands of dollars. The Veterans, although hard at work fund-raising, didn't have that kind of money. Would the dream die simply because they couldn't get the ship from Suisun Bay to San Pedro?

Then there was the problem of spare parts. The bill authorizing the transfer of the ship also allowed for the transfer of "any unneeded equipment from other vessels in the National Defense Reserve Fleet in order to assist placing the *Lane Victory* in operating condition." Once again, interpretation was a problem. The word "unneeded" would later cause a major rift in the Maritime Administration and result in unnecessary confusion and heartache for Joe Vernick and his group.[1] But at the beginning the Veterans could have any and all the spares they wanted.

---

[1] Maritime Administrator John Gaughn approved donating spare parts to the *Lane Victory*. Another official at the Maritime Administration, however, felt that spare parts should be kept in the Fleet in case the Victory ships were activated. At the same time, an employee assigned to Marad's San Francisco office voiced his concern to the Inspector General regarding control of spare parts taken off ships. In the bureaucratic lexicon, any obstacle, no matter how small, makes an issue "controversial," a word with frightful implications, to be regarded with suspicion and subjected to the full bureaucratic "process." This is what happened to the sound and practical proposal for putting useless spare parts to good use in a good cause. The *Lane Victory*'s access to spare parts was held in abeyance until all the "controversies" were investigated.

Left, volunteers from the U.S. Merchant Marine Veterans remove sealing from one of the hatches to the Lane Victory. *Below, with the help of a floating crane from Mare Island, they remove spare booms from the* Panamerican Victory.

The logical thing was to load the spare parts on the ship before it left Suisun Bay. Otherwise there would be expensive truckloads of equipment to transport from the Reserve Fleet to Los Angeles. Easier said than done.

Years before, spare parts for the Victory ship program were stored on the *Panamerican Victory*. This ship was located at the end of a row of ships at the north end of the fleet. Two rows of ships to the south was the *Lane Victory,* also located at

the end of a row. The Reserve Fleet had a floating crane which had the capacity to handle most of the spares. But there was a problem of reach. Most of the spare parts were located inside cargo hatch #4 on the *Panamerican Victory*. The boom on the Reserve Fleet's crane couldn't reach that far. The best alternative would be to borrow a floating crane from the Navy at Mare Island. It would have the reach and the capacity to handle

The Mare Island floating crane underway with a barge full of spare parts being transferred from the Panamerican Victory *to the* Lane Victory.

heavier loads. But one doesn't just borrow a crane from the United States Navy. Not usually.

Enter Captain James Nolan. A former master for States-Marine Lines and a former San Francisco Bay Pilot, James Nolan is also a Captain in the Naval Reserve. He taught piloting to Navy shiphandlers at Little Creek, Virginia and seemed to know everyone in the Navy and most people in the other branches of the service. As former master of the *SS Jeremiah O'Brien*, he is interested in maritime history and making ships into museums. With a few phone calls he arranged to not only borrow the floating crane for as long as necessary, but with an "Oh, by the way," learned that the Navy had a tug

The crane barge alongside the Lane Victory. *It took one week and several hundred hours of volunteer labor to transfer and safely stow all the spares. Photo by Jane Weidringer.*

traveling down the coast to Long Beach in the near future. As long as their tug was going there anyway, they would be happy to tow the *Lane Victory* to Los Angeles free of charge and at no cost to the taxpayers!

Now everyone concentrated on accumulating the spare parts. Several trips were made to the fleet to locate and remove spares from similar ships. Once gathered, they were stowed on the *Lane Victory*. More than 10,000 volunteer hours plus travel time to and from Southern California was spent staging spares before the final departure. The culmination was a one-time, now-or-never effort. Once the ship was out of the Reserve Fleet, the opportunity would be gone. The Maritime Administration provided the stowage plan for the *Panamerican Victory*. Indicating where each spare was located, when combined with a Marad inventory list it gave the Veterans the number, description and location of every spare on board. A work party was sent to the Reserve Fleet to mark the spares being transferred to the *Lane Victory*. Each box, part and piece of equipment was spray-painted to make it easy to identify.

In the early months of 1989 "Operation Spare Parts" got underway. The Veterans' work crew arrived from Southern California on a Sunday. The following day, as they stripped the covers off the hatches on the *Panamerican Victory*, the Navy's floating crane from Mare Island arrived. Towering over the ship, it quickly removed propellers, shafts, motors and countless other necessary parts to keep the *Lane* operating in her new life as a museum ship. Then the crane and barges of parts were shifted alongside the *Lane* and the process was reversed. Parts were carefully loaded inside the hatches and on deck, blocked for the sea voyage, and the hatches covered up again. By Friday the crane was gone and the *Lane Victory* was almost ready for the voyage south. She had 1,200 tons of spare parts on board.

In May 1989, the soon-to-be-memorial was placed outboard of one of the rows of ships at the fleet. It was the third and final time she would leave Suisun Bay. A towing bridle,

With the spare parts securely stowed on board, the ship was moved outboard of one of the rows at the fleet, left. Here the towing bridle was rigged and other final preparations made for the tow to San Pedro.

Towing day and one of the Navy's tugs from Mare Island is alongside, above, ready to help the Lane Victory *out of the fleet. Left, the tug* Narragansett *takes a strain on the towing bridle as the voyage south begins. Left photo courtesy Jim Nolan.*

Underway in San Francisco Bay (San Francisco in the background) the Lane Victory *heads for her new home — San Pedro. Courtesy Jim Nolan.*

insurance wire and other equipment for the trip to Los Angeles were rigged. The ship was ready. Everyone was jubilant.

Then came word of the oversight on H.R. 2032.

Joe Vernick: "We got ready to take possession of the ship. We found out we couldn't take it because the Congressional Act said it was being given to an unamed nonprofit organization. It didn't stipulate our name. So we had to go back to the Maritime Administration . . . that was real hectic . . . just at that time Jim Nolan got the Military Sealift Command to tow the ship down here."

The date was set. The ship would leave on June 8. But to whom did it belong? Could the Veterans get the bill amended in time?

Joe Vernick: "So we were going back and forth with the Maritime Administration. They finally transferred it . . ."

John Smith: ". . . just the day before it was scheduled to leave the Reserve Fleet."

On June 7, 1989, the United States Merchant Marine Veterans of World War II received the "pink slip" to the *Lane Victory*. Technically a Deed of Gift, it stated, "Notice — The S.S. LANE VICTORY is owned by, and is the exclusive property of, U.S. MERCHANT MARINE VETERANS OF WORLD WAR II (Recipient), which is solely responsible for this vessel." It was the first time in history that the U. S. government gave a Deed of Gift to a nonprofit corporation.

And now, it suddenly dawned on the Los Angeles Harbor Department that the Veterans were serious. What had been idle talk a few months earlier was suddenly a reality. They had a ship. They were towing it down the coast. They wanted a berth in Los Angeles Harbor.

17

BERTHING PAINS

W hen the *Lane Victory* arrived in Los Angeles harbor on June 12, 1989, all hell broke loose. To begin with, the Harbor Department claimed they knew nothing about the ship and wanted nothing to do with it.

The Merchant Marine Veterans feared such a reaction. But they knew if they waited for the Harbor Department to decide on a berth, they would never get an answer. Towing the ship into Los Angeles Harbor without permission was one way to force the issue. Once the ship was there, the Harbor Department would have to give them a place to put it. *Fait accompli* is the Latin term for it, loosely meaning "it's done." It was a bold move but at the beginning it looked like it would backfire.

The Los Angeles Harbor Department refused to acknowledge *fait accompli*. In other cases it waived fees and provided free pilotage for unique ships, but in the case of the *Lane Victory* it not only insisted on payment but wanted it in

A close-up view of the powerful USNS Narragansett *as she arrives in Los Angeles harbor with her valuable tow. Photo by C..L. Johnson.*

Through the efforts of Capt. James Nolan, a "tow of convenience" was arranged with the U.S. Navy at no cost to the taxpayers. Right, the USNS Narragansett *arrives with the* Lane Victory. *Photo by C.L. Johnson.*

advance. Unable to anchor because there was no power on board to raise the anchors once they were let go, the ship was forced to drift in the harbor, held out of harm's way by the tug that brought her in.

At the time, the Merchant Marine Veterans were in a meeting. Word reached them quickly that until they came up with pilotage fees, their ship would drift around the harbor. Who knew what kind of trouble she would get into? Suspending the meeting, the veterans quickly wrote out a check for the requisite $270 and hand-carried it to the Harbor District.

Joe Vernick: "They wouldn't leave us in, 'Get out. We don't want you here."

Mark Owens, who made his first trip as third mate on the *Lane Victory* in 1968, was now a Los Angeles Harbor Pilot. Unfortunately, he was off duty the day the ship arrived. "They ran afoul of the harbor department. Partly because the harbor department is so difficult to deal with in general and partly because they were so narrow-minded as to what they wanted.

"Our chief pilot at the time thought if he stiffed them they'd just go away. When they showed up outside with the ship and they were calling for the pilot, he was sitting in the office like, 'I'm not going to send one.'

"So finally Captain Doug ---- went out and got him in.

"I was off and a few days later I showed up at work and here's my ship."

Joe Vernick: "John and I had been talking to them a year or two before we had the ship, about getting the *Lane Victory*. They told us cold, 'There's not a single inch of space for you guys.'"

Finally the veterans were permitted to tie the ship up at Berth 55 — for one week only.

Joe Vernick: "One of our chief engineers, Harry Goldstick used to tell me, 'Joe you're never going to get it. You're crazy, the government's never going to give you guys a ship.'

"When the ship came in on June 12, he was there. The tugboats were moving it to the pier. He says, 'You know what, Joe, I see it and I still don't believe it.'"

The Harbor Commission was offended. Public Relations Director and spokesperson Julia Nagana said, "They were towed down from San Francisco, essentially without a place to go. They had no prior authorization."

Fait accompli.

The battle for a permanent berth became explosive. Joe Vernick, watching the ship arrive at its new berth said, "The Los Angeles Harbor Commission has given us permission to dock it here at Berth 55 until June 19. After that we don't know where we'll go. The government has given us this one million dollar ship, and we can't find a home for it."

Julia Nagana replied, "They have exactly one week, and then they'll have to move the ship at their own expense. They will have to find another location." She suggested the ship be towed to the outer harbor where it could be anchored at no charge. Otherwise the Harbor District would charge an average of $931 per day for tying up the *Lane Victory* at any of the berths under its control.

The Merchant Marine Veterans might have accepted the fee charge were it for space at Berth 87-89. Located next to the Los Angeles Maritime Museum, it was the perfect spot for a "museum ship." Nearby is a statue honoring merchant seamen, erected by the splinter group that left the organization several years earlier.

"Berth 87 to 90 is definitely out of the question," said Nagana, anticipating the request.

The Harbor Department had ideas other than museums. The site housed a container cargo terminal. Demand for such space is high — and profitable. Although recently vacated by its tenant, there were others interested in it. Mark Richter, assistant director of property management for the port said the Harbor Department could hardly afford to relinquish the terminal at a time when it could barely handle the existing containerized shipping trade, not to mention increases projected for the future.

To relieve some of the pressure, the port offered two other sites, one along Cerritos Channel in Wilmington and another at the foot of Avalon Boulevard at the location of a future recreational and commercial complex for the residents of Wilmington.

Joe Vernick had dealt with this type of "accommodation" before. The Cerritos channel site was miles from nowhere and the Avalon Boulevard location was years from being completed.

Wilmington is a seaman's town. But the city proper is not near the piers. Shipping berths in Wilmington are reached after traveling through acres of container terminals, warehouses and bare lots piled with industrial refuse.

Joe Vernick responded in a rare burst of anger, "They want to send us out somewhere where we'll never be heard of again. The people who made Los Angeles Harbor valuable are the Merchant Marine. Through this harbor passed hundreds of thousands of troops. The least that we want is a central location for the vessel, which it deserves. They say it's too valuable a piece of property. I say who the hell made it valuable? The Merchant Marine."

Ira Distenfield, president of the Los Angles Board of Harbor Commissioners patiently explained the bottom line, "I am extremely supportive of them having the ship and I'm also supportive of that ship being put on harbor property in a way that would give the community an opportunity to enjoy it. But we can't put it on property that has the ability to be rented for the purpose that it was entrusted to us."

The Veterans countered with the argument that the terminal should be abandoned because it is the only industrial site remaining on a stretch of waterfront that includes the port's World Cruise Center, Ports O' Call Village and the Cabrillo Marina.

The San Pedro Chamber of Commerce came in on the side of the ship. Leron Gubler, executive director of the Chamber: "The ship would fit in well with what we're trying to do in the way of tourism. You've got this shipping terminal right in the middle, which isolates the World Cruise Center from the rest of those activities."

The Harbor Department rather petulantly replied, "Our feeling is that we certainly have not committed the San Pedro waterfront exclusively to tourist and visitor activities."

"It is utterly disgraceful," replied Joe Vernick. "They are sitting on $50 million to $60 million in profits, and they're so reluctant to give us a helping hand."

The *San Pedro News-Pilot* put the situation into perspective in an editorial on June 16, 1989.

> The ship deserves to be in Los Angeles Harbor near the Maritime Museum and near other people-oriented attractions now situated on the west bank of the Main channel.
>
> The Harbor Commission is confusing its role, we believe, if it allows the profit motive to govern the decision of whether or not

to allow the vessel to be sited at Berth 87, a part of the area left vacant last month with the loss of Evergreen Marine Corp.

The small 3.06 acre parcel the association is seeking is only a part of the 25 acre container yard.

It would make excellent parking for an attraction such as the Liberty [sic] ship museum and monument.

Additionally, it could be used to advantage as overflow parking for the Maritime Museum, which has limited parking and which at times hosts events bringing hundreds of visitors to the area.

The port annually extracts millions of dollars net profit from the many and varied users of its facilities.

Millions of dollars are still being held in accounts for unbudgeted projects in the future.

Money would seem to be one of the lesser considerations.

If we are to believe in former Harbor Commissioner Ira Distenfield's stated department philosophy that the port is there for the people, we wonder to what better use the land could be put.

The merchant mariners need only 550 feet of space alongside the dock at Berth 87 to spot the Lane Victory.

The land required is only a small corner of the available container terminal.

The port could still make its millions by leasing the other acreage on the parcel.

Thousands of people would make the trip to San Pedro to visit the ship museum, promoted as a floating monument to the seamen who died for their country.

The port already has 190 acres sitting vacant on Terminal Island and it is contemplating creating another 300 acres with materials dredged from the harbor floor.

It seems to us that the commission is being pretty small over a 3.06 acre parcel, which itself is a pretty small piece of the many miles of shoreline the port has available to it.

The week of free use at Berth 55 was up on June 19th. On June 20th the ship was still there. The Merchant Marine Veterans called a press conference.

Getting right to the point, Joe Vernick addressed the assembled reporters. "We're going to stay right here. We have no place to go. We're orphans." Once again stressing the suitability of Berth 87, he said it would be only fitting to have the *Lane Victory* at that berth as a memorial "dedicated to the thousands of merchant mariners that perished fighting for freedom to make this harbor what it is today."

Nagana replied for the Harbor Commission. "It is unfortunate that the port is being accused of being insensitive to this project. We're sympathetic to their needs and we are concerned, but we do need to maintain the efficient operation of the port."

Port officials were busy trying to lease the space out to a commercial operator. Assistant director for property management for the Harbor Department, Mark Richter, rationalized the issue. Acknowledging that the terminal brings in about $2 million a year in revenue to the port, he said, "But the compensation is not the point. The point is that we are short of cargo space and we're hardly in a position to declare a terminal of this kind surplus."

Cargo space equals revenue which equals compensation — i.e. profit.

The politicians waded in, successfully straddling the issue.

Congressman Anderson supported the Veterans' desire, but qualified it by recognizing that the Harbor Department had its own concerns to take care of.

Los Angeles councilwoman Joan Milke Flores, who represented the Harbor District at the time, offered some verbal support, saying she would like to see the ship berthed near the Maritime Museum. But, recognizing where the authority lay, concluded with ". . . it is really up to the port."

Mayor Tom Bradley, who had been made an honorary member of the Merchant Marine Veterans of World War II, wrote stating that he was supporting the Harbor Department's decision.

John Smith said, "We're fighters. We've been fighting for forty-five years."

Joe Vernick was adamant. "I want to see the ship down here before I kick the bucket. It's just something we want to do because we deserve it. That's my whole life, getting that ship here for a memorial."

Other veterans' groups came in on the side of the mariners. Herb Norch, representing the U.S. Navy Armed Guard World War II Veterans wrote to Mayor Tom Bradley.

> I am a member of U.S. Navy Armed Guard WW II Veterans along with 9,200 members that served aboard Liberty ships, oil tankers and Victory ships in WW II along with our Merchant Marines in all parts of the world supplying vital equipment, supplies and fuel to help win the war.
>
> It was very sad to learn that your great city and port of Los Angeles cannot find a decent home for the SS Lane Victory to be used as a museum. I know that San Francisco and Baltimore each have a WW II Liberty ship and it was the best thing that ever happened to bring alive their waterfront and show our younger generation there was good people that built and sailed on these great ships. And also that at one time, United States was number one in shipping and it would be self-supporting and help with the economy in Los Angeles. I know you have the great support of Armed Guard members along with the destroyer-escort Sailors Association, Tin Can sailors Association and disabled American Veterans. I can assure you that it would be a great tourist attraction.
>
> As you have read in your local papers, the Merchant Marine Veterans of WW II are now recognized by the Veterans Administration as Veterans and are entitled to the same benefits that other veterans that served in the armed forces of United States. I pray and hope that you give this ship her rightful place in history by giving her honor in berthing her at the port of Los Angeles. Thank you very much for taking the time to know how I and many others feel about this matter.

Support poured in: Electronic Televisions, CNN cable vision, The News Media, Printed Media, Chevron Oil Company and the I.L.W.U.

The impasse lasted for two weeks. Finally, on June 27, relations improved. There was a meeting and a last-minute compromise agreement between the harbor officials and the seamen. The Harbor Commission agreed to allow the *Lane Victory* to be moored at nearby Berth 52 where it could stay at no charge until renovated and converted to a floating museum and memorial.

"We've kind of cleared the air a little bit," said Vernick. "They're going to work with us, and we'll work with them."

Nagana used the opportunity to doggedly address the issue of Berth 87. She said it "was absolutely out of the question, and it still is."

Joe Vernick: "For the time being they're adamant about 87 and we've acquiesced. Right now, we have a berth and I'm satisfied. At least we won't have to worry about having the sword of Damocles hanging over our head."

In his usual positive fashion, the following day he began a letter with the ringing statement, "The *Lane Victory* is now home!"

On August 4 a letter was sent to councilwoman Joan Milke Flores of the 15th District of Los Angeles. Her constituents asked her to submit a resolution in the Los Angeles City Council for Berth 87 for the *Lane Victory*. Jim Davis of the Veterans met with the councilwoman and was assured that she would submit the resolution.

Interviewed in 1990, Joe Vernick said, "It's been a constant struggle with the harbor people. Even right now we're still negotiating."

Because of the temporary need for Berth 52 for a special shipment of cargo, the ship was moved to Berth 177 in Wilmington. The move took place on November 15, 1989. Wilmington Transportation provided the tugs at no cost. The services of the pilot, Capt. Mark Owens, were also provided free of charge.

Capt. Owens: "Later they said the city would not help them in any way, but that they wouldn't necessarily try to interfere with them. So the gist of that was that any off-watch pilot that wished to, assisted them in their moves. So they just scheduled them for when I was off. Any time they want to move it I get a call and we just make it work. I moved it over to 177. I moved it once before that. I moved it three times."

"When we made that shift over to 177 they had all kinds of people on board. I'm trying to get around, I forget why I wasn't working the bridge wings. I was on the deck below for some reason, running from bridge wing to bridge wing you know, 'Excuse me, excuse me, excuse me, excuse me.'

"It was a lot of fun. All kinds of help. Every other guy had a VHF [walkie-talkie]. And every time I said something you'd hear it all over the ship.

"When we shifted those first times, there was no power whatsoever on the ship. To heave up the lines they'd have to take a bight on it with a handy-billy and heave it up a little bit at a time. I'd try to pinch one end [of the ship] or the other in so they could get those lines tight while they heave up on the others.

"But all these guys in their late sixties, early seventies out there heaving on it.

"I'm telling you, it was a riot. 'You just tell us what you want done, Cap.'

"'Don't hurt yourself, please.'"

A special cargo shipment required that the ship move to Pier 177. Here she is just leaving the berth at Pier 52. Photo by Bill Loenhorst.

In February the *Lane Victory* returned to its home berth

at Pier 52. This berth was provided through the good graces of Richard Holdaway, President of Kaiser International. There was never a charge for its use during the entire time the ship was there.

The first anniversary celebration of the ship was held on October 21. It was attended by Congressmen Glenn Anderson, Dana Rohrabacher and many other dignitaries.

Congressman Rohrabacher was the newest member of the team. His feelings were strongly stated in the letter he sent after the celebration:

> Dear Mr. Vernick:
> Thank you for inviting me to participate with you in honoring Congressman Glenn Anderson last Saturday. I am particularly grateful for the opportunity you gave me to introduce my colleague from the House of Representatives.
> Events such as this serve to focus attention on your efforts to establish the *S.S. Lane Victory* as the Merchant Marine Memorial Museum. With your persistence and commitment you will be successful.
> Again, thank you for including me in the company of such fine people, particularly the Merchant Marines Veterans who were the logistical backbone of the Allied victory in World War II. Your gallantry is legendary.

Meanwhile, Councilwoman Flores submitted her resolution to the committee and then to the Los Angeles City Council. Again, in typical political fashion, by the time the Flores resolution passed, it was watered down. No longer was there a mention of Berth 87. In final form it passed as a resolution of general support rather than one specifically allowing use of Berth 87.

> Item No. 27 89-2034
> Commerce, Energy and Natural Resources Committee report on berthing of the vessel SS Lane Victory in Los Angeles Harbor as a memorial museum of the U.S. Merchant Marine service.
> Recommendations for Council action:

The size of the flag flown at the first anniversary celebration symbolized the faith of the crew in the project., which would succeed beyond all expectations. Photo by Bill Loenhorst.

Adopt the resolution (Flores-Farrell) expressing the following on behalf of the city council:

1. Recommend to the Harbor Department that the SS Lane Victory be berthed in Los Angeles Harbor, in a locale with easy public access and adequate parking accommodations where it will serve as a memorial museum and benefit the residents of Los Angeles and all of Southern California.

2. Extend the City of Los Angeles highest degree of respect, admiration and gratitude to all of the valiant Merchant Mariners and their representative association, the U.S. Merchant Marine Veterans of World War II.

A similar resolution was given to the Los Angeles Board of Supervisors, with Supervisor Deane Dana introducing the resolution to the full board. It passed unanimously. The tide was turning.

On December 1, 1989, headway was made on a permanent berthing space. The Flores resolution brought some action. The Los Angeles City Council asked the Harbor Department to negotiate with the Veterans to find a site in San Pedro for the *Lane Victory*.

Joan Milke Flores: "Locating the distinctive ship the *SS Lane Victory* in the Los Angeles Harbor will help to educate and inform the public about our merchant marine and the role they have in U.S. history."

The issue of berthing was finally resolved (at least the Harbor Department thought so) with the Los Angeles Harbor Department agreeing to allow the ship a permanent berth in exchange for the veterans giving up their demand for the coveted space at Berth 87. The Flores-Farrell resolution went through the city council's Industry and Economic Development Committee where it was unanimously approved. Then the city council itself endorsed the resolution with unanimous approval. It required the *Lane Victory* organization to submit an application for "a permanent berth in San Pedro, in a locale with easy access to the public and adequate parking accommodations."

John Smith: "We agreed, sort of an unwritten agreement, that if we'd quit hollering and make a fuss about that [Berth 87-89] they would give us this ten year lease. If we hadn't fought for that we probably wouldn't have anything. We went for the highest goal and in return they fed us a bone. This is a good bone, at least it's not all that bad. But without the fight we'd have nothing."

Then came a demand from the Harbor District for fees for using the berth. It was an ill-timed slap in the face. Public opinion was strongly on the side of the *Lane Victory*.

Joe Vernick: "They sent us a letter from the harbor department. Sure we could have the berth but it would cost us seven thousand something per month and after five years fourteen thousand."

The Veterans quickly went into action, bringing in every politician they knew.

Joe continues: "Then we started getting all these letters. We sent letters proving that the *Jeremiah O'Brien* pays nothing, the *Star of India*, the *John W. Brown*, not only do they not pay for berthing space but they get free power and water. All those letters were sent there [to the harbor district] and letters of support from admirals and other knowledgeable people. They finally saw that . . . and Joanne Flores our councilwoman told them to go back and rethink their request . . . 'After all,' she said, 'this is a nonprofit organization. It's an honor to have these people. This represents a memorial.'"

"Then the commissioners said the harbor had no right to send that letter to us."

As far as the Merchant Marine Veterans were concerned, the Berth 87-89 issue wasn't dead, but merely shelved. As Joe Vernick said, "We'll get our berth eventually. We're tough, persistent old seafarers. This is our goal."

18

FROM DEAD SHIP TO LIVING MUSEUM

eanwhile, the ship slowly came to life.

By January, 1990 the sanitary system was operational with flush toilets and hot and cold wash water. This included a sewage collection and disposal system. No longer did the crew have to use port-a-potties on the dock. The gun crew quarters in the after house were converted into a ship's office. Electrical power was brought on board. Although the *Lane* was a DC [direct current] ship, electrical circuits for AC [alternating current] power were connected in the new office and throughout the midship house. Cargo booms, winches and related equipment were removed from no. 3 hold, installed and put in operating condition. The lifeboats were taken out of the hold and placed in their davits.

American President Lines donated the labor and paint to restore the stack to that company's original markings — a white eagle bracketed by four white stars on a red band with blue

With lifeboats in place and American President Lines' colors on the stack, the Lane Victory *looked much as she did while operating in the 1950s.*

above and below it. Their Sailor's Union of the Pacific shore gang did the job with pleasure, fondly recalling the days when they sailed on such ships.

A security system was installed which included bilge sensors, a gangway annunciator pad, and office burglar alarms. A walkway was painted throughout the ship so that visitors could follow it and see as much as possible yet not get lost. This required building stairways into cargo holds 1, 4 and 5, and installing watertight doors in the lower holds.

One of the main deck staterooms was stripped and converted into a ship's store. Known as the "Slop Chest" it was staffed by volunteers from the Victory Belles. Merchandise includes windbreakers, shirts, hats, mugs, steins, books, cushions, tote-bags, key chains, pens, coffee cups, and other souvenirs.

Capt. Mark Owens: "When I first saw that ship it was just like it came out of the fleet. No better than that. And they re-rigged it and got it going in the face of everyone telling them that they couldn't. They machined up all the bushings for the booms and they drug all that machinery out on deck. I'm really impressed with them."

The original radio antenna was installed. The ship's radio transmitters and receivers were put into operation and in 1989 the *Lane Victory* amateur radio station came on line. One of their first accomplishments was to make contact with Merchant Marine Veteran's Regional Vice President E. J. Hines, Jr. in Charleston S.C. That year's hurricane Hugo left the state devastated. The phone lines were down and there were no communications. Harry Goldstick, call sign WA6JTM, quickly got through on the ham circuit and Joe Vernick was able to talk

U.S. Merchant Marine Veterans World War II

K
E
C
W

P.O. Box 629
San Pedro, CA 90731   **S.S. LANE VICTORY**

Above, the call card for the ship's amateur radio station. Right, volunteers Emmet Harvey and Bob Luckenbill in the radio shack in May, 1990. Both photos courtesy Lane Victory.

immediately with Hines. He was relieved to find out that all was well with the South Carolina chapter.

In early 1990 the U.S. Merchant Marine Veterans of World War II were recognized as a legitimate organization by the Internal Revenue Service which granted them "nonprofit" status.

Immediately, the *Lane* began "giving back" to the community. The ship became a practice platform for the Los Angeles Fire Department. The first exercise was May 27, 1990 with Chief Thomas E. McMaster in charge and there were exercises in June and July. During each exercise fifteen companies and three rescue ambulances, in addition to five fire boats, participated. This enabled the fire department to build a command structure and walk through simulated shipboard fires.

An unforeseen, and very lucrative bonus of having the ship in Los Angeles was its proximity to Hollywood and the film industry. Having a World War II vintage ship in their own back yard served as inspiration to producers and directors. In short order the *Lane Victory* became a backdrop and sometimes center of attention for movies and television. She appeared on Murder, She Wrote; Hunter; Quantum Leap; Back to Paradise; Naked Gun; Loose Cannon; Double Impact and was used by Lorimar, Paramount Pictures, Warner Brothers and Golden Era Productions in some of their films. The fees generated from the film industry were a welcome addition to the Veterans' treasury.

Capt. Jim Nolan, serving as maritime consultant to the organization, began working on the process of having the ship made into a National Historical Landmark.

July 20, 1990 from the Department of the Interior, National Park Service.

Dear Mr. Vernick:

We are pleased to inform you that the National Park Service has completed the study of the property identified on the enclosed sheet for the purpose of nominating it for possible designation as a National Historic Landmark. We enclose a copy of the study report. The National Park System Advisory Board will consider

Like most movie stars, the Lane Victory *has worn many costumes in her film career. Top photo courtesy C.L. Johnson, all others from* Lane Victory.

the nomination during its next meeting, at the time and place indicated on the enclosure. The Board will make its recommendation to the Secretary of the Interior based upon the criteria of the National Historic Landmarks Program.

You have 60 days to submit your views in writing, if you so desire. After the 60 day period, we will submit the nomination and your comments to the National Park System Advisory Board's Historic Areas Committee, which will then inform the full Advisory Board of the Committee's recommendations at the Board's meeting. The Secretary of the Interior will then be informed of the Board's recommendations for his final action.

Now the city of San Diego became interested in having the ship.

Joe Vernick: "We got two letters from two congressmen. They'd love to have us. Right alongside of the *Star of India* and the *Berkeley*. They'd love to have us down there."

John Smith: "The member down there is somewhat like Abe Rapaport, he's somewhat abrasive. Pushy type, but a do-er, nonetheless. He has his own group in San Diego. Before he really got connected with the *Lane Victory* he withdrew from the American Merchant Marine Veterans [the first splinter group to leave]. But they don't have anything, although they had little meetings. He joined us . . . became a charter life member. He's helping us. He takes a port that's been favorable you see . . . So Joe and I went down there a few weeks ago at his request when the

Capt. James Nolan at the wheel of one of the jeeps he placed aboard for display in the ship's cargo hold.

Russian ships were in . . . the three Russians. He had the connections . . . he's well known in veterans' affairs."

The trip to San Diego was a pleasant change from Los Angeles. Not only was the *Lane Victory* group the center of attention, they were actively courted. It was a new and very pleasant experience.

John Romeo, head of the San Diego branch of the Merchant Marine Veterans hired a car for the occasion.

Joe Vernick: "A big white stretch limousine with black windows."

Acting as chauffeur, John Romeo put Joe Vernick and John Smith in the back. Driving up to the gate at the San Diego Naval Base where the Russian ships were berthed, he told the security guard, "I've got Admiral Vernick and Capt. Smith in the back here."

John Smith: "There was an officer in the same mobile shack, to screen people because this was a very important day. So he called the officer out and the officer saluted us and told us go into the VIP parking.

"We had an appointment there the first day with Capt. Edwards; he's the Superintendent of their ship repair base at San Diego. We had, I think, like five or ten minutes of his time scheduled and soon as we got there he called in his aide and talked about the *Lane Victory*. He got interested. John Romeo was talking about the *Lane Victory*. He attached himself to us now in a strong way, he's pushing in all directions for us. So instead of having a ten minute social visit, the captain poured us coffee, and sat down. He told his aide, 'Now take notes about the *Lane Victory*.'

"So he got the dimensions, the size, because we had mentioned drydocking as one of our problems. He says, 'Is there much moss around the hull and the waterline?'

"Moss is more difficult to get off than rust or scale. It mushes, you got to scrape it off. So it's a little more labor. And little details about the length of the hull, condition of the hull, very knowledgeable engineer, Capt. Edwards is.

Joe Vernick right, and John Smith during a rare quiet moment in the ship's office. Courtesy *Lane Victory.*

"It extended over an hour. With his aide there. Since then Joe talked to him a couple more times.

Joe Vernick: "We sent him blueprints."

John Smith: "He asked for drydocking prints.

"The captain did tell us that he'd be working hard to get us into drydock there. But because of the Persian Gulf situation[1] I don't know how it'll be . . . good for us or bad for us . . . you know . . . we don't know because everything changes when you get a war condition.

"Then we went to a congressman, who didn't happen to be in, but his aide came out and they introduced us. Instead of asking for support with the ship, he says, 'Well, in case you're having trouble with the harbor up there and you may not have a dock, you can get a dock down here.'

"He says 'We'll work on it.'

"So there's a thousand foot of space between the *Berkeley* and the fish wharf in San Diego, you know, empty. Normally it's empty. Once in a while there'll be a purse seiner or something that pulls in there, but normally it's empty. So we made pictures of that empty space and the other ship. What a logical place to be for this ship."

"We got more involved with this. He [John Romeo] wanted us to meet the mayor, a lady he knows on a first name

---

[1] In August 1990 Iraq invaded Kuwait. A multi-national coalition under a United Nations mandate went to war against Iraq in January 1991.

basis, named O'Conner. We didn't have time, so we went up to the Veteran's Affairs Council. These harbor commissioners, the harbor supervisors of San Diego county have nominated five veterans of different organizations, the American Legion, the Veterans of Foreign Wars and other organizations to represent them on a new Veterans' Affairs Council for about two years. And it's a powerful group. There's forty-some veterans' groups in San Diego County and these five that are appointed by the supervisors can select four others to make a committee of nine. They got so much power in San Diego County that if they want to block off a street, or have a parade or have a swap meet or what ever they want, the county, they'd do anything for the veterans. There's an awful lot of veterans there in San Diego, retired. So this Veterans' Affairs Council, they came out and asked us down to show slides of the *Lane Victory*, which I did. I'm going back to the full forty-three organizations at their meeting, that umbrella group, every veterans' organization to show the slides again. They have such enthusiastic accord and, believe me, if we needed a dock that group would get us one. If they were here in this harbor [Los Angeles] they'd have this dock long ago for us. The supervisors and the city council and everybody has high respect for them.

"There was one other incident that happened that day. The Russian ships came in."

Joe Vernick: "This guy [John Romeo] gave him a Merchant Marine flag of his own design. The Commander, Kvatov, of the Pacific Russian Fleet, gave him a big hug and kissed him on the mouth and presented him with a Russian hat, a sailor's cap."

John Smith: "They had limos waiting to take the Russians to another meeting. They were only going to give us a couple of minutes to get this flag presented — present him with the flag and thank you very much and get in the limos and go. But the Russian Admiral, he shook hands with John Romeo and the admiral not only held one hand, but he put the other hand on his wrist and he talked to him about the merchant marine 'cause his father died in World War II. They were talking about that and it was translated and the admiral, the American admiral and the captains . . . the doors on the limos were open and they were waiting. They're prancing around like they had to go to the bathroom, while Admiral Kvatov held his hand. He talked for over ten minutes, twelve minutes actually, to be exact. This was just tremendous. That opened a lot of eyes in the Navy people."

Joe Vernick: "The flag now hangs at the submarine base in the submarine museum in Vladivostok."

Congressman Anderson was displeased when he heard the ship might go to San Diego.

Joe Vernick: "This is his pet project. When he heard something about San Diego, he blew his top. He went up to the Harbor Commission and told them, 'I worked very hard to get this project here.'

"Even his aide called me. 'Glenn Anderson is all shook up because he heard that you might go to San Diego.'"

A step toward permanency was National Historic Landmark Status. It came in December, 1990 and put the *Lane Victory* in the same status as the Statue of Liberty and the battleship *USS Arizona*. Less than 100 ships have been so honored.

In conferring the status, James Delgado, head of the U.S. Parks Service's National Maritime Initiative, said, "They were essential to our victory in [World War II]. The *Lane Victory* is the only unaltered Victory ship left and the only one being preserved as a memorial."

John Smith: "This really increased our prestige and enthusiasm. The turnaround happened when the lease was final, a major turnaround.

"We had lost volunteers. We lost some of the spirit of the early day volunteers. We lost a lot of financial donations because the people said, 'You don't even have a permanent berth. Why should we contribute our local money and goods to you when you may not even be around? You may have to go back to the fleet, 'cause you don't have any permanency.'

"Once this leasing was arranged, then the volunteers came flocking back, the money came in, the membership grew and so it was an automatic uphill venture from then on."

The local community favored the project.

"The people were for us," says Joe Vernick, "the Homeowners Association, the Chamber of Commerce, everybody. You know we had the fire department, we had the police department practice searching for narcotics with their dogs from the harbor department, we had Sea Cadets from the Navy League coming aboard now, we had boy scouts and members of the unified school systems. The *Lane Victory* was getting to be quite well known."

John Smith: "I was out to a club meeting . . . a local club called the Bilge Club. It's a group of executives from the waterfront community here. It's been in existence for thirty some odd years, quite a successful club. They had a luncheon meeting and several different people were there from different organizations. They asked, 'When can we have meetings aboard the *Lane Victory*? Here we are in a rented auditorium, having a meeting, all waterfront people. When can we get an auditorium on there for our meetings.'

"And the Binnacle Club became interested, the Marine Square Club which was a waterfront Masonic Club wanted to meet here. Several other waterfront organizations, even the Propeller Club told me that they were totally interested when we got an auditorium and could arrange catered luncheons. So that future was assured. That meant more members, more publicity, more support.

With all the interest from San Diego and the local community, the Los Angeles authorities suddenly decided that the *Lane Victory* might not be such a bad thing after all.

The Merchant Marine Veterans held firm to their conviction. John Smith: "We were still trying to get a better berth, Berth 87 which we long fought for. It was ideal for us. It was perfect and it was perfect for the city of San Pedro because it was developing as a main tourist area."

John Smith and Joe Vernick saw the future of the ship in this way: "Everything is on a very optimistic note."

The "optimistic note" permeated the ship and her workers. On any day of the week volunteers could be found working at various projects. The deck department took the cargo gear, including the jumbo booms, out of the lower hold, rigged them and put them in place. The engine department re-bricked the boilers. Decades of grey paint were chipped off, exposing the bare metal underneath, which in turn was primed and painted, making the ship look as good as the day she was launched. One white-haired volunteer dressed in a Santa Claus suit for Christmas — the rest of the year he could be found chipping paint on the winches and hatch combings.

Weekends were special times. The volunteers started gathering on Friday afternoon. Many of them stayed on board until Monday morning. Saturday and Sunday were workdays, typically fourteen and sixteen hours long. It wasn't unusual for the crew to be told two or three times to knock off for a coffee break before they would actually do it. The author saw crewmembers working on deck after dark, by flashlight, simply because they wanted to finish the job at hand.

The one meal everybody attended was Saturday lunch. Isaac Givens, formerly Second Cook and Baker on the *Lane Victory* and later pastry chef on the *Lurline*, Matson Lines' famous passenger ship, was the star chef. A typical Saturday meal included trout (both fried and baked), mashed potatoes, vegetables, soup, punch, berry pies, fresh rolls, miscellaneous pastries, coffee and condiments. Or it might consist of turkey, dressing, potato salad, cranberry sauce, pastries, vegetables, soup and chocolate pie. The food was always good, the camaraderie contagious.

Weekends attracted the most visitors. Following the yellow lines on deck they were seen in all parts of the ship, peering into rooms, admiring the neatly-made bunks, listening to an explanation of the radio room equipment or the navigation gear. They especially enjoyed the displays in the museum located

Re-bricking the boilers, left, was one of the more difficult jobs tackled by the engine department.

Right, I. Roy Coats assembles the after steering station.

Rigging the cargo gear included welding one of the jumbo booms, left. Courtesy Lane Victory.

Right, the jumbo was then installed and the process of re-rigging it began. Courtesy Lane Victory.

Not every ship carries its own Santa Claus. When not dressed for Christmas Stan Tokich could be found chipping and painting on deck. Courtesy Lane Victory.

in No. 4 upper 'tween deck. Here were found the artifacts of ships and shipping, the history of the *Lane Victory* and the U.S merchant marine.

John Smith: "That part of the future, to my knowledge, is sure, the permanent berth. So the future is assured. We know the quality of the ship. I don't know how it could be so good after being in the water forty-five years. Remarkable. So we're not afraid of that and [we have] the beautiful spare parts program down there in storage and the enthusiasm that is building up."

Joe Vernick: "We've been fortunate, really, to make progress like we have. One of our former Vice-presidents, Jerry Werner, thought up this idea of the charter life membership which is five hundred dollars. We've got about three hundred of them sold. Membership has been growing and we're been

Isaac Givens, left, served as cook on the Lane Victory *early in its career and was later pastry chef on the* Lurline. *Right, some of the desserts for Saturday's noon meal. Both photos courtesy* Lane Victory.

The ship's museum quickly became a tourist attraction and a tribute to the U.S. Merchant Marine. Courtesy Lane Victory.

getting small donations here and there so we're making ends meet.

John Smith: "We turn in about twelve hours a day, seven days a week. We're all volunteers. No one gets paid."

Joe Vernick: "To me it's a memorial for thousands of merchant mariners that died during the war fighting for the liberty, freedom and security that we now enjoy. That's what this ship represents."

John Smith: "I agree with those words exactly. I also want to add that the ship itself, being a sort of a future home of merchant mariners, a future rendezvous point, a future sort of USO type operation for seamen and the historical reference, is like a landmark. It's a historical thing. The machinery, the hull, the construction, the deck gear, all the break-bulk cargo system is a historical thing for the public to enjoy."

Joe Vernick: "And we've had a lot of people. We've had almost a thousand people in one of our last events that we had aboard here. Admiral Alvar Gomez was aboard. Congressman

Glenn Anderson, councilwoman Flores, we had a lot of dignitaries from government including Navy people. They all came and sent beautiful thank you letters afterward. We had close to a thousand people.

"John and I were talking the other day and I said, 'Can you believe this? Here we have this ship and look at all these people. We never dreamt that it would develop this way. It's almost frightening.

"It's going to be a wonderful memorial museum. Don't forget, we lost 7,000 merchant mariners during World War II. We don't have cemeteries, like the Army and Navy. Our men lie at the bottom of the seven seas. That's why the ship is so important. It's a memorial — the only memorial — dedicated to those merchant marines who died for their country."

The *Lane Victory*'s berth at San Pedro is entirely fitting.

Joe Vernick: "It was built within half a mile of where it rests today. After 45 years, it has come full circle. Many fellows who worked on this vessel are still around and live in the area. They are helping us now. It's going to be around for a long time, I can assure you of that."

The months and years ahead would be filled with accomplishment. There were a few disappointments along the way, but for the *Lane Victory* and her crew, the best was yet to come.

19

Eight Days a Week

Amemorial to merchant mariners is one thing, an active living maritime museum is another, quite different, thing. It was always the intent of the U.S. Merchant Marine Veterans of WWII to not only create a memorial and museum of the *Lane Victory*, but to bring her back to life — for the ship to once again sail under her own power. This meant overcoming a mountain of technical hurdles. Times had changed. Coast Guard and other regulatory bodies viewed ships much differently than they did when the *Lane* last sailed in the 1960s and the *Lane* had to meet the new standards.

One of the most complicated problems was electrical. When the ship tied up to Kaiser International Corporation's Berth 52 they were allowed to plug into the berth's 480 volt, 3 phase alternating current electrical system. But most of the ship's services required direct current. One of the ship's volunteers, who owned an electrical equipment business, built and delivered an AC-to-DC rectifier so that the ship could use its pumps and other equipment. That solved the problem of current to the ship's existing systems, but modern equipment, such as fluorescent lighting and electronics could not be used. The volunteer then delivered several 480 volt AC transformers, with switch panels, to change the 480 volt AC to 120 volt AC, providing the ship with an adequate supply of both DC and AC current. With power available, major AC wiring installations were made in the deck house and cargo holds. Receptacles were installed so that portable modern equipment such as public address systems, radios, TVs, power tools or computers could be used.

A host of other changes were made:

— engine and boiler rooms surveyed and essential overhauls on pumps, compressors, generators, valves and instruments.

— installation of a new sea-water-to-fresh-water evaporator with related pumps and piping.

— installation of a new high volume auxiliary circulator pump and motor.

— creation of a new machine shop in no. 3 hold including lathe, drill press, cut-off saw, shaper, milling machine, pipe threader, welder, shelving, lockers, bins, racks, tool boards and an engineer's office. This allows the ship to create its own parts for equipment that is no longer manufactured.

— because of new environmental laws, the ship was required to install a 30,000-gallon waste water storage tank and a water treatment plant so that all waste water could be discharged into the city sewage system or pumped overboard while at sea. This necessitated installing new piping for the galley and restrooms, blanking off all original overboard drains and installing new drain lines to the storage tank.

— installation of a replacement turbine boiler feed water pump.

— four new modern refrigeration compressors put into operation.

— installation of a high volume DC-driven, combination fire and bilge pump, for emergencies or when the ship is at a location without shore power (such as at anchor).

— installation of a 224 amp, 480 volt diesel-driven AC generator on deck. This serves as a back-up AC power source if shore power and ship's power are not available.

— installation of a new oily-water separator so that bilge water can be pumped overboard.

— installation of a DC-to-AC motor generator set with controls so that the ship will have AC power for essential services when the ship is away from the shore AC supply.

— installation of a compressed air supply system with suitable outlets.

— installation of a filtration system to convert dock-side fresh water to purified water for the ship's high pressure steam boilers.

— installation of new drinking fountains.

— acquisition, installation and restoration of a complete complement of ship's guns which are fully operable. These are used to simulate firing sounds of real wartime battles during the ship's cruises.

— installation of a new cathodic protection system to help prevent hull corrosion.

Active ships are drydocked every two years. The *Lane* was last drydocked when she was prepared for lay-up in 1971. No one really knew what the bottom looked like after twenty years in the lay-up fleet. Moss, seaweed, mussels and barnacles could be dealt with: simply scrape them off. But what about the hull plating? How badly deteriorated would it be after more than twenty years in the brackish water of Suisun Bay without regular applications of protective paint? In 1992 the organization

Before and After bow shots of the Lane Victory *in drydock. The hull was in excellent condition requiring a minimal amount of repairs. Courtesy the* Lane Victory.

decided to "bite the bullet" and scheduled the ship for drydocking at the Southwest Marine docks at nearby Terminal Island. On April 30 Wilmington Transportation Company provided two tugs, at no charge, which towed the ship to Southwest Marine. Anxiously, the crew watched as the ship was centered over the keel blocks, then raised out of the water. She looked good to them, but what would the Coast Guard and American Bureau of Shipping (ABS) say?

Inspectors from both agencies went over the ship from stem to stern, from truck to keel. The final result: "She's in excellent condition."

The only required repairs were minimal including 266 feet of seam welding. The propeller shaft and rudder shaft bearings showed a minor amount of wear-down, but the shafts themselves were fine. In addition, one hundred fifty-five pound zincs were bolted in key locations on the hull to prevent corrosion. The hull was blasted from keel to low load line, coated with two coats of International primer, then two coats of anti-fouling paint. A final coating of special anti-fouling paint known as Premier Pro-Tech that inhibits the growth of marine organisms was donated by the manufacturer, Premier Paint Co. of Burke, Virginia, arranged by Capt. James Nolan. The hull was also blasted from low-load line to the cap rail, primed and painted with two coats of Alkyd Storm Gray.

The drydocking successfully completed, the organization could now realistically proceed with two major projects they had long planned: 1) day cruises with paying passengers, and 2) attending the 50th Anniversary of the D-Day landings in Normandy, scheduled for June 6, 1994.

To make the ship more interesting and attractive to the public, no. 2 cargo hold was converted into a museum for objects too large to display in the existing museum built earlier in no. 4 'tween deck. The display included five military jeeps, ships' whistles and other nautical memorabilia. Later, the centerpiece of this museum would be the triple expansion, 1,000 horsepower steam engine built in 1920 and used during the filming of 20th Century Fox's classic 1966 picture "The Sand Pebbles."[1]

The museum in no. 4 upper 'tween deck continued to grow. The gift shop moved from its former small main deck crew room to a larger, professionally-designed store with attractive display space. Exhibits in the museum expanded to include fifty showcases with artifacts. Maritime banners and flags from every state in the U.S. hang from the overheads, and fifteen scale models of World War I and II ships, tugs, passenger vessels and a German submarine fill the tops of display cases. The center of the museum seats 150 for meetings.

To carry passengers and comply with OSHA and U.S. Coast Guard and environmental regulations, eight inflatable life rafts and brackets, two modern radars, a radiotelephone and a public address system were installed. With these items in place the ship was almost ready for its inaugural cruise.

First, to be sure everything operated properly, came sea trials. These were held on September 10, 1992. With a full complement of Coast Guard, ABS and other regulatory body inspectors on board, the ship left her berth under her own power

---

[1] In 1996 the engine was aboard being restored and made operable.

for the first time in more than twenty years. Crossing Los Angeles Harbor, then out to the open sea, the speed was gradually increased to full ahead as engines, piping, electrical systems and navigation equipment were checked and rechecked. Turns were made to test the rudder and steering gear; the engine was put full astern to ensure its ability to stop the vessel. Reentering the harbor, both anchors were tested and the ship returned to her berth, a broom flying at the mainmast in time-honored tradition indicating a clean sweep of all trials. The proud ship was ready for passengers.

Certified to carry 900 passengers including crew, the *Lane Victory* made her inaugural cruise on October 3, 1992. Bob Lace, current president of the *Lane Victory* organization: "This was the first time that a Victory ship in Southern California took a cruise under its own power. Everybody had worked so hard. There were guys aboard in their 60s and 70s who absolutely cried."

Since then she has made numerous day-long trips without the slightest problem.

A typical day cruise on the *Lane Victory* begins with boarding passengers at 7 a.m. Greeted at the gangway by Joe Vernick, president emeritus of the organization, they are directed to the offshore side of the main deck where a continental breakfast of orange juice, coffee, sweet rolls and muffins is laid out. Members of the "Yellow Houn' Dawg Blues Band" bring their instruments aboard, setting up under an awning on top of no. 4 hatch. Around 8:45 crew members station themselves at boxes of life preservers strategically located around the ship and demonstrate their use as an explanation of how to wear them is given over the public address system. By then the tug is in place, the pilot on board. Sharply at nine the lines are let go and the ship eases away from her berth as the American flag is transferred to the steaming gaff and the band strikes up "Anchors Aweigh."

Frequently the ship provides extra entertainment during day cruises. Here a mime plays Charlie Chaplin. Courtesy Lane Victory.

Once well away from the dock the tug is let go and the ship cruises at slow speed toward the exit of Los Angeles Harbor. Frequently, a Los Angeles City fireboat will accompany the ship to the entrance, her nozzles spewing a majestic salute as the sunlight bounces rainbows off the boat's arcing geysers. When clear of the harbor breakwater, speed increases and the course is set for Catalina Island, twenty-six miles away. The band lapses into Dixieland jazz and popular songs of the World War II era.

Now the drama begins. As cruise directors, Bob Lace and Cliff Hagenbuch laid out a full day's entertainment, with Bob narrating events on the ship's public address system as they unfold. A day cruise on the *Lane Victory* is not just an ocean voyage to nowhere. It is a re-creation of life aboard a merchant ship during World War II. At some point in the cruise an announcement is made that a German spy has been seen aboard! Passengers are requested to keep a lookout for him. Later it is announced that the spy was captured, but he may have gotten a message off on the ship's radio giving the *Lane*'s location to the Luftwaffe. The spy, dressed in a Nazi uniform, is paraded in handcuffs from bow to stern amid good-natured booing and hissing from the passengers.

Meanwhile, the ship nears Catalina and cruises the lee side of the island while John Smith, Vice-President of the organization, who lived there for several years, explains its history and points out landmarks. Lunch is at noon. Cruise Director Clint Johnson has arranged a lavish buffet catered by Ante's restaurant of San Pedro. A typical menu might include sliced roast turkey, baked ham slices, lasagna and meat balls, diced

An "enemy" plane flies past. Note the markings on the fusilage.

potato salad, pasta salad, green salad with a choice of dressings, rolls and butter, dessert, fresh fruit, cake or cookies, coffee, wine, beer, soft drinks.

About the time everyone is dozing from the effects of the gargantuan lunch, an announcement comes over the public address system: "Bogies have been sighted on the radar! Gunners to your stations!" The gun platforms are cleared of all passengers and the Armed Guard mans the ship's defenses. Soon, a formation of propeller-driven planes is spotted (The Condor Squadron Based at Van Nuys Airport). Within scant minutes the planes break formation and begin "straffing attacks" on the ship. The Armed Guard goes into action, firing the ship's antiaircraft guns and 5-inch cannon. As the planes fly past at mast level their Luftwaffe markings are clearly visible.

Again and again they attack and are repeatedly beat off by the accurate firing of the ship's guns. Bullets are heard ricocheting across the deck. Smoke from the planes' engines indicate direct hits by the *Lane*'s crew. Soon, aircraft with World War II American markings enter the fray, chasing the enemy planes in dogfights across the sky. Eventually the entire squadron forms up and flies over the ship in salute as everyone applauds.

Bob Lace puts the cuffs on the captured "Nazi spy," Bob Swank. Courtesy Lane Victory.

Under "attack," the Lane Victory *valiantly fights back, her gun crews giving as good as they take.   Courtesy* Lane Victory.

Of course, all the firing is simulated, but the *Lane* has been so involved with the movie industry that some of the "magic" has rubbed off.   The drama is very realistic.

Returning to Los Angeles Harbor in the afternoon, the tugs come alongside, gently nudging the *Lane Victory* into her berth.   While the ship is tying up, a raffle is held.   First prize is two tickets to the next cruise, with items from the ship's store being offered as additional prizes.   As the passengers go ashore they are individually thanked by Joe Vernick and John Smith. Many of them will return on future cruises.

Comments from those that have made the cruise have been enthusiastic: "Super.   Great.   Good music.   Stirring. Outstanding.   Fantastic.   Made my day.   Crew Worked hard. Brought back many memories.   A real nostalgia wallow. Sensational.   More than expected."

The 50th Anniversary of the D-Day landings was a major historical milestone.   The governments of the Allied powers —

the United States, Great Britain and France — planned a week-long series of events to mark the anniversary of the landings at Normandy in 1944. Hundreds of thousands of people, including contingents of veterans and military groups, would descend on Northern Europe in late May and early June. The climax of this great gathering would be the convergence of heads of state, military, ships and planes off Normandy on June 6, 1994. The president of the United States, the queen of England and the president of France would review the armada. Commemorative ceremonies in the English ports and in France and solemn remembrances in the cemeteries that honored those who died in the invasion filled the days preceding the event.

Originally, three World War II merchant ships from the United States planned to return to Normandy for the 50th Anniversary — the *John W. Brown*, the Liberty ship museum from Baltimore, the *Jeremiah O'Brien*, the Liberty ship museum from San Francisco and the *Lane Victory*. The *O'Brien* would sail south from San Francisco and join up with the *Lane Victory*. Off Baltimore the *Brown* would join them, forming "The Last Convoy" of merchant ships to cross the Atlantic.

One of the many problems facing the *Lane* for such a long voyage in the open ocean was the absence of enough ballast in the holds for safe operation in rough weather. Calculations called for a minimum of 2,000 tons of clean, easily stowed and environmentally safe ballast. At first all the organization could locate was about 100 tons of concrete piles. The remainder was elusive. Then, the ship received a call from a U.S. Navy shipyard superintendent in Long Beach. The result was two Navy tugs towed the *Lane* to the yard where they loaded 2,000 tons of five-ton concrete drydock keel blocks into the ship's holds and then towed the ship back to San Pedro. As John Smith succinctly put it, "Problem solved."

But there were many other difficulties to overcome. The enormity of the project was mind-boggling. All systems on the ship must be in perfect working order and pass the stringent requirements of the Coast Guard. Volunteers worked long hours to get everything operating as when the ship was new: engines, turbines, pumps, electrical systems, air compressors, refrigeration, plumbing, navigational electronics. Spare parts were loaded for repairs that might be needed during the voyage: impellers, rotors, windings, electric brushes, piping, wire rope, mooring lines, electronic tubes, transistors, blocks, hatch boards, tarps, hatch wedges and hundreds of other items. Then came the supplies: cleaning brushes, brooms, cleanser, soap, pots, pans, boiler compound, fire hose, nuts, bolts, nails, wrenches, pliers, hammers, batteries, wire, rags, hand cleaner, paint, paint brushes, thinner, grease and oil, towels, toilet paper, detergent, to mention a just few. Food was ordered to feed a crew of fifty for five months: coffee, flour, spices, cooking oil, sugar, canned good, meats, vegetables. And fuel to get the ship to Europe and back. Properly licensed and certified crew had to be arranged for. Everything had to pass Coast Guard, ABS and FCC (Federal Communications Commission) inspection. The *Lane* approached every organization it knew to donate the needed items.

As the sailing date in April 1994 approached, the *John W. Brown* dropped out of the convoy. Upon drydocking, it was found she had too many rivets that needed replacement or repair and the cost of making her seaworthy was prohibitive. That left two ships in the convoy.

The financial obstacles of the *Lane Victory* still appeared insurmountable. In addition to the requested donations, the trip was budgeted to cost over a million dollars. Cash was needed to pay Panama Canal fees and purchase fuel, food and supplies during the trip. Where would they get it? Time was running out. They had begged, borrowed and leveraged everything possible. Now they needed hard cash. Joe Vernick and John Smith quietly went to work. The *Jeremiah O'Brien* sailed on April 18 for Panama. As she passed Los Angeles two days later, the crew of the *Lane* worked feverishly to get their ship ready. The *O'Brien*, a Liberty ship, could only make ten knots. At her normal speed of sixteen, the *Lane* could easily catch up at the Canal or in the Caribbean. But still they needed a financial windfall. The final decision depended on money. Bob Lace:

"The shipyard bill blew most of the proceeds [from the scrap ship sale] and did not account for provisions, agent's fees, insurance, and equipment to meet the various government agencies' requirements to make the trip."

Then, a miracle. On April 21 they received a letter from the Norris Foundation:

> Dear Mr. Vernick:
>
> It is with great pride that the Trustees of the Norris Foundation present you with a check in the amount of $250,000 to be used by the S.S. Lane Victory in her historic voyage and participation in the 50th anniversary of the invasion of Europe by the Allied Forces. We would like to express our gratitude to the Merchant Marines for all they have given our nation and for the remarkable job they have done in restoring the S.S. Lane Victory in preparation for this important voyage.
>
> Following our meeting yesterday, I realize why the Allies were so successful on the beaches of Normandy fifty short years ago. It was because of men like those, serving on the S.S. Lane Victory, who knew they could complete their mission and accomplish their goals regardless of the obstacles they might face.

Now, the *Lane* could go. Bob Lace: "The sudden appearance of the $250,000 from the Norris foundation telescoped the activity in a frenzied manner with many last minute decisions based on speculation." Plans were finalized, stores and fuel were taken on board and the ship sailed amid great jubilation and excitement. The *Lane* would catch the *O'Brien* somewhere off the East Coast.

Then a catastrophe. John Smith explains what happened: "While enroute, the ship's two boilers were discovered to have fuel oil in the [boiler water] sight glasses. After taking emergency measures, the ship slowly limped into nearby Acapulco. The cause of the oil contamination was found to be a fuel oil storage tank's steam heating coils which had a leak in the return piping thus bringing oily water to the boiler feed water system."

Heated feed water becomes steam which operates the ship's turbines. It is fed to the turbine through water tubes. The boiler water must be absolutely pure. Any residue in the boiler water, such as the oil, coats the inside of the water tubes and acts as insulation. This results in the tubes getting too hot, and, on other ships, has caused violent explosion.

John Smith: "Facilities at that port were inadequate to do a thorough job of boiler cleaning and because of the lost time made it impossible to make the date in Normandy, so the ship was ordered to return to San Pedro by the Board of Directors."

Anticipated for more than two years, the voyage was suddenly over, almost as soon as it started. The crew was devastated. They had almost literally moved mountains, expended enormous effort and overcome every obstacle. Joe Vernick: "I and the board got terrible criticism because of our decision to return the *Lane* rather than proceed to Normandy. Members who were aboard wouldn't talk to us and some still say that the *Lane* should have continued to Normandy and that we didn't want the *Lane* to go."

John Smith: "It was a blessing in disguise. If that had happened in the Atlantic Ocean a thousand miles from any help, without power, the ship could have been lost. We're fortunate it happened where it did."

Joe Vernick: "It could have broken down in the Atlantic and ended up in a European port and good-bye to the *Lane*. Our concern was in the safety of our volunteer crew and preserving our National Historic Landmark."

The ship returned to its dock but the Monday morning quarterbacking continued. Joe Vernick: "There will forever be mixed feelings about not going to Normandy."

It was a wrenching disappointment, but being undone by an old fuel heating system doesn't diminish the *Lane*'s incredible achievement or bring anything but admiration for the devotion, hard work and enthusiasm of her volunteers. Theirs was a gallant triumph against near-impossible odds. In activating a 50-year old ship and preparing it for a voyage halfway around the world, they accomplished what few can do.

Upon the *Jeremiah O'Brien*'s return from the Normandy events, the *Lane Victory* crew invited them to spend a night tied up next to their ship. The *Lane* covered all the expenses and had a party for the entire crew and some shoreside VIPs.

The *Lane* and the *O'Brien* are sister ships, in spirit if not in fact. They face the same challenges in restoring and preserving our maritime heritage and they understand each other. So, it was a warm, if, for the *Lane*, slightly bittersweet, occasion.

The *O'Brien*'s staff invited the *Lane Victory* to join them at the planned celebration for the Liberty ship's return to San Francisco and the two ships proceeded in convoy up the coast. Entering San Francisco Bay the *Lane* took a position of honor, sailing as the lead ship of the great maritime cavalcade that welcomed the *O'Brien* home. She stayed for three days, tied ahead of the *O'Brien*, as enthusiastic visitors toured both ships.

But 1994 turned out to be another banner year for the *Lane*, after all. The campaign for a suitable berth had been ongoing from the time the ship arrived in Los Angeles Harbor in 1989. Finally, the Los Angeles Harbor Department bowed to the irresistible force that was the Merchant Marine Veterans and agreed to build a location at Berth 94. This prestigious location is next to the cruise ship berth and the Catalina boat landing. There was ample parking. The berth was easy to find, being directly under the Vincent Thomas Memorial bridge, a well-known San Pedro landmark. In October of 1994 the *Lane* moved to Berth 94 with a gala ribbon cutting ceremony attended by harbor officials and the wife of deceased congressman Glenn Anderson who had been such a strong advocate of the ship. At long last the *Lane Victory* had a home.

Bob Lace: "We had proven that we were an attraction and reliable as an entity. They [the Harbor District] knew that the *Lane Victory* was an added attraction to the harbor picture and gave us the first year water rental free."

In 1995, U.S. Army Air Force Veterans organized a nationwide fly-in of vintage aircraft to Long Beach airport to

On October 23, 1994, the ribbon was cut for the Lane*'s new berth at Pier 94 in San Pedro. Left to right are: Ezunial Berts, Executive Director, Worldport, L.A.; John Smith, Lee Anderson, wife of Glenn Anderson, Capt. Larry Welsh, Joe Vernick and Councilman Rudy Svorinich. Courtesy* Lane Victory.

commemorate the end of World War II. Flyovers were scheduled to honor the *R.M.S. Queen Mary* and the *Lane Victory* which was anchored nearby. Major publicity was generated for the two World War II ships and the pilots who were traveling to several rendezvous airports enroute to another major celebration in New York.

Recognition continued accruing to the *Lane Victory*. In December of 1994 she was invited to take part in the annual parade of lighted yachts at Los Angeles Harbor at Christmas time. For the 1995 parade the ship was named as the judging station for the event.

The *Lane* was again drydocked in 1995, this time with far less anxiety, fewer repairs and less cost.

After several years of planning with the San Diego Maritime Museum for a joint celebration, one was finally staged on June 14 to 17, 1996. The *Lane* steamed to San Diego and was given a berth of honor at their Embarcadero near the San Diego Maritime Museum's three vessels, the *Star of India*, a British 3-masted bark built in 1854, the double-ended San Francisco ferry *Berkeley*, a vehicle and passenger ferry boat built in 1898, and the beautiful, operable steam yacht *Media*, build in 1904. Like the *Lane Victory*, these vessels are fully restored. The *Lane* fit right in. Advance publicity was well-laid out and special tickets were printed for visits to all four vessels with the funds generated shared equally. It was a bustling occasion as over 8,000 visitors came aboard and enjoyed the historical gathering. Future plans call for it to be an annual event.

Joe Vernick: "The goodwill trip to San Diego helped the attitude towards the board. We would like to make trips which the members enjoy since they have activated the *Lane* with no near ports to go to."

John Smith: "It was a great success."

The *Lane* has also become quite a movie star and filming activities have been a major source of income for the restoration, maintenance and operation of the ship. Aside from filming at the home wharf, the ship has been moved to the outer harbor several times and for ten days to the old Todd shipyard and to Wilmington and Long Beach for special background scenes. The crew enjoy these occasions and have become quite used to seeing "real" movie stars. The logistics (and expense) of movie-making often bemuse them. During the filming of the movie "Outbreak" the ship was hired to go to San Francisco for a special scene. This consisted only of the vessel passing under the Golden Gate Bridge. It took ten trips in and out to get the right shot and the ship was then sent home.

About fifty Hollywood films have been done on board since the *Lane*'s arrival in 1989. Recent ones included:

Outbreak	A Walk in the Clouds
Super Dave Osborne	Carnasaur (Video Game)
Op Center	American Tiger
Gun for Hire	Down Periscope

The Pest

Road to Ruin

Weber BBQ (commercial)

Native Land

General Hospital (twice)

Moving Target

The Owl

Come See Paradise

Gulf Storm Calendar

Max Monroe, Loose Cannon

Story Book One

Toshiba Camera (commercial)

Deep cover

Tequila & Bonnetti

G Force

Story of Book One

JAG

Bay Watch Nights

Max Factor (commercial)

Quantum Leap (second time)

Rapid Fire

Unsolved Mysteries (twice)

The End

I Wonder Why (music video)

Naked Gun 2½

G Force

Eagles Against the Sun

KTTV Weather News

Three Ninjas

MacGyver

Mann and Machine

Hunter (second time)

Looking to the future, Joe Vernick wonders: "Although things are going along well, what will happen within the next five years? Who will be around to take the ship out? Will it eventually end up as a floating museum, maybe even turned over to L.A. Harbor to operate the *Lane*, similar to the *Queen Mary*?"

John Smith: "Physically, the ship could be around for a hundred years. Structurally she's sound, mechanically she's sound. Our finances are in good shape. But a big concern is getting volunteers with seamen's papers. Any time we cruise, whether it be to Catalina or San Diego or around the world, the Coast Guard requires that we have a full complement of properly licensed and certified seamen.

"We need to change the name of our organization. Being called The U.S. Merchant Marine Veterans of World War II is cumbersome and limits us. We go out in the community looking for volunteers and many of the people we talk to think they can't help because they didn't serve in World War II or the merchant marine. We need a name that isn't so limiting."

Bob Lace: "The future plans call for expanding our membership, training programs consistent with Coast Guard approval, working with other merchant marine groups to unify under some common banner without giving up independent operations, continuing to work for legislative action in behalf of the merchant marine and programs to perpetuate the organization as a memorial and remain solvent in the process."

Whatever the outcome, the U.S. Merchant Marine Veterans of World War II continue the never-ending job of maintaining and preserving the *Lane Victory*. Now, the challenge is to shepherd the development of an active living museum ship, and to bring it into the twenty-first century.

As Joe Vernick welcomes visitors, now numbering in the thousands, he hears them talk about the ships they sailed on or their wartime experiences. The expressions on their faces, sometimes punctuated with a few tears, are eloquent testimony that the Merchant Marine Veterans and the *Lane Victory* have transported them, for a few moments, back to a time when they were young, when they fought in a great cause, and life was full with the promise of unknown adventure. It is what they have worked to achieve.

John Smith: "Many of us are in our eighties. This ship keeps us alive. It gives us a purpose for living. I think that's why so many of us have lived so long."

Now, they look to the future. As families bring their children to learn something of their country's history, a new generation takes up the challenge of preserving and bringing that history to life.

Richard Goby, passenger: "[My grandson and I] both have 9-year-old attitudes. This is incredible. It's my first time on a ship like this, but we'll be back. Every kid ought to be aboard this ship. This is history."

Grandson: "This is better than Christmas presents."

Joe Vernick: "We have a great ship in better condition than it was fifty years ago. And I hope it will be around another fifty years."

20

QUOTES WITHOUT COMMENT

I. Roy Coats (Calship foreman): "There was never a day that went by that I didn't wish that I had another two hours left on the shift so I could complete what I had started."

Don MacLean (Calship worker): "Oh, definitely. Definitely. You really worked. No question about it. It was funny . . . the shipyard was full of war effort. There was no question about it. And so was the merchant marine."

Isaac Givens (cook): "You know, it's a funny thing what that sea does to you. In the length of time at sea and in them storms and things, regardless of how prejudiced a guy was, that sea changed him. When he come back he was a changed man. And I tell all the people, seamen are a different species from the people who work ashore. See, if everybody could go to sea and stay at sea like we did out there, this world would be changed a lot.

The Lane Victory *underway on one of her many cruises to Catalina.* *Courtesy* Lane Victory.

"A lot of times you couldn't sleep for three or four days and the crew got all upset. The whole crew gets upset, you know. But, then you in them storms and things.

"I think the ocean and the whipping of them waves. Waves out there high as this ship sometimes and you didn't think you was going to come back . . . see how the waves take the ship and toss it around, whip it around, and you in a storm for three or four days and you're scared, you don't know whether you gonna come out or not, you know.

"And a lot of times when I went out there I said, 'When I get home I ain't comin' back out here.' I get home and go right back out here again."

"It was good to me. Yeah."

"Swede" Jansson (engineer): "She vas yust like, yust like a new ship, you know. You could do anything wid her, she vas steaming all over and good. Very good."

Isaac Givens: "This is our ship. This ship belongs to us. The government didn't give it to a corporation, they give it to the merchant marine veterans. There was no corporation there

Max Jones, the ship's chief steward, tends to something delectable on the galley range. Courtesy Lane Victory.

during World War 11. No, it was merchant marines out there, the merchant seamen went to sea, that's right."

"Swede" Jansson: "Ve had like a family on that ship. It vas a hell of a good crew, I'll tell you, captain. It vas a hundred percent SUP crew and they vas a really good crew you know."

Frank Filas: "Like I say, we had a pretty happy ship, no question about that. And we weren't even in a hurry to go home. Some guys get homesick, want to go home after a trip or two over there, but no, we, stay out there. We're having a ball and making a good buck you know, stay out there."

Gil MacMillan (second mate): "As I remember it was a great ship. I enjoyed the trip."

John Mena (third mate): "It was a good bunch of guys. I guess when you live with the same guys constantly regardless of where they come from or what their opinions are, you get

In the left photo Red Burton, on the left and,Chuck Gardner at the operating platform. Right an engineer, right, explains the boiler controls to Bill Mumford, left and Bud Hein. Both photos courtesy Lane Victory.

The world is at the doorstep of the Lane's *radio crew. Just a few taps on the key . . . Courtesy* Lane Victory.

close. So we had a rag tag outfit, but they were close. And they knew what they were doing."

Physical inspection report from Pacific Coast Transport Company:

To say that a ship looks like the Lane *Victory* continues to be a short hand method of saying that a ship looks like an excellent ship.

From an article in a 1970 edition of *Mayday* magazine:

Since being activated for the Vietnam Sealift in October, 1966, the *Lane Victory* made 14 voyages, loading in every major West Coast port and also carrying ammunition from the East Coast through the Panama Canal to Southeast Asia. Her first master was Capt. Edward MacMichael, retired Pacific Coast District Ship's Operations Officer. Capt. Edward Wentworth has been with the ship for the past three years. Saddened by her deactivation, he packed his gear slowly, "One of the best ships in the Pacific," he said.

Interviewer: "Why do you work on the ship?"

Fran Smith (gift shop): "I love it."

Interviewer: "Why do you love it?"

Fran Smith: "Well, sitting home going to clubs and this and

The ever-cheerful Fran Smith tends the register in the gift shop. Courtesy Lane Victory.

that, it gets boring after awhile, year after year. Everybody's so pleasant here. And it's just that I feel good and I feel younger now. I'm gonna be seventy-three and I just feel good. I go home and I got aches and pains something terrible. Come over here and you forget about it. And the men and women here are so nice. And Saturday we have the lunch you know. And it's just refreshing."

Isaac Givens: "Well, the sea keeps you young. That sea, that ocean keeps you young. I think that's what it is. It's the ocean out there."

The Lane Victory *on cruise with all her combat medals proudly on display under the ship's name board. Courtesy* Lane Victory.

Interviewer: "Why do you work on the *Lane Victory?*"

Bill Gordon (volunteer): "Well, I love it.

Sheila McIntyre (volunteer): "Because my husband dragged me down here. I got started coming down with him and listened to all the fellows tell their stories, sea stories. They'd never had a place to get together and share their experiences and that's what got me interested. So I started writing stories about them. Giving the articles to the newspaper [*The Anchor Light*].

"Now it's like working full time. Sometimes the pressure gets to you. You know I went ahead and worked 'till one o'clock last night to get caught up.

"I really have enjoyed it. I enjoy the people. And I like doing the PR work."

Bob Lace, right, president of the Board of Directors, and Clint Johnson, Secretary, discuss the finer points of making a cruise to Catalina successful for 800-plus passengers. Courtesy Lane Victory.

Capt. Olson (visitor): "Isaac Givens' wife told me that until the *Lane* came along he was just kind of deteriorating at home. But when he started working on here this kind of brought him back to life again. It does that for a lot of people."

Overheard in the engine room: "This is our machine shop, we can make just about anything you need."

The ship's Dixieland jazz band has been a part of every event and cruise since the ship arrived from the Reserve Fleet. Top photo courtesy Lane Victory.

The gun crew is made up of Armed Guard veterans and ex-Navy gunners. Courtesy Lane Victory.

Bill Vincent (volunteer): "I sailed one tanker and most everything else was Liberty ships except the one Victory ship. The Victory ship was one just like this except we carried 1,500 troops down in number three hold.

"Libertys were slower than a Victory. Victory's gotta be twice as fast as a Liberty.

"Well, I'll tell you what. I guess I'm a fool like all the rest of them. I just get up and get down here and volunteer and do all this damn slave labor this early in the morning. You couldn't do it

Capt. Larry Welsh, master of the Lane Victory. *Courtesy* Lane Victory.

for money. I wouldn't do it for money. Anyway, I volunteered. Then I got the newspaper, read the newspaper they had lifetime memberships and I said, 'Hell I want a lifetime membership.' So I took out a lifetime membership."

"Swede" Jansson: "Vell, I like to see *Lane Victory* still be alive. I like to see her in a steaming condition. She vas the best Victory I had. And I'm glad she's still alive."

Mark Owens (harbor Pilot): "The ship was rather special to me. It was my first ship on a license. And to have that particular ship show up so many years later as a museum. I really want to see them succeed. I was very happy to be able to donate something to them."

Interviewer: "Why do you work on the *Lane Victory*?"

Mary Anne Struyk (volunteer): "Because of my husband being a merchant marine and, I don't know, I just kind of took up the cause when we joined the club . . . the organization.

"Isaac (Givens) was in the office one day and I said, 'If I'm not on the ship I sort of feel guilty, like I should be here.'

"And he says, 'Well you've got it in your blood, you know.

"So I think that's what happened."

Interviewer: "Why do you work on here?

Hal Runnels (volunteer): "It's part of my life. I love the sea. I started out as a cabin boy before World War II for Matson, on the old *Maui*, hauling cattle to Hilo, for Parker Ranch."

John Struyk (volunteer): "I sailed Victorys for MSTS. I shipped Army Transport during the war, then went back in '56 and sailed the *McGraw,* the *Dalton* and the *Towell.*

"I always liked to work on ships. I worked in the shipyard for about three years. It's something to do. I like it. I mean, it beats just laying around.

John Smith: "If I worked this hard when I was working for a living, I'd be a millionaire."

'Swede" Jansson: "*Lane Victory* was in my book . . . I had quite a few Victorys. I had about ten of them. And *Lane Victory*, she vas a vork horse. Even now, vhen I was up in Port Chicago on der Knot ship. I told this guy . . . not a deep sea

The Lane Victory *at her permanent berth, Pier 94, under the Vincent Thomas Memorial Bridge.* *Courtesy* Lane Victory.

seaman, he called it a boat. All the crew call a Knot ship a boat, you know. The boat. Because they be on the crewboat, you see. So, they see them grey ones laying on the side [across the delta at the Suisun Bay Reserve Fleet], he say, 'yeah, vat is that?'

"That Victory ships,' I said. 'And you can take them out today. They got the best ship in the fleet if they fix them up."

John Smith: "As a personal thing, just walking on this ship, sometimes I get like goosebumps, trembling with enthusiasm. Something comes over me to see this old ship. I'm sure a lot of our members get the same way. It's wonderful."

Interviewer: "Why do you come down here and cook every week?"

Isaac Givens: "Because I love it."

APPENDICES
BIBLIOGRAPHY
INDEX

APPENDIX A

NUTS & BOLTS

Name: SS *Lane Victory.*
Official Number: 248094.
Construction: Welded steel, full scantling.
Power: Steam turbine.
Length, overall: 455 feet 3 inches.
Length between perpendiculars: 436 feet 6 inches.
Beam: 62 feet.
Depth of hold: 38 feet.
Mean Draft, loaded: 28 feet.
Gross tonnage: 7,612.
Net tonnage: 4,555.
Displacement tonnage: 15,200.

Design: Straight, raked stem with a paravane skeg fitted on the forefoot, cruiser stern, V-shaped bow, 62-foot parallel midbody. Transverse framing on 36-inch centers. Double bottom tanks which carry fuel oil, salt water ballast and reserve feed water. Two complete decks running from stem to stern, a forecastle deck over no. 1 hold and a first platform deck in holds number two and three. The ship is subdivided by seven full watertight bulkheads that extend to the main deck with the exception of the forepeak bulkhead which extends to the forecastle deck.

Narrative description of the Lane *Victory*.

The *Lane Victory* was designed as a general cargo ship, carrying cargo in five holds, three forward and two abaft the midships machinery space.

No. 1 hatch measures 22'4" by 25'.
No. 2 hatch measures 22'4" by 24'.
No. 3 hatch measures 22'4" by 36'.
No. 4 hatch measures 22'4" by 36'.
No. 5 hatch measures 22'4" by 24'.

The main deck is flush and has on it a forecastle deck, a midships house and a small poop deck.

There are three masts, each with a masthouse. Cargo rigging serves each hatch from the masts. The foremast is located on the forecastle deck and is 100' 8" high. It serves no. 1 hatch. The mainmast, measuring 109' 4" is located at frame 52 and supported by standing rigging which serves holds no. 2 and no. 3. Kingposts at the forward end of the midships house also serve no. 3 hold while kingposts at the after end of that superstructure serve no. 4 hatch. The 104' 11" mizzenmast at frame 122 and supported by standing rigging serves holds no. 4 and no. 5. Hatches no. 2, no. 3 and no. 4 then are double rigged, that is, with cargo gear serving both ends of each hatch. The fourteen cargo booms are rated at five tons each. Each boom is supported with a single-part topping lift. The cargo runners are a single-part cargo fall of 5/8-inch diameter improved plow steel wire rope. Completing the five ton boom rig are 5-part 4-inch sisal vangs with upper and lower wire rope pendants. Roller bearing blocks are used throughout on cargo gear.

The ship also carries two large booms, termed "Jumbo" or heavy-lift booms, rated at thirty tons and fifty tons. The larger boom is located at the after end of the main mast and serves hatch no. 3 while the smaller is at the forward end of the mizzenmast and serves no. 4 hatch. The 30 ton boom is equipped with 9-part cargo falls and an 11-part topping lift both of 3/4 inch diameter wire rope. Seven-part 4 1/2 inch sisal vang tackle with upper wire rope pendants is hand operated over the winch gypsy heads. The fifty ton boom, with 11-part cargo falls and 11-part topping lift of 1-inch diameter wire rope and 7-part 5 inch sisal vangs is operated similarly to the thirty ton boom. The overboard operation of the heavy lift booms includes a third vang with flounder plate.

The Lane Victory has fourteen electric motor-driven cargo winches clustered in two groups of four around the main and mizzenmasts with two located forward and two aft of the superstructure. Ten single-drum, two-speed winches serve the thirty and fifty ton booms. Each winch is driven by a fifty horsepower, watertight, enclosed motor. The winches have control equipment, resistors and brakes arranged on a common bedplate under waterproof enclosures. The single speed winches have a capacity of 7,450 pounds at 220 feet per minute. The 2-speed winches have a capacity of 7,450 pounds at 220 feet per minute in high gear and 19,000 pounds at eighty-five feet per minute in low gear. All winches are operated through pedestal controllers conveniently located near the hatchways. The one-speed double reduction herringbone gear winches have 18- by 20-inch drums and are manufactured by the American Hoist and Derrick Co, of St. Paul, Minnesota; they are driven by 50 h.p., 230 volt, 180 amp, 600 revolutions per minute motors manufactured by the Allis-Chalmers Manufacturing Co. of Norwood, Ohio. The double-speed, reduction herringbone gear winches, with 20- by 20-inch drums, are also manufactured by American Hoist & Derrick, with motors by Allis-Chalmers.

The anchor windlass is an electric motor-driven, horizontal shaft type on the forecastle deck. Manufactured by the Hesse Ersted Iron Works of Portland, Oregon, the windlass is capable of raising two anchors simultaneously from a thirty fathom depth of water at a chain speed of thirty feet per minute. The windlass motor, an Allis-Chalmers compound wound type, is rated at 60 h.p., 230 volts, 226 amps, and 600 r.p.m. Warping heads on the wildcat shaft of the windlass provide the facilities for handling mooring lines. The ground tackle includes two 9,500 lb. cast steel best bowers (anchors), in the hawsepipes, and one 3,420 lb. stream anchor stowed on the main deck aft. The anchors were manufactured by the Columbia Steel Co. of Pittsburg, California. The anchor chain is 300 fathoms of 2 1/8-inch diameter stud link cast steel chain, manufactured by the Paciflc Chain & Manufacturing Company. Insurance wires include a ninety fathom, 1 °-inch diameter wire rope stream line; a 130 fathom, 1 3/4-inch diameter wire rope towline; two seventy-three fathom 1-inch diameter wire rope hawsers; two seventy-three fathom wire rope warps; and two seventy-three fathom lengths of 8-inch sisal rope. All of the wire ropes are mounted on reels located on the weather deck.

Other deck machinery includes an electric warping capstan on the main deck aft, with its machinery below. The smooth-barrel, reversible vertical-motor driven capstan was manufactured by the McKlernan-Terry Corp. of Harrison, New Jersey. It produces a line pull of 20,000 lbs at a rope speed of 30 feet per minute. The capstan motor is a 35-h.p., 230 volt, 138 amp, 600 r.p.m. manufactured by Allis-Chalmers.

There are four twenty-four-foot steel lifeboats, two motor-propelled, with a total combined capacity of 124 persons, stowed in gravity-type davits manufactured by the Welin Davit & Boat Corp. of Perth Amboy, New Jersey. An electrical winch, also manufactured by Welin, is provided for each davit and is driven by motors manufactured by Westinghouse. During wartime, in addition to the lifeboats, four twenty-person life rafts, mounted on skids fore and aft of the midships house, and two fifteen person life floats, mounted aft on the deckhouse, were also available for lifesaving.

The vessel was armed with eight single 20mm Oerlikon guns, a 3-inch, 50 caliber gun forward, and a 5-inch, 38 caliber gun was recently reinstalled aft. The majority of the space in the poop deckhouse was for the ship's twenty-eight-member armed guard, which manned the guns. Their quarters and mess were at the main deck level, while below, accessible by trunk, is the magazine, with shell hoist.

Accommodations are provided for sixty-two officers and crew in the midships house. In 1944 they were described as:

"The captain's stateroom and office are on the cabin deck, starboard side. The quarters for deck officers, engineers and radio operators are on the cabin and boat decks. The quarters for the crew are on the main deck. The officer's mess and pantry are located at the after end of the deckhouse on the starboard side of the boat deck. The crew's mess and pantry are located below the officers' mess. The galley is located at the after end of the deckhouse on the main deck. The hospital is on the port side on the main deck. The quarters for both the officers and crew are comfortably and conveniently arranged. Built-in berths are provided for the officers' and crews' staterooms and pipe berths for the hospital."

The galley is equipped with electric ranges. Other galley equipment includes: two steam jacketed kettles manufactured by Legion Utensils of New York, New York, a Hobart mixer, manufactured by that Troy, New York company, a vegetable peeler manufactured by the Anstice Co. of Rochester, New York, and a refrigerator manufactured by the Star Metal Manufacturing Corporation of Philadelphia. There are also refrigerators in the officers' pantry and aft pantry. Steward's stores, dry stores, and refrigerated stores are located on the second deck, amidships.

Wartime issued radio equipment remains on board. It includes: high frequency, low frequency, emergency frequency transmitters, high receiver, low receiver, alarm signal keyer, auto alarm, and crystal receiver, all manufactured by the Radiomarine Corporation of America, of New York, New York, and the radio receiver and radio direction finder in the chart room. The torpedo indicator, manufactured by the Electro-Protective Corporation of Newark, New Jersey, and the gyroscopes, bearing pelorus stands, and bearing repeater compasses, all manufactured by the Dodge Division of the Chrysler Corporation of Detroit Michigan, are aboard. The bridge is completely outfitted and conforms to the standard 1944 description of a Victory, with standard magnetic compass in a compensating binnacle, a Navy-type flagboard located on the wheelhouse top, sounding machine and boom, engine room telegraphs, bells, gongs, fog horn, rudder angle indicator, echo depth sounder, clinometer, and brake sounding machine. Telephones for shipboard communication, manufactured by the Alwin Products Corporation of Jersey City, New Jersey, remain in working condition. The ship's wartime issue Maytag washers, in working condition, and the machine shop, in the engineering spaces, with a lathe, drill press, and grinder, as well as all spare parts, complete the fully functional, operational appearance of the ship.

Ventilation below decks is naturally supplied through four 36-inch cowls, two 24-inch cowls, and two 18-inch cowls, with each kingpost also serving as an exhaust trunk from the holds with 30-inch diameter Breidert exhaust heads installed at the top of each kingpost. Two 20,000 cubic-feet-per-minute axial flow supply fans with ducts lead to several terminals in the machinery spaces, with a single 12,000 c.f.m. axial flow fan with ducts leading from the heated space.

The propulsion machinery is housed midships, with a cross-compound, double-reduction geared, impulse-reaction type marine steam turbine unit rated at 6,000 shaft horsepower, manufactured by Allis-Chalmers, driving a single screw at a speed of 100 revolutions per minute. The shafting, forged steel and sixteen inches in diameter, runs aft to the manganese bronze, four blade, right hand screw. Manufactured by the Koppers Company of Baltimore on March 1, 1945, the 18-foot, 3-inch diameter screw weighs 30,170 lbs., has a pitch of .6 and drives the vessel at a maximum speed of 16.3 knots. Steam is provided by two sectional-header, single pass design boilers manufactured by Babcock-Wilcox. Rated at 525 psi, with an operating pressure of 465 psi, the boilers produce 27,500 pounds per hour at 750 degrees, with a furnace volume of 450 cubic feet. The boilers are twelve sections wide and are 39 feet 6 inches athwartship by 11 feet 8 inches fore and aft, and 21 feet 3 inches overall height to the top of the economizers. Fitted with interdeck superheaters

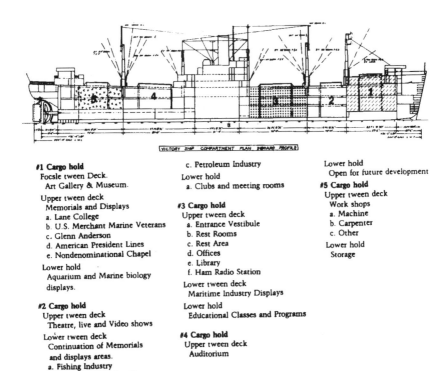

VICTORY SHIP COMPARTMENT PLAN INBOARD PROFILE

#1 Cargo hold
Focsle tween Deck.
Art Gallery & Museum.
Upper tween deck
Memorials and Displays
a. Lane College
b. U.S. Merchant Marine Veterans
c. Glenn Anderson
d. American President Lines
e. Nondenominational Chapel
Lower hold
Aquarium and Marine biology
displays.

#2 Cargo hold
Upper tween deck
Theatre, live and Video shows
Lower tween deck
Continuation of Memorials
and displays areas.
a. Fishing Industry
b. Maritime Administration

c. Petroleum Industry
Lower hold
a. Clubs and meeting rooms

#3 Cargo hold
Upper tween deck
a. Entrance Vestibule
b. Rest Rooms
c. Rest Area
d. Offices
e. Library
f. Ham Radio Station
Lower tween deck
Maritime Industry Displays
Lower hold
Educational Classes and Programs

#4 Cargo hold
Upper tween deck
Auditorium

Lower hold
Open for future development

#5 Cargo hold
Upper tween deck
Work shops
a. Machine
b. Carpenter
c. Other
Lower hold
Storage

This early plan of the intended uses of the cargo holds was tempered by time and the realities of changing demands and conditions. Nonetheless, much of it has come to pass.

and economizers, each boiler is fired with three double-front mechanical-atomizing oil burners with water-cooled side walls and refractory in the front and rear walls and floors.

Electrical power is provided by an inboard and outboard turbo-generator, the turbines manufactured by the Moore Steam Turbine Company of Wellsville, New York, and the generators manufactured by the Crocker-Wheeler Corporation of Ampere, New Jersey. The three-wire marine direct current generators produce 300 kilowatts, with 120 and 240 volts and 1250 amps at 1200 rpm. The ship also has emergency diesel generators in the engine room and in the emergency diesel room. The steering gear, a slide electrohydraulic, double-ram type, is manufactured by the McKiernan-Terry Corporation, and is located aft.

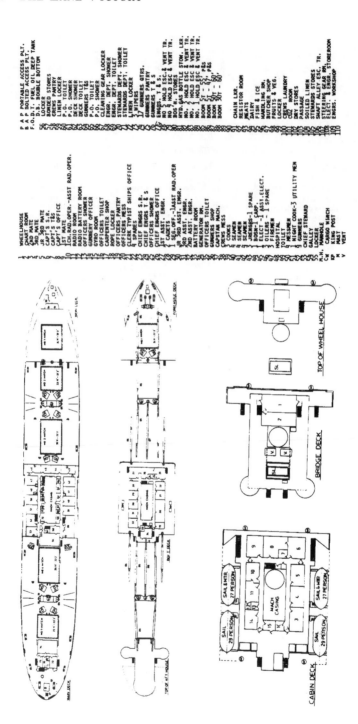

Appendix B

THE VOYAGES OF
THE *LANE VICTORY*

Ports of call:　　　　Long Beach, California
　　　　　　　　　　　　Port Hueneme, California
　　　　　　　　　　　　Manus, Admiralty Islands
　　　　　　　　　　　　San Francisco, California

Crew:
Master	G. M. Cramer
Chief Mate	Joseph Pierson
Second Mate	Robert Bushong
Third Mate	Ernest Sharp
Junior Third Mate	Donald Runyon
Purser	James C. Walsh, Jr.
Chief Radio Operator[1]	Frank Adams
Second Radio Operator	Syndey Cooly
Third Radio Operator	Albert Lind
Carpenter	Clifford Newkirk
Boatswain	Antonio Ferreira

---

[1] Wartime operations called for a twenty-four hour radio watch, hence three radio operators.

AB (Able-bodied Seaman)	Felix Onorato
AB	Cecil Mathis
AB	Ted Lister
AB	David Beta
AB	Charles Nafle
AB	Lee Reasoner
AB	William C. Boatman
Deck Maintenance	Theodore Dargil
OS (Ordinary Seaman)	Lawrence Stohl
OS	John Morrison
OS	James Curtis
Chief Engineer	James Scott
First Assistant Engineer	Bernard Gunn
Second Assistant Engineer	James Kasseroff
Third Assistant Engineer	Vernon Richardson
Junior Third Assistant Engineer	Francis Hughes
Acting Licensed Jr. Engineer	James Simmons
Acting Licensed Jr. Engineer	Richard Jones
Acting Licensed Jr. Engineer	Paul Wierman
Chief Electrician	Clifford Brown
Assistant Electrician	James McCullough
Oiler	Joseph Berlotat
Oiler	Jack Marirish
Oiler	Harry Hibler
FWT (Fireman Water Tender)	Raymond Brunk
FWT	William Redline
FWT	Arthur Brown
Wiper	William McHale
Wiper	Roy Ismert
Wiper	Harold Davis
Chief Steward	Jack Marris
Chief Cook	Walter Allen
Night Cook & Baker	Ernest Kloetzli
Second Cook	Raymon Hines
Assistant Cook	Arthur Kurt
Messman	Joseph Pleri
Messman	Edward Baesch, Jr.
Messman	James Thronsburg
Messman	George Allen
Utility Messman	Ad Y. Boswell
Utility Messman	William Page
Utility Messman	Sydney Emmert
Messman	Oda Winn
Messman	Arthur Bryant

Engine Cadet	James Menlove
Deck Cadet	Warren N. Ernest
Oiler	Richard Reisner

Armed Guard crew:

Lieutenant	Ted L. Wilson
Gunner's Mate Second Class	Emil G. Wahlund
Coxswain	Wayne J. Stafford
Gunner's Mate Third Class	Patrick J. Hurley
Seaman First Class	William G. Bosely
Seaman First Class	Junior J. Feldkamp
Seaman First Class	Clarence C. Fields
Seaman First Class	Joseph J. Figuizzi
Seaman First Class	James O. McCown
Seaman First Class	William L. Scroggs
Seaman Second Class	Russel W. Sandercook
Seaman Third Class	Alvin R. Krause

Joined at Los Negros in Admiralty Islands:

Gunner's Mate Third Class	Roy A. Bundtrock
Seaman First Class	Howard A. Balding
Seaman First Class	Paul M. Bostwick
Seaman First Class	Bruce 0. Wilbur
Seaman First Class	Richard T. Harris

VOYAGE 2 — AUGUST 30, 1945 TO FEBRUARY 27, 1946

Ports of Call:	San Francisco, California
	Guam, Marianas Islands
	Taipan, Marianas Islands
	Honolulu, Territory of Hawaii
	San Francisco, California

Crew:

Master	G.W. Cramer
Chief Mate	Joseph Pierson
Second Mate	John Buckley
Third Mate	Victor Archer
Junior Third Mate	Thomas McLarin
Radio Operator	Frank Adams
Carpenter	Clifford Newkirk
Boatswain	Bradford Dalton
AB	Vernon Smith
Deck Maintenance	Carl Nelson
AB	Manuel Medina
AB	Robert Adams

AB	Peter Faroone
Deck Maintenance	Harry Jenson
AB	Arne Andersen
AB	John Smith
OS	Paul Faroone
OS	Carl Merci
OS	Jimmie Guthrie
Deck Cadet	Warren Ernest
Purser	Michael Rapport
Chief Engineer	James Scott
First Assistant Engineer	Vernon Richardson
Second Assistant Engineer	Robert Oster
Third Assistant Engineer	Francis Hughes
Junior Third Assistant	Paul Wierman
Junior Engineer	Ivor Jones
Junior Engineer	Richard Reisner
Junior Engineer	Everett Fletcher
Chief Electricain	George Keefe
Second Electrician	Jack Morrish
Oiler	William McHale
Oiler	Harold Davis
Oiler	Harry Ellsworth
FWT	Wayne Coad
FWT	Guy Graham
FWT	Socrates Cliotes
Wiper	Loren Vockrodt
Wiper	Ray Sherman
Wiper	Kenneth Gelhaus
Engine Cadet	James Menlane
Chief Steward	Lee Norr
Chief Cook	Michael Michalik
Second Cook & Baker	Lawrence O'Clair
Galleyman	Lyle W. Busby
Saloon Messman	Dean McKay
Petty Officer's Messman	Louis Ramsey
Bedroom Utility	Solomon Smith
Saloon Pantryman	William Mason
Crew Messman	Rogue Villarosa
Second Cook & Baker	Richard L. Hise

Armed Guard crew:

Gunner's Mate Third Class	Barney M. Nordstrom
Seaman First Class	Charles Giangualano

VOYAGE 3 — MARCH 6, 1946 TO MAY 18, 1946

Ports of Call: San Francisco, California
Shanghai, China
San Francisco, California

Crew:

Master	Ralph L. Moon
Chief Mate	Kenneth F. Rambo
Second Mate	Constantine Fullman
Third Mate	John Gosslen
Junior Third Mate	Kristian D. Ebeniveche
Radio Operator	Bryan R. Jones
Purser	Anton Straub
Carpenter	Clifford Newkirk
Boatswain	Willie Kahl
AB	Anthony Lorenzo
AB	Richard Myers
AB	Willie Dirkson
AB	Ea Jang Kumyay
AB	Edward Ulrick
AB	Edward J. Keeling
Deck Maintenance	Kenneth Makaiwi
Deck Maintenance	Solomon Bishaw
OS	Arlcson J. Tudor
OS	Delbert L. Gossett
OS	Harry Dobbs
Chief Engineer	Joseph J. Russell
First Assistant Engineer	John Henkins
Second Assistant Engineer	Buck J. McFarland
Third Assistant Engineer	Edgar Morningster
Junior Third Asst. Engineer	Edward G. Warren
Junior Engineer	Andrew Acosta
Junior Engineer	Andrew Rodriguez
Junior Engineer	Jack C. Fair
Electrician	Kenneth R. Christie
Second Electrician	Donald H. Rovanpera
Oiler	Harold O. Davis
Oiler	Wayne H. Coad
Oiler	Richard Pennington
FWT	Samuel M. Erickson
FWT	Warren M. Vockrodt
FWT	Kenneth J. Gclhaus
Wiper	Francis P. Dufrante
Wiper	James E. Grey

Wiper	Joe Machak
Chief Steward	Leroy Lee Norr
Chief Cook	Charles E. MacDonald
Second Cook & Baker	Milton Wright
Third Cook	William T. Price
Saloon Messman	Dean E. Kruger
Messman	Eugene A. Tinker
Saloon Pantryman	Cyrus W. Brandenburg
Messman	Wing Bee Yee
Utility Messman	Robert L. Ashley
Utility Messman	Thomas D. Craig
Messman	Robert M. Bruce
Messman	Leo J. Wilturner
Deck Cadet[2]	Earnest Warren
Engine Cadet	James L. Menlo
Oiler	Otis D. Dunn
Deck Cadet	Enos J. Dickson
Engine Cadet	Lester E. Hurrelbrink
Deck Cadet	Angus W. Gafkin
Workaway[3]	George L. Klor

VOYAGE 4 - JUNE 18, 1946 TO SEPTEMBER 21, 1946

Ports of call: San Francisco, California
Manila, Philippine Islands
Legaspi, Philippine Islands
Bulan, Philippine Islands
San Francisco, California

Crew:

Master	Ralph L. Moon
Chief Mate	Kenneth Rambo
Second Mate	Stanley Young
Third Mate	Kristian Benneche
Junior Third Mate	Marion Gove
Radio Operator	Rene Gasse
Carpenter	Clifford Newkirk
Bosun (Boatswain)	Willie Kahl

---

[2] More than one deck and engine cadet are shown in the official logbook. This merely indicates that some signed off and others signed on. The ship wouldn't normally carry more than one of each.

[3] A "workaway" is someone hired in a foreign port to work as a crewmember until the ship reaches its first United States port where, by law, he must sign off. Workaways are seldom carried on American-flag merchant ships.

Deck Maintenance	Jack Gasson
Deck Maintenance	Finne Davis
AB	Angelo Foster
OS substituting as AB[4]	Leo Lasanen
OS substituting as AB[4]	Peter Forakis
AB	Charles Manduk
AB	Emery Bowers
OS substituting as AB[4]	Elwin Phillips
OS	James Calloway
OS	Robert Biagini
OS	Phillips Caruso
Purser	James C. Walsh, Jr.
Chief Engineer	James E. Scott
First Asssistant Engineer	Vernon Richardson
Second Assistant Engineer	Glenn Walker
Third Assistant Engineer	Edward O'Brien
Junior Engineer acting Junior Third Assistant Engineer[4]	William Goddard
Oiler Acting Junior Engineer[4]	Andrew Acosta
Junior Engineer	Richard Pennington
Junior Engineer	Ishamael Blankenship
Chief Electrician	Kenneth Cristy
Assistant Electrician	Jack Fair
Oiler	Albert Brown
Oiler	Coenraad Kommene
Oiler	Chen Ah Ching
FWT	John McNeil
FWT	Axel Patman
FWT	Richard Grose
Wiper	Thomas Holmes
Wiper	Alexander Leonesio
Wiper	Michael Indelicato
Chief Steward	Edward Fegan
Chief Cook	Earl Kilpatrick
Second Cook & Baker	Everett Ateman
Assistant Cook	Roy Whitlock
Messman	William Collins
Messman	Robert Bruce
Saloon Pantry	Russell Carlson
Messman	Francisco Sanchez

---

[4] When it is difficult to fill higher ratings such as AB or Third Assistant Engineer, the Coast Guard will occasionally allow those of lower ratings to be substituted.

BR (Bedroom Utility)	William Kramer
BR	Apolonio Galaggae
Messman	Eladio Balanga
Messman	James Witcher
Deck Cadet	Howard Donegan

VOYAGE 5 - DECEMBER 4, 1946 TO MARCH 3, 1947

Ports of call: San Francisco, California
Manila, Philippine Islands
Cebu, Philippine Islands
Jimenez, Philippine Islands
Legaspi, Philippine Islands
Tabaco, Philippine Islands
Donsol, Philippine Islands
Los Angeles, California
San Francisco, California

Crew:

Master	Ralph L. Moon
Chief Mate	Kenneth Rambo
Second Mate	John Neidlinger
Third Mate	Marshall Howard
Junior Third Mate	Lloyd Waller
Radio Operator	Russell Bohl
Carpenter	George Moniz
Bosun	Willie Kahl
Deck Maintenance	Leo Sigert
Deck Maintenance	Sidney Perkins
AB	Peter Tringale
AB	Walter Jones
AB	Leland Nichols
AB	Harlan Farmer
AB	Arthur Conaty
AB	Thomas Moore
OS	Herbert Fox
OS	Howard Doty
OS	Wallace Rauley
Purser	Robert Throop
Chief Engineer	Vernon Richardson
First Assistant Engineer	John Reeves
Second Assistant Engineer	Richard Jones
Third Assistant Engineer	Paul Wierman
Junior Third Asst. Engineer	Russell Barron
Junior Engineer	Richard Pennington

Junior Engineer	Everett Fletcher
Junior Engineer	Harry Kolstad
Chief Electrician	Victor McDonald
Assistant Electrician	Leroy Snow
Oiler	Thomas Anderson
Oiler	George Buddell
Oiler	James Hughes
FWT	Harry Drosia
FWT	Albert Torres
FWT	Marshall Pidge
Wiper	Walter Thayer
Wiper	Henry Souza
Wiper	Jose Gonzales
Chief Steward	John Witt
Chief Cook	Ray Wilson
Second Cook	J.D. Martin
Assistant Cook	Alfred Mantelli
Messman	Clarence Turner
Messman	Hugh Fulston
Messman	James Dennis
Messman	Bill Long
Messman	Joseph Ray
Messman	Doo Chan Park
Wiper	Malcolm Turner

VOYAGE 6 - MARCH 7, 1947 TO JULY 7, 1947

Ports of call: San Francisco, California
Portland, Oregon
Karachi, India
Colombo, Ceylon
Singapore
Davao, Philippine Islands
Cebu, Philippine Islands
Manila, Philippine Islands
Hong Kong
Shanghai, China
Jinsen, Korea
Fusan, Korea
Kobe,Japan
Yokohama, Japan
San Francisco, California

Crew:

Master	Ralph Moon
Chief Mate	Martin Schwarzbach
Second Mate	John Neidlinger
Third Mate	Marshall Howard
Junior Third Mate	Lloyd Waller
Radio Operator	Russell Bohl
Carpenter	George Moniz
Bosun	Willie Kahl
Deck Maintenance	Eldon Webb
Deck Maintenance	Sydney Perkins
AB	Peter Tringale
AB	Joseph Mackey
AB	Andy Cordova
AB	Walton Jones
AB	Kenneth Spencer
AB	Arthur Conaty
OS	George Mosley
OS	Wilburn Strawn
OS	Mathew Lampi
Purser	Robert Throop
Chief Engineer	Vernon Richardson
First Assistant Engineer	John Reeves
Second Assistant Engineer	Richard Jones
Third Assistant Engineer	Paul Wierman
Junior Third Engineer	Miles De Somer
Junior Engineer	Everett Fletcher
Junior Engineer	Harry Kolstad
Junior Engineer	Richard Pennington
Chief Electrician	Charles Holmes
Assistant Electrician	Billy Mc Guire
Oiler	John Oboleurcy
Oiler	Edwardo Gomez
Oiler	Ralph Miller
FWT	Leonard Smith
FWT	Alphonse Grijalva
FWT	Marshall Pidge
Wiper	Walter Thayer
Wiper	NoelJones
Wiper	Benjamin Rice
Chief Steward	McKinley Jones
Chief Cook	John Howell
Second Cook	J.D. Martin
Assistant Cook	James Crawford

Messman	Lavon Booker
Messman	Clifford Oscarson
Messman	Wilford Lucas
Messman	Roland Crane
Messman	Hugh Fusion
Messman	Eddie McGregor
Wiper[5]	Ralph Lethlean
Assistant Electrician	Charles Anderson
Messman	Earl Zafft
Messman	Elmo Berndsen
Oiler	Gasper Vavaro
Wiper	Kenneth Sanders
Wiper	Manuel Conty
Wiper	John Tillman

VOYAGE 7 - JULY 8, 1947 TO MARCH 29, 1948

Ports of call: San Francisco, California
Los Angeles, California
New York, New York
Baltimore, Maryland
Rauma, Finland
Grangemouth, Scotland
Norfolk, Virginia
Venice, Italy
Naples, Italy
New York, New York
Tocopilla, Chile
Cristobal, Canal Zone
Alexandria, Egypt
Port Said, Egypt
Cagliari, Sardinia
Port Said, Egypt
Suez, Egypt
Singapore
Sasebo, Japan
Honolulu, Territory of Hawaii
Long Beach, California
San Francisco, California

---

[5] Usually the foreign articles are signed a few days before the ship sails for its first foreign port. At this time the names of the crew are entered in the official logbook. Occasionally some of the crew decide they don't want to make the trip after all. If the master agrees, they can sign off. Their replacements' names are then entered in the logbook as they are signed on. The ratings after messman Eddie McGregor in this list joined the ship in that manner.

Crew:[6]

Master	Ralph L. Moon
Chief Mate	Leroy Smart
Second Mate	Gilman McMillan
Third Mate	Howard Marshall
Junior Third Mate	Lloyd Waller
Radio Officer	Ross Andrews
Carpenter	Elmer Richardson
Bosun	Leon Warywoda
Deck Maintenance	Eldon Webb
Deck Maintenance	J. Paul Johnston
AB	Asa Butler
AB	J. Mackey
AB	William Berger
AB	Richard Rodgers
AB	S. Cornett
AB	C. Dawson
OS	William Du Charme
OS	Harold Dine
OS	Roy Johnson
Cadet	Warren Kiernan
Purser	C.G. Morales
AB	Henry Johansen
Junior Third Asst.Engineer	Sherwood Anderson
Chief Engineer	Vernon Richardson
First Assistant Engineer	William Fisher
Third Assistant Engineer	Jack Clayton
Junior Engineer	C. Fletcher
Junior Engineer	R. Pennington
Junior Engineer	Henry Fem
Chief Electrician	W. Condon
Oiler	S. Joseph
FWT	J. Blefgen
FWT	P. Hughes
Wiper	T. Figueroa
Wiper	William Conlow
Wiper	R. Tcxeira
Engine Cadet	J. Hughes
Second Assistant Engineer	E. Theobald

---

[6] The reasons for the unusually long crew list are the length of the voyage and the number of times the ship returned to United States ports. While an American merchant seaman can't sign off a ship in a foreign port, he can in a U.S. port. Many on this voyage took advantage of that opportunity.

Oiler	William Waughn
FWT	J. WJlburn
Oiler	William Shaffer
Second Electrician	O. Luoma
Chief Steward	N. Litcofsky
Chief Cook	W. Kidd
Second Cook	G. Deering
Third Cook	P. Pimienta
Messman	L.Burkhardt
Messman	C. Clayton
Messman	J. Caldera
Messman	S. Dewey
Mcssman	J. Torres
Messman	J. De Leon
Second Cook	R. Fitch
Messman	R. Foshee
Messman	C. Edwards
Mcssman	J. Bowen
Messman	R. Faircloth
Wiper	A. Geo
Wiper	J. Rice
Wiper	George Gilmore
FWT	W. Driggers
Oiler	T. Haynes
OS	J. Mathews
OS	G. Patterson
Deck Maintenance	C. Wilbur
Radio Operator	R. Colman
AB	N. Larsen
Chief Mate	L. Huff
Third Mate	C.Gabriel
AB	H. Tuneson
AB	N. Vayda
AB	M. Mc Kinnon
OS	L. Holm
OS	J. Hyde
OS	G. Mauley
Deck Maintenance	G. Button
Deck Maintenance	G. Burnnell
Deck Maintenance	B. Megrue
Bosun	L. Paugi
Second Assistant Engineer	W. Fischofer
AB	R. Herwick
OS	F. Ralon

Second Cook	F. McGrath
Third Cook	W. Davis
Messman	P. Abel
Messman	J. McWilliams
Messman	E. Beavers
Messman	G. Velez
Messman	R. Betancourt
Messman	D. Denibar
FWT	G. Jones
Oiler	H. Sayer
Wiper	O. Tiniofejens
Wiper	F. Beyer
Wiper	F. Rodriguez

VOYAGE 8 — APRIL 6, 1948 TO MAY 11, 1948

Ports of call: Oakland, California
Yokohama, Japan
Honolulu, Territory of Hawaii
San Francisco, California

Crew:

Master	Edward C. Dumouchelle
Chief Mate	John C. McNeill
Second Mate	Howard L. Peterson
Third Mate	Harry H. Aldrich
Junior Third Mate	Morris A. Jacobson
Radio Operator	Roy F. Coluran
Carpenter	Elmer A. Richardson
Bosun	Joesph Lii, Jr.
Deck Maintenance	George Muller
Deck Maintenance	Stanley Olson
AB	Victor F. Smart
AB	John Donnelly
AB	Richard G. Williams
AB	Raymond C. Johnson
AB	Alex Promet
AB	Kemp J. Beuker
Ordinary Seaman	Eddie Tofoya
OS	Robert L. Chamberlain
OS	Jesus C. Puluzi
Purser	Anton W. Straula
Chief Engineer	Peter J. Fitzpatrick
First Assistant Engineer	Joseph A. Sedenio

Second Assistant Engineer	Manuel Soto
Third Assistant Engineer	Howard K. Priestley
Junior Third Asst. Engineer	Gustav D. Schulz
Junior Engineer	Clement Dang
Chief Electrician	Walter F. Condon
Second Electrician	Walter V. Shalica
Oiler	John J. Spelman
Oiler	George Hobbs
Oiler	Michael Bestik
FWT	Woodrow Love
FWT	James H. Everett
FWT	Delbert M. Fleming
Wiper	Antone Fernandez
Wiper	Charles Martriss
Wiper	Hans Christensen
Chief Steward	Chris Thomas
Chief Cook	Charles S. Gflliean
Second Cook & Baker	Isaac B. Givens
Pantry Utflity	Clyde Morris
Messman	Manuel L. Garnier
Messman	Antonio 0. Paniagua
Messman	Roble Chese
Messman	Salvador Sanchez
Messman	Lester Skaggs

VOYAGE 9 - OCTOBER 10, 1950 TO FEBMARY 12, 1951

Ports of call: Oakland, California
        Yokohama, Japan
        Inchon, Korea
        Pusan, Korea
        Wonson, Korea
        Pusan, Korea
        Hungnam, Korea
        Pusan, Korea
        Hungnam, Korea
        Pusan, Korea
        Sasebo, Japan
        Inchon, Korea
        Taechau, Korea
        Sasebo, Japan
        San Francisco, California

Crew:

Master	Marinus Olson
Chief Mate	William Chilcoat
Second Mate	Paul Oupe
Third Mate	Gilman C. MacMillan
Junior Third Mate	Robert E. Bennett
Radio Operator	Arti Aro
Bosun	Bart E. Guranich
Carpenter	George J. Monez
Deck Maintenance	James E. Tippett
Deck Maintenance	Joseph Jagodzinski
AB	John H. Muncy
AB	Jorgen A. Nielsen
AB	Raymond Driscoll
AB	Torbjorn Lindau
AB	Philip Y. Jang
AB	James A. Sanker
OS	Harper M. Lewis
OS	Robert J. Spicer
OS	George J. Johnson
Purser	Ray A. Fuflbright
Chief Engineer	John P. Bayer
First Assistant Engineer	Charles C. Cook
Second Assistant Engineer	Phflip Lellman
Third Assistant Engineer	Lloyd Trembley
Junior Third Asst. Engineer	Barker B. Daniel
Licensed Junior Engineer	Clarence Harrison
Chief Electrician	Karl F. Wasenius
Second Electrician	John H. Linday
Oiler	Johan T. Isaksen
Oiler	Michael Carbonella
Oiler	David L. Lisher
FWT	Karl E. Pederson
FWT	Luis A. Cubillos
FWT	Charles 1. Stokes
Wiper	William Cambea
Wiper	Akien Nakayama
Wiper	Theodore Colon, Jr.
Chief Steward	Honorio Baldeoia
Chief Cook	Rogellus Norwood
Second Cook	Lester P. Budrow
Assistant Cook	William H. Beltz
Saloon Messman	Edward Ramsburg
Crew Messman	Eduardo Herrera

Crew Messman	Yiu Ming
Petty Officer's Messman	Frank O'Brien
BR	Pedro Juarez
Pantryman	Eladio Mayoral

VOYAGE 10 — FEBRUARY 23, 1951 TO AUGUST 24, 1951

Ports of Call:
San Francisco, California
New Orleans, Louisiana
Los Angeles, California
Ulsan, Korea
Pusan, Korea
Moji, Japan
Pusan, Korea
Moji, Japan
Pusan Korea
Moji, Japan
Sasebo, Japan
Pusan, Korea
Yokohama, Japan
Okinawa, Ryuku Islands
Olongopo, Philippine Islands
Manila, Philippine Islands
Saigon, French Indo-China
Rangoon, Burma
Kohsichang, Siam
Saigon, French Indo-China
Manila, Philippine Islands
Guam, Marianas Island
San Francisco, California

Crew:

Master	Marinus Olson
Chief Mate	Frank Ellis
Second Mate	Joseph Edwards
Third Mate	Jack R. Bowden
Junior third Mate	James J. Clark
Radio Operator	Arti Aro
Bosun	Joseph E. Johnson
Carpenter	Dale Richardson
Deck Maintenance	Albert J. Walker
Deck Maintenance	William Geyer
AB	Laurits Haun
AB	John Haos
AB	Herbert Tuarson

AB	Groziu Drensky
AB	Harold Meditz
AB	John Bray
OS	Charles A. Gonyas
OS	William R. Noble
OS	Paul J. Miller
Purser	Willard F. Lyon
Chief Engineer	John Bayer
First Assistant Engineer	Robert Jacobsen
Second Assistant Engineer	Thomas Dunlap
Third Assistant Engineer	John Tracy
Junior Third Asst. Engineer	Roger Halquen
Junior Third Asst. Engineer	Michael Carbonella
Chief Electrician	Ronald N. Harper
Second Electrician	Julio N. Diaz
Oiler	Ralph E. Cajeas
Oiler	Nick Loflo
Oiler	Joseph G. Wadsworth
FWT	Morris A. Perry
FWT	John F. Best
FWT	Charles Fleethaxn
Wiper substituting as FWT	John P. Timlin
Wiper	James A. Patton
Wiper	John Westine
Wiper	Ray McIntyre
Wiper	Ray Napier
Chief Steward	Henry Baldwin
Chief Cook	Rogellus Norwood
Second Cook	George Deering
Assistant Cook	Ernest Owens
Messman	Julio Magno
Messman	Edward Herrera
Messman	Peter Spatalo
Messman	Ming Yiu
Messman	Pedro Juarez
Messman	Santiago Canas

VOYAGE 11 — AUGUST 25, 1951 TO FEBRUARY 19, 1952

Ports of Call: San Francsico, California
Gulfport, Mississippi
Wilmington, California
Sasebo, Japan
Pusan, Korea

Masan, Korea
Yokohama, Japan
Moji, Japan
Pusan, Kora
Kunsan, Korea
Sasebo, Japan
Naha, Okinawa
Pusan, Korea
Kunsan, Korea
Yokohama, Japan
Portland, Oregon

Crew:

Master	Marinus Olson
Chief Mate	Frank R. Ellis
Second Mate	James L. Singleton
Third Mate	William Laudenschlager
Junior Third Mate	John D. Mena
Radio Operator	Ronald R. Piatt
Bosun	Alfred Dorego
Carpenter	Birger Gjeseth
Deck Maintenance	Alfred M. Saar
Deck Maintenance	Joseph Holomalia
AB	Martin Boschman
AB	Henry B. Johnson
AB	Peter Torres
AB	Laurence J. Reagan
AB (waiver)	Albert J. Stefanouritz
OS	Russell W. Perry
OS	George E. Silva
OS	Fernando E. Panizo
AB	Frank Tuccari
Purser	Willard F. Lyon
Chief Engineer	John P. Bayer
First Assistant Engineer	Robert A. Jacobsen
Second Assistant Engineer	William L. O'Donnell
Third Assistant Engineer	William F. Wurzler
Junior Engineer	James Kastrosny
Junior Engineer	Lester H. Stoeln
Chief Electrician	Clarence D. Boggs
Second Electrician	Paul L. Juery
Oiler	Sven H. Arbin
Oiler	Armand Champagne
Oiler	Robert C. Beam
FWT	Autonis Savant

FWT	Manuel Dacunha
FWT	Henry Diserens
Wiper	John E. Palmquist
Wiper	James Marsala
Wiper	Manuel Narciso
Chief Steward	Honorio Baloeira
Chief Cook	Rogelles Norwood
Second Cook	James B. Shorter, Jr.
Assistant Cook	Clyde B. Talbot
Messman	Julio Magno
Messman	Eduardo Herrera
Messman	Pedro Juarez
Messman	Charles Thomas
Messman	Bonifacio Aure
Messman	Share Kew Lew
Purser	Peter A. Low
Bosun	Edward A. Lewis
Purser	George Peter Kelder
Second Assistant Engineer	Alexander E. Has
Second Electrician	Gilbert Monrreal

VOYAGE 12 — FEBRUARY 23, 1952 TO APRIL 14, 1952

Ports of call:
Portland, Oregon
Wilmington, California
Cristobal, Canal Zone
Liverpool, England
Philadelphia, Pennsylvania

Crew:

Master	Marinus Olson
Chief Mate	Frank R. Ellis
Second Mate	Loren C. Carlson
Third Mate	Harold N. Holbrook
Junior Third Mate	Colin Nickelsen
Radio Operator	Jack D. Gripp
Bosun	Jacob Beckel
Carpenter	George N. Harris
Deck Maintenance	Thomas S. Green
Deck Maintenance	Dalmer D. Giyle
Deck Maintenance	Olaf W. Kittel
AB	John E. Luoma
AB	Sidney Everidge, Jr.
AB (Acting)	Dale E. Nichols

AB (Acting)	Victor E. Carlson
AB (Acting)	Robert J. Dueber
AB (Acting)	Gordon D. Ferrell
OS	Ronald E. Combs
OS	Edward R. Zboralski
OS	John H. White
Purser	Paul H. Wilson
Chief Engineer	Richard A. Dominguez
First Assistant Engineer	William A. Clark
Second Assistant Engineer	Ronald L. Duffis
Thrid Assistant Engineer	Jerome Doherty
Junior third Assistant Engineer	James D. Stilleke
Licensed Junior Engineer	Walter R. Woodward
Chief Electrician	John L. Thurston
Second Electrician	James F. Murray
Oiler	William H. Griffen
Oiler	Alexander D. Hughes
Oiler	Harvey A. Parker
FWT	John J. McGee
FWT	John A. Blefgen
FWT	Charles Emberry
Wiper	Raymond O. Jeannot, Jr.
Wiper	James P. Hayden
Wiper	James N. Davis
Chief Steward	Harry L. Rouleau
Chief Cook	Nick Villa
Second Cook	Gerald L. Bradley
Assistant Cook	August Farmer
Messman	Stuart B. Walsh
Messman	Roy E. Butler
Messman	Albert Robinson
Messman	Clarence Thomas
Messman	Charles E. McCullar
Messman	James McChrystal

VOYAGE 13 — APRIL 17, 1952 TO MAY 15, 1952

Ports of call: Philadelphia, Pennsylvania
                        Bremerhaven, Germany
                        Philadelphia, Pennsylvania

Crew:
Master   Marinus Olson
Chief Mate   Frank R. Ellis

Second Mate	Loren C. Carlsen
Third Mate	Ingvald B. Haugland
Junior Third Mate	James L. Orfe
Radio Officer	Jack D. Gripp
Bosun	Jacob Beckel
Carpenter	Antonios Malios
Deck Maintenance	Thomas S. Green
Deck Maintenance	Olaf W. Kittel
Deck Maintenance	Veikko O. Kaasimen
AB	Sidney Evveridge, Jr.
AB	John E. Luoma
AB	Gunnar A. Modig
AB	Eugene M. Gerardiello
AB	John E. Jansson
AB (12 month)	Victor E. Carlson
OS	Edward R. Zboralski
OS	Rafael F. Fernandez
OS	August Schulzc
Purser	Paul H. Wilson
Chief Engineer	Richard A. Dominguez
First Assistant Engineer	William A. Clark
Second Assistant Engineer	Francis W. Hoffman
Third Assistant Engineer	Jerome Doherty
Junior Third Assistant Engineer	James D. Stilleke
Licensed Junior Engineer	Roland L. King
Chief Electrician	John B. Larkin
Second Electrician	Oscar Bergstrom
Oiler	Andrew C. Queirolo
Oiler	Kenneth McKenzie
Oiler	Richard W. Teetor
FWT	Harold M. Lyngroth
FWT	Harold E. Bocc
FWT	Gosta B. Holmquist
Wiper	Santiago O. Bahon
Wiper	Aidan B. Hart
Wiper	Alphonse A. Asaro
Chief Steward	Harry L. Rouleau
Chief Cook	Gerald L. Bradley
Second Cook & Baker	Wilfred B. Stewart
Assistant Cook	Pao San Nee
Messman	Albert Robinson
Messman	Clarence Thomas
Messman	Gaston Manilone
Messman	Roy E. Butler

Messman	Carlos M. Ortega
Messman	Manuel Estrada

VOYAGE 14 — MAY 10, 1952 TO JUNE 27, 1952

Ports of call: Philadelphia, Pennsylvania
Gibraltar
Trieste
Gibraltar
New York, New York

Crew:

Master	Marinus Olson
Chief Mate	Frank R. Ellis
Second Mate	Loren C. Carlsen
Third Mate	Ingvald B. Haugland
Junior Third Mate	James L. Orfe
Radio Officer	Angel M. Gutierrez
Bosun	Richard A. Johanson
Carpenter	Antonios Malios
Deck Maintenance	Jens P. Kjeldsen
Deck Maintenance	George W. King
Deck Maintenance	Veikko O. Kaasinen
AB	William J. Muirhead
AB	Holger K. Jensen
AB	Gunnar A. Modig
AB	Eugene M. Gerardiello
AB	John E. Jansson
AB	Carl A.B. Hansen
OS	Xenefon Combos
OS	Rafael F. Fernandez
OS	August Schulzc
Purser	Paul H. Wilson
Chief Engineer	Richard A. Dominguez
First Assistant Engineer	William A. Clark
Second Assistant Engineer	Francis W. Hoffman
Third Assistant Engineer	Jerome Doherty
Junior Third Assistant Engineer	James D. Stilleke
Licensed Junior Engineer	Leslie M. Clark
Chief Electrician	John B. Larkin
Second Electrician	Kenneth McKenzie
Oiler	Andrew C. Queirolo
Oiler	Joseph M. Conway

Oiler	Richard W. Teeter
FWT	Harold M. Lyngroth
FWT	Robert M. Clark
FWT	Gosta B. Holmquist
Wiper	Santiago O. Bahon
Wiper	Aidan B. Hert
Wiper	Alphonse A. Asaro
Chief Steward	Gerald U. Willett
Chief Cook	Gerald L. Bradley
Second Cook	Albert Miles
Assistant Cook	Obie Hendricks
Messman	Pedro Q. Collazo
Messman	Leonardo Vargas
Messman	Charles Sobel
Messman	Giuseppe Giampietro
Messman	Charles M. Ortega
Messman	Manuel Estrada

VOYAGE 15 — JUNE 24, 1952 TO JULY 20, !952.

Ports of call: New York, New York
Bremerhaven, Germany
New York, New York

Crew:

Master	Marinus Olson
Chief Mate	Frank R. Ellis
Second Mate	Loren C. Carlsen
Third Mate	Ingvald B. Haugland
Junior Third Mate	James L. Orfe
Bosun	Richard A. Johansen
Carpenter	Antonios Malios
Deck Maintenance	Thomas Dougher
Deck Maintenance	Louis Beckman
Deck Maintenance	Harold R. Meditz
AB	Holger K. Jensen
AB	Carl A.B. Hansen
AB	William J. Muirhead
AB	John E. Jansson
AB	Torsten A. Henricson
AB	William J. Smith
OS	Xenefon Combos
OS	Roger B. Cunnane, Jr.
OS	Joseph R. Wolfe

Purser	Paul H. Wilson
Chief Engineer	Richard A. Dominguez
First Assistant Engineer	William A. Clark
Second Assistant Engineer	Frank E. Morrison
Third Assistant Engineer	Jerome Doherty
Junior Third Assistant Engineer	Emilio Docampo
Radio Officer	Angel M. Gutierrez
Licensed Junior Engineer	Frank P. Warwick
Chief Electrician	Anthony Petrovich
Second Electrician	Robert M. Clark
Oiler	Bentti M. Airikka
Oiler	Francis Grech
Oiler	Albert M. Bloecher
FWT	Salaiman Kalil
FWT	Emil A. Svahn
FWT	Gosta B. Holmgrist
Wiper	Alphonse A. Asaro
Wiper	Santiago O. Bahon
Wiper	Wilfred B. Sweeney
Chief Steward	Gerald U. Willett
Chief Cook	Valentin Rego
Second Cook	Anado V. Lumbaca
Assistant Cook	Julius Lazarus
Messman	Manuel Estrada
Messman	George Mazanskas
Messman	Magon F. Hernandez
Messman	Pedro Q. Collazo
Messman	Leon A. Feldman
Messman	Henry Maldonado

VOYAGE 16 — APRIL 10, 1953 TO JULY 10, 1953.

Ports of call:	New York, New York
	Balboa, Canal Zone
	San Pedro, California
	Yokosuka, Japan
	Inchon, Korea
	San Francisco, California

Crew:	
Master	G. M. Keymer
Chief Mate	Louis F. Mercedes
Second Mate	Joseph Nasta
Third Mate	Charles Brunswick

Junior Third Mate	Carl G. Rugge
Radio Officer	William R. Harvey
Bosun	Gustay Olson
Deck Maintenance	Castulo Reyes, Jr.
(promoted to bosun)	
Deck Maintenance	Luis Santiago
AB	Joseph Russell
AB	Severino Correa
AB	John G. Miller
AB	Vlaho Zec
AB	William J. Papine
AB	Gustav E. Davidson
OS	Arthur J. Lewis
OS	Ernest U. Mazyck
OS	Lester E. Martin
Chief Engineer	Shirley G. Shields
First Assistant Engineer	Theodore Richards
Second Assistant Engineer	Louis M. Hart
Third Assistant Engineer	James V. Brennan
Junior Third Assistant Engineer	Frank A. Brown, Jr.
Junior Engineer	George McKeever
Chief Electrician	Joseph Skotion
Second Electrician	Francis J. Nay
Oiler	Francisco Moran
Oiler	Juan V. Zabala
Oiler	Edward J. Walka
FWT	David B. Regin
FWT	Eduardo M.M. Hernandez
FWT	Edward J. Brady
Wiper	Juan Marquez
Wiper	James H. Fairman
Wiper	Michael J. Paul
Chief Steward	James T. Simpson
Chief Cook	James A. Ross
Second Cook & Baker	Jaslin Dixon
Third Cook	Cefferino Ondaro
Messman	Lester Randolph
Messman	Lewis Reed
Messman	William Speed
Utility	Pedro S. Montesinos
Utility	Ramon Velez
Utility	Sydney B. Turbee
Second Electrician	Jospeh A. Parduski

Bosun	William E. Groves
Junior Third Mate	Malcom McKenzie Cross

VOYAGE 17 — JULY 11, 1953 TO OCTOBER 15, 1953

Ports of Call: San Francisco, California
Yokohama, Japan
San Francisco, California

Crew:

Master	G. M. Keymer
Chief Mate	L. F. Mercedes
Second Mate	Jack Kennedy
Third Mate	Malcolm M. Cross
Junior Third Mate	Henry Pederson
Radio Operator	William R. Harvey
Bosun	James W. Mossman
Deck Maintenance	Richard E. Dowem
Deck Maintenance	Oscar Stewart
AB	Mitchell E. Henson
AB	Joseph Toth
AB	Joseph G. Brown
AB	Marvin Minor
AB	Edward J. Sanford
AB	Russell H. Rose
OS	Charles E. Edwards
OS	Louis J. Shank
OS	Richard F. Robinson
Chief Engineer	Shirley G. Shields
First Assistant Engineer	Theodore Richards
Second Assistant Engineer	Frank J. Burch
Third Assistant Engineer	Joseph A. Francisovich
Junior Third Assistant Engineer	Frank A. Brown, Jr.
Junior Engineer	Francisco G. Moran
Chief electrician	Robert L. Whitman
Second Electrician	Joseph A. Parduski
Oiler	Edward J. Walka
Oiler	Thomas H. Hindson
Oiler	Woodrow W. Shea
FWT	Herman J. Gilkeyson
FWT	Eduardo M.M. Hernandez
FWT	Jussi Luoma
Wiper	George M. Bottorff

Wiper	Juan Marquez
Wiper	Edward G. Miller
Chief Steward	Frank Sullivan
Chief Cook	James A. Ross
Second Cook & Baker	Robert L. Peterson
Messman	Horace Rucker
Messman	Pedro S. Montesinas
Steward's Utility	Elmore Day
BR Utility	William Speed
Utility	Roscoe C. Stanley
Utility	Golden R. Cargile
Messman	Connie L. Eaves
Third Cook	Wilkerson Robinson
Junior Third Assistant Engineer	John Mendez
Third Cook	Ceferno Ondaro

VOYAGE 18 — OCTOBER 9, 1966 TO JANUARY 26, 1967.

Ports of call:

San Francsico, California
Subic Bay, Philippine Islands
Cam Ranh Bay, South Vietnam
Qui Nhon. South Vietnam
Nha Be, South Vietnam
Subic Bay, Philippine Islands
San Francisco, California

Crew:

Master	Edward A. McMichael
Chief Mate	Charles A. Carlson
Second Mate	Steele
Third Mate	R. Robertson
Radio Officer	Joseph Nelson
Purser	A.C. Todd
Bosun	Marvin Luster
Carpenter	Carl Payden
AB	Myron Johnson
Deck Maintenance	Richard Lee
Deck Maintenance	Jules Foin
Deck Maintenance	Robert Blair
AB	Leon Lewis
AB	William McMAnus
OS	Stephen Mattos
AB	Drensky
AB	Pettibone

OS	O'Haga
AB	Victor Anderson
OS	Walter Bindig
Chief Engineer	Walter Drabina
First Assistant Engineer	John Jansson
Second Assistant Enginer	Clyde Taft
Third Assistant Engineer	Orval Lytle
Day Third Assistant Engineer	Warren Huff
Chief Electrician	Lewis Gros
Second Electrician	Adrian Blumquist
Oiler	Stig Karlsson
Oiler	John C. Jurgenson
FWT	Albino Verrares
FWT	Cabert Dobbins
Wiper	James Trapple
Wiper	George Hanisco
Wiper	Darrell Brown
Chief Steward	Clyde Briedlander
Chief Cook	Byrd Morton
Second Cook	James Sheridan
Assistant Cook	Anthony Yuknevich
Messman	Howard C, Woodard
Messman	Nathan Soloman
Messman	Christian Jack
Messman	Jake Winfred Reed
Messman	Norman Haeckel
Oiler	Ira P. Sears
Carpenter	Leroy Johnson

VOYAGE 19 — JANUARY 27, 1967 TO MAY 5, 1967.

Ports of call: San Francisco, California
San Diego, California
Port Hueneme, California
Bangkok, Thailand
Manila, Philippine Islands
Kaoshiung, Taiwan
Naha, Okinawa
Yokohama, Japan
Oakland, California

Crew:
Master Edward A. MacMichael
Chief Mate Charles A. Carlson

Second Mate	William S. Wellman
Third Mate	Keith O. Marsh O.
Radio Operator	Leroy Bridwell, Jr.
Purser	Jake Werb, Jr.
Bosun	Robert L. French
Carpenter	Carl A. Payden
Deck Maintenance	Michael Yoka
Deck Maintenance	Paul E. Hauan
AB	Eugene O. Alberti
AB	Patrick A. Healy
AB	Wayne M. Bentley
AB	George H. Songer
AB	Johannes Troost
AB	Dennis R. Murphy
OS	Fred H. Nierhake
OS	Gregory A. Rivers
OS	Onofre A. Jaquez
Chief Engineer	Philip S. Morgan
First Assistant Engineer	Robert M. Stevens
Second Assistant Engineer	Knud E. Schmehl
Third Assistant Engineer	Orval Lytle
Third Assistant Engineer	Ronald D. Ross
Chief Electrician	Laurence A. Blakeslec
Second Electrician	Ronald R. James
Oiler	William A. Walker
Oiler	Michael W. Mayoski
Oiler	Earl Richardson
FWT	Albino A. Varares
FWT	Allen B. Jaffe
FWT	David W. Franklin
Wiper	Kenneth A. Page
Wiper	Philip H. Brecht, Jr.
FWT	Craig L. Dato
Chief Steward	Tom Sorensen
Chief Cook	Larry R. Bemis
Assistant Cook	Jake W. Reed
Second Cook & Baker	Lloyd O. White
Messman	James G. Love
Messman	David L. Latendresse
Wiper	Timmy A. Horn
Messman	Charley Shoopman
Messman	Stephen V. Lusby
Messman	William D. Weaver

Deck Maintenance	William R. De Verna
Messman	Esel D. Stallard (joined in Bangkok)

VOYAGE 20 — MAY 6, 1967 TO AUGUST 2, 1967.

Ports of call:	Oakland, California
	Stockton, California
	Long Beach, California
	Yokohama, Japan
	Manila, Philippine Islands
	Qui Nhon, South Vietnam
	Manila, Philippine Islands
	Oakland, California
	San Francisco, California

Crew:

Master	Edward Wentworth
Chief Mate	John W. Hanify
Second Mate	George H. Clyburn
Third Mate	Thomas W. Nation
Third Mate	William M. Cunningham
Radio Operator	Leroy Bridwell
Purser	Edward W. O'Hara
Bosun	Robert L. French
Carpenter	Earnest L. Powell
Deck Maintenance	Wayne M. Bentley
Deck Maintenance	Jacky L. Miller
Deck Maintenance	Viekko O. Kaasinen
AB	Richard M. Cameric
AB	James A. McCormick
AB	George A. Songer
AB	Johannes Troost
AB	Teddy L. Kinder
OS	Robert J. Elasko
AB	Otis King
OS	Reynaldo Williams
OS	Jeffery Quinn
OS	Richard M. Pauly
Deck Maintenance	John Reyes
AB	Robert J. Oliver
OS	Arnold T. Scales
Chief Engineer	Philip S. Morgan
First Assistant Engineer	Lee D. McKinney

Second Assistant Engineer	Jeoffrey W. Wright
Third Assistant Engineer	William Croxall
Day Third Assistant Engineer	Milton W. Kornylak
Day Third Assistant Engineer	Dixon R. Stroup
Chief Electrician	Lawrence A. Blakeelee
Second Electrician	Sulo A. Toivonan
Oiler	Earnest L. Tucker
Oiler	Michael William Mayosky
Oiler	Willaim A. Ward
FWT	Chester O. Shaw
FWT	Adrian S. Blomquist
FWT	Leon T. Trout
Wiper	Walter S. Partica
Wiper	Harold C. Hornbeck
Wiper	Arthur Carre
Chief Steward	Morris Grundland
Chief Cook	Francis J. Radonich
Second Cook	Lloyd O. White
Assistant Cook	James G. Love
Assistant Cook	Jake Winifred Reed
Officer's BR	Arnie L. Whitfield
Steward Utility	Steven V. Lusby
Saloon Pantry	Donald J. Jones
Messman	George F. Moore
Saloon Messman	Jerome Hohenstein
Messman	Eric Klungreseter

VOYAGE 21 — AUGUST 3, 1967 TO OCTOBER 31, 1967.

Ports of call:
San Francisco, California
Coos Bay, Oregon
Newport, Oregon
Westport, Oregon
Longview, Washington
Seattle, Washington
Vung Tau, Vietnam
Newport (Saigon), Vietnam
Vung Tau, Vietnam
San Francisco, California
Richmond, California

Crew:

Master	Edward D.Wentworth
Chief Mate	Robert L. Hendricks
Second Mate	Frederick S. Lane

Third Mate	James E. Miller
Third Mate	Robinson Brugman
Radio Operator	Earnest E. Hudson
Purser	Edward W. O'Hara
Bosun	Robert L. French
Carpenter	James H. Thompson
Deck Maintenance	Jacob J. Lichtman
Deck Maintenance	William A. Cafferty
AB	Herbert A. Pusey
AB	Clyde C. Panning
AB	Donald J. Scott
AB	John A. Holley
AB	John R. Brackenbush
Ab	Donald E. Cordell
OS	Ruben Moos
OS	Claude H. Liebfreid
OS	David L. Letich
Chief Engineer	Phillip S. Morgan
First Assistant	Nestor O. Striike
Second Assistant Engineer	James E. Wiseman
Third Assistant Engineer	Robert L. Jones
Third Assistant Engineer	George B. Hemas
Chief Electrician	Lawrence A. Blakeslee
Second Electrician	Peter Kaneps
Oiler	Charle R. Hotchkiss
Oiler	Charles J. Splain
Oiler	Earnest L. Tucker
FWT	Leon T. Trout
FWT	Jesse Vrans
Wiper	Walter S. Partica
Wiper	Harold C. Hornbeck
Wiper	Edmond P. Atkins
Chief Steward	Morris Grundland
Chief Cook	Francis J. Radonich
Second Cook & Baker	Lloyd O. White
Assistant Cook	Jerome Hohenstein
Officer's BR	Arnie L. Whitfield
Messman	Richard C. Soehngen
Messman	Edward C. Keyes
Messman	Julie S. Rossetti
Steward's Utility	George F. Moore
Engine Cadet	Theodore F. Lopez
Messman	Allan A. Morey
FWT	Jackie Longmier
Deck Maintenance	Alexius Wingenbach

Chief Mate	Robert L. Hendricks
Deck Cadet	Ted F. Lopez

VOYAGE 22 — NOVEMBER 1, 1967 TO DECEMBER 20, 1967.

Ports of call:
Richmond, California
Pearl Harbor, Hawaii
Honolulu, Hawaii
Pearl Harbor, Hawaii
Kwajalein, Marshall Islands
Guam, Marianas Islands
San Diego, California
Long Beach, California
San Francisco, California

Crew:

Master	Edward A. McMichael
Chief Mate	Frederick S. Lane
Second Mate	James E. Miller
Third Mate	Robinson Brugman
Radio Operator	Delbert E. Holton
Purser/pharmacist	Edward W. O'Hara
Deck Cadet	Steven J. Alexander
Bosun	W. L. Olmey
Carpenter	Clyde W. Leek
Deck Maintenance	Confessor Lopez
Deck Maintenance	Victor Anderson
Deck Maintenance	Ronald E. Carlson
AB	James R. Breen
AB	Joseph G. Brown
AB	Richard B. Williams
AB	Samuel J. Burlow
AB	John A. Holley
AB	Douglas Ullrich
AB	Walter F. Raephel
OS	Richard Valentine
OS	Dustin T. Roop
OS	Thomas N. Kahaleiwi
Chief Engineer	Philip S. Morgan
First Assistant	Nestor O. Skriiko
Second Assistant	Norman J. McDonnel
Third Assistant	Robert L. Jones
Third Assistant	George B. Hemus
Engine Cadet	James L. Stone
Chief Electrician	Lawrence A. Blackslee

Oiler	Charles R. Hotchkiss
Second Electrician	John J. McNulty
Oiler	Ira P. Shears
Oiler	William A. Ward
FWT	Earnst L. Tucker
FWT	Leon T. Trout
FWT	Chester O. Shaw
Wiper	Ronald Shaw
Wiper	Craig L. Dato
Wiper	Gregory A. Rivers
Electrican	Charles R. Harding
Chief Steward	John B. Walquist
Chief Cook	Lloyd O. White
Second Cook	Lloyd O. White
Assistant Cook	Juan J.B. Olmos
Officers' BR	George L. Rogers
Officers' Pantry	Donny M. Rutherford
Officers Messman	Edward C. Keyes
Messman	Robert R. Thompson
Messman	Armando Soto
Steward's Utility	Raymond Busher
Chief Cook	Francis J. Radonich
Steward's Utility	George F. Moore
Officers' BR	Robert A. Erickson
Chief Steward	Morris Gremen
Deck Maintenance	Ronald E. Carlson

VOYAGE 23 — DECEMBER 21, 1967 TO FEBRUARY 23, 1968.

Ports of call: San Francisco, California
Port Chicago, California
Sattahip, Thailand
Bataan, Philippine Islands
Oakland, California

Crew:

Master	Edward D. Wentworth
Chief Mate	Frederick S. Lane
Second Mate	James E. Miller
Third Mate	Robinson Brugman
Radio Operator	Delbert E. Holton
Purser	Edward O'Hara
Bosun	Will M. Omley
Carpenter	Clyde M. Luke
Deck Maintenance	Confessor Lopes

Deck Maintenance	Ronald E. Carlson
Deck Maintenance	Douglas W. Chesshire
AB	James R. Breen
AB	Walter W. McDougall
AB	Samuel J. Berlow
AB	Vincent S. Spiewak
AB	Douglass Ullrich
AB	Walter F. Raethel
OS	Richard Valentine
OS	Dustin T. Roop
OS	Thomas N. Kahaleiwi
Chief Engineer	William M. Hutchenson
First Assistant Engineer	Nestor O. Skriiko
Second Assistant Engineer	Norman J. McDonnel
Third Assistant Engineer	Raymond C. Saylo
Third Assistant Engineer	Joseph E. McKenna
Chief Electrician	James P. Irvin
Assistant Electrician	John McNulty
Oiler	Charles R. Hotchkiss
Oiler	Bobby G. Nelson
Oiler	William A. Ward
FWT	Ernest L. Tucker
FWT	David W. Franklin
FWT	Bert W. Howard
Wiper	Richrd Allino
Wiper	Raymond W. Babb
Wiper	David A. Wardingly
Chief Steward	Larry R. Bemis
Chief Cook	Lloyd O. White
Second Cook & Baker	Bobbie W. Sterns
Assistant Cook	Roy Pruett
Messman	Simion Omeja
Messman	Ronald S. Cross
Messman	John M. Mikulick
Messman	William Howard
Messman	Norman K. Holley
Cadet	James R. Agnew

VOYAGE 24 — FEBRUARY 24, 1968 TO APRIL 25, 1968

Ports of call: Oakland, Calffornia
Newport (Saigon), Vietnam
Naha, Okinawa
Oakland, California

Crew:

Master	Edward G. Wentworth
Chief Mate	Fredecrick C. Lane
Second Mate	James E. Miller
Third Mate	Neils Moldrop
Third Mate	Leonard Richardson, Jr.
Radio Operator	Delbert E. Horton
Purser	Edward O'Hara
Bosun	William Reber
Carpenter	Clyde W. Luk
Deck Maintenance	William J. Corrigan
Deck Maintenance	Ronald E. Carlson
Deck Maintenance	Alan Stockton
AB	James R. Breen
AB	Walter W. MacDougall
AB	George H. Songer
AB	Floyd Weber
AB	Francis T. Williams
AB	William M. Walls
OS	Jackie L. Miller
OS	Melvin L. Daniels
OS	Michaael J. Leon
Chief Engineer	Phillip S. Morgan
First Assistant	David M. McDowell
Second Assistant	Norman J. McDonnel
Third Assistant	Felix F. Florence
Third Assistant	Steuart B. Brock
Third Assistant	George Preece
Chief Electrician	Horst H. Schmidt
Assistant Electrician	Lawrence A. Blackley
Oiler	Charles R. Hotchkiss
Oiler	George W. Skinner
Oiler	Andrew Stromsnes
FWT	Avino A. Varrares
FWT	Harold Goldberg
FWT	Chester 0. Shaw
Wiper	Edwardo Salgeuro
Wiper	Christian C. Jack
Wiper	Roger Benaridez
Chief Steward	Morris Grundland
Chief Cook	Harold C. Cladius
Second Cook & Baker	Jan Mantel
Assistant Cook	Jerry D. Olmstead

Messman	James C. Sadler
Messman	U. T. B. Kalma
Messman	Stanley Kuk
Messman	Marcus A. Reynoza
Messman	J. D. Sharp

VOYAGE 25 — APRIL 26, 1968 TO JULY 9, 1968.

Ports of call:

Oakland, California
San Francisco, California
Port Chicago, California
Guam, Marianas Islands
Subic Bay, Philippine Islands
Cam Ranh Bay, Vietnam
Raymond, Washington

Crew:

Master	William Murray
Chief Mate	James E. Miller
Second Mate	Leonard W. Ricketson
Third Mate	James E. Trexler
Third Mate	Neils Moldrup
Radio Operator	Delbert E. Horton
Purser	Robert L. Davis
Bosun	William H. Reber
Deck Maintenance	Raymond J. Corrigan
Deck Maintenance	Franics Lukaszewski
Deck Maintenance	Charles L. Greshom
AB	Thomas H. Vail
AB	Wayne M. Bently
AB	Ian M. Gunn
AB	Floyd Weber
AB	Alfred A. Salamat
OS	Richard A. Bem
OS	Amandys Meier
OS	Roberto E. Prado
Chief Engineer	Phillip S. Morgan
First Assistant Engineer	David M. McDowell
Second Assistant Engineer	Norman J. McDonnel
Third Assistant Engineer	Frank P. Stanbuck
Third Assistant Engineer	George E. Preece
Chief Electrician	Horst H. Schmidt
Second Electrician	Lawrence A. Blackslee
Oiler	Rudolph Pajnich

Oiler	George W. Skinner
FWT	Arthur D. Wyatt
FWT	Lawrence Ochsenhirt
FWT	Albino A. Varrares
Wiper	Frederick L. Wash
Wiper	Norman Trujillo
Chief Steward	Morris Grundland
Chief Cook	Harold C. Cloudis
Second Cook & Baker	James O. Lacey
Assistant Cook	Ralph M. Beller
Messman	Marcus A. Reynoza
Messman	Eusebio S. Cama
Messman	James C. Sadler
Messman	William R. McClemore
Messman	Ronald B. Rey

VOYAGE 26 — JULY 11, 1968 TO SEPTEMBER 27, 1968

Ports of call:
Raymond, Washington
Tacoma, Washington
Seattle, Washington
Everett, Washington
Manila, Philippine Islands
Qui Nhon, South Vietnam
Buckner Bay, Okinawa
Naha, Okinawa
Oakland, California

Crew:

Master	Edward D. Wentworth
Chief Mate	George H. Clayburn
Second Mate	Neils Moldrup
Third Mate	Michael K. Owens
Radio Operator	Roy A. Curtis
Purser	Edward W. O'Hara
Bosun	Willima B. Sellers
Carpenter	James R. Breen
Deck Maintenance	Leo A. Chezek
Deck Maintenance	Lafe J. Purvis
Deck Maintenance	Edwin W. Winsee
AB	William E. Alfred
AB	Johhny L. Peterson
AB	Robert E. Murrey
AB	Floyd Weber
AB	Alf Reider Loken

AB	Benjamin J. Ivy
OS	Arthur H. Anderson
OS	Edward M. Lonergan, Jr.
OS	Park S. Olson
Chief Engineer	Charles R. Beale
First Assistant Engineer	David M. Mcdowell
Second Assistant Engineer	Gilbert H. Meighan
Third Assistant Engineer	Frank P. Stambuck
Chief Electrician	Horst Schmidt
Oiler	Rudolph Padsnick
Oiler	Gabrial Maes
Oiler	Peter Kaneps
FWT	Arthur D. Wyatt
FWT	Carol Davis
FWT	Albino A. Varrares
Wiper	James C. Sadler
Wiper	Marcus A. Reynoza
Wiper	Thomas M. Riff
Chief Steward	Harry Rodrigues
Chief Cook	James D. Cloyd
Second Cook & Baker	Carl S. Morgan
Assistant Cook	Arnie L. Whitfleld
Messman	Michael R. Gamble
Messman	Howard Lev. Torpey
Messman	Esuvo S. J. Calma
Messman	James M. McTiernan, Jr.
Messman	Elwood H. Reever
Messman	Rolf F. RiUing
Wiper	James M. Nissing

VOYAGE 27 — SEPTEMBER 28, 1968 TO JANUARY 20, 1969.

Ports of Call: Oakland, California
San Francisco, California
Sunnypoint, North Carolina
Cristobal, Canal Zone
Balboa, Canal Zone
Subic Bay, Philippine Islands
Cat Lai, South Vietnam
Suyong, Korea
Pusan, Korea
Long Beach, California

Crew:

Master	Edward D. Wentworth
Chief Mate	George W. Retzer
Second Mate	James E. Miller
Third Mate	Robinson Brugman
Radio Operator	Delbert E. Holton
Purser/pharmicist	Edward W. O'Hara
Midshipman (Deck)	Clarence C. Bushert, Jr.
Bosun	Edward. H. Momohara
Carpenter	James R. Breen
Deck Maintenance	Ralph W. Mason
Deck Maintenance	Sabino Y. Rodriguez
Deck Maintenance	Albert W. Kinney
AB	Harold L. Fuller
AB	Johnny L. Petterson
AB	Darwin R. Robinson
AB	Crawford Robertson
AB	Richard R. Lewis
AB	Louis Gaitan
OS	Armand E. La Croix
OS	James M. Homer
OS	Robert S. Bently
Chief Engineer	Raymond R. Burnham
First Assistant Engineer	James P. Nevins
Second Assistant Engineer	Frank B. Stambuck
Third Assistant Enginerr	Charles W. McCormick
Midshipman (Engine)	Charles J. Reinhardt
Chief Electrician	George Lichtenberger
Acting Second Electrician	Stig H.L. Karlsson
Oiler	George W. Skinner
Oiler	James P. Staples
Oiler	John C. Zipey
FWT	Arthur D. Wyatt
FWT	Albino A. Varares
FWT	Percy O. Anderson
Wiper	J. Dodge
Wiper	John L. Coney
Wiper	J.H. French
Chief Steward	Morris Grundland
Chief Cook	Lawrence T. Langan
Second Cook & Baker	Homobono L. Acosta
Assistant Cook	David J. Steele
Messman	Joseph R. Blanchard
Messman	Stanley Kuk

Messman	Alexander Guerrero
Messman	Conrado C. Tejuco
Messman	Michael J. Haven, Jr.
Messman	Frank Bruno
Acting Second Electrician	John L. Koney
Second Assistant Engineer	James P. Nevins

VOYAGE 28 — FEBRUARY 19, 1969 TO MAY 19, 1969.

Ports of call:
Long Beach, California
San Diego, California
Oakland, California
Pearl Harbor, Hawaii
Honolulu, Hawaii
Qui Nhon, South Vietnam
Poro, Philippine Islands
Bataan, Philippine Islands
Manila, Philippine Islands
Subic Bay, Philippine Islands
Naha, Okinawa
Inchon, Korea
Yokosuka, Japan
Yokohama, Japan
Oakland, California

Crew:

Master	Edward Wentworth
Chief Mate	George W. Retzer
Second Mate	James E. Miller
Third Mate	Eli Donabedian
Third Mate	Frank Miller
Radio Operator	Delbert E. Holton
Purser	Edward W. O'hara
Bosun	Zemon J. Pinto
Carpenter	John E. Gaumer
Deck Maintenance	Erick P. Larson
Deck Maintenance	Howard E. Christian
Deck Maintenance	John Justice
AB	Harold Byrkner
AB	Elmer L. Smith
AB	William T. Bailey
AB	William H, Harwell
AB	Donald R. Potts

OS	Robert E. Moresy
OS	Ervin J. Cousal
OS	Dorman F. Phelps
Chief Engineer	Forest H. Lunn
First Assistant Engineer	James P. Nevins
Second Assistant Engineer	Walter L. Scribner
Third Assistant Engineer	John E. Greenwalt
Third Assistant Engineer	Ude Strickmann
Third Assistant Engineer	Bertram Smith
Chief Electrician	Horst H. Schmidt
Assistant Electrician	Walter L. McCrarey
Oiler	Curtis D. White
Oiler	Michael W. Mayoski
Oiler	James P. Staples
FWT	Arthur D. Wyatt
FWT	Albino A. Varrares
FWT	William E. Snow
Wiper	Joseph W. Kraeoer
Wiper	Edwin J. Gregory
Wiper	George F. Moore
Chief Steward	Leo V. Schmitt
Chief Cook	Joseph Bolcak
Second Cook & Baker	Frank H. Montano
Assistant Cook	Edward E. Hale
Messman	Marcelino Olivere
Messman	Homobon Acosto
Messman	Ernest Cruz
Messman	Frank Swartz
Messman	Robert H. Lee
Messman	Lawrence P. Reynolds

VOYAGE 29 — MAY 20, 1969 TO JULY 31, 1969.

Ports of call:
Oakland, California
Port Chicago, California
Cam Ranh Bay, South Vietnam
Cat Lai, South Vietnam
Manila, Philippine Islands
Seattle, Washington

Crew:

Master	Eugene R. Spencer
Chief Mate	Robert O. Reinhart

Second Mate	Frank Miller
Third Mate	Eli Donabedian
Third Mate	Roy E. Fuller
Radio Officer	Robert E. Williams
Purser	Edward W. O'Hara
Bosun	Douglas P. Kapule
Carpenter	John K. Gaumer
Deck Maintenance	Peter T. La France
Deck Maintenance	Hom Moon You
Deck Maintenance	James G. Olds
AB	Hugo Maki
AB	Carl A. Perry
AB	Charles W. Stienfort
AB	Pasquale P. Menisi
AB	Holger O. Johansen
AB	Leo D. Bennett
OS	Carol R. Thornsberry
OS	Ernest Cruise
OS	James G. Love
Chief Engineer	Forrest H. Lunn
First Assistant Engineer	Edwin L. Tillotson
Second Assistant Engineer	Herbert Bannister
Third Assistant Engineer	William A. Ward
Third Assistant Engineer	Udo Strickmann
Third Assistant Engineer	Dennis Tison
Chief Electrician	Horst H. Schmidt
Second Electrician	Ernest L. Tucker
Oiler	John C. Jurgensen
Oiler	Michael W. Mayoski
Oiler	James P. Staples
FWT	John W. Boyle
FWT	Patrick Lego
FWT	George W. Skinner
Wiper	Carlos Bravo
Wiper	Paul R. Peitzcker
Wiper	Joseph W. Kraber
Chief Steward	Lynn Schniden
Chief Cook	Jose Beltran
Second Cook & Baker	Paul Cecil Petti
Assistant Cook	George M. Babbs
Messman	Frank W. Schwartz
Messman	Stanley Kuk
Messman	Jacob Swinkels
Messman	Michael P. Jones

Messman   Maurice S. Van Meter
Messman   Lawrence P. Reynolds

VOYAGE 29 — MAY 20, 1969 TO JULY 31, 1969.

Ports of call: Oakland, California
Port Chicago, California
Cam Ranh Bay, South Vietnam
Cat Lai, South Vietnam
Manila, Philippine Islands
Seattle, Washington

Crew:

Master	Eugene R. Spencer
Chief Mate	Robert O. Reinhart
Second Mate	Frank Miller
Third Mate	Eli Donabedian
Third Mate	Roy E. Fuller
Radio Officer	Robert E. Williams
Purser	Edward W. O'Hara
Bosun	Douglas P. Kapule
Carpenter	John K. Gaumer
Deck Maintenance	Peter T. La France
Deck Maintenance	Hom Moon You
Deck Maintenance	James G. Olds
AB	Hugo Maki
AB	Carl A. Perry
AB	Charles W. Stienfort
AB	Pasquale P. Menisi
AB	Holger O. Johansen
AB	Leo D. Bennett
OS	Carol R. Thornsberry
OS	Ernest Cruise
OS	James G. Love
Chief Engineer	Forrest H. Lunn
First Assistatn Engineer	Edwin L. Tillotson
Second Assistant Engineer	Herbert Bannister
Third Assistant Engineer	William A. Ward
Third Assistant Engineer	Udo Strickmann
Third Assistant Engineer	Dennis Tison
Chief Electrician	Horst H. Schmidt
Second Electrician	Ernest L. Tucker
Oiler	John C. Jurgensen
Oiler	Michael W. Mayoski

Oiler	James P. Staples
FWT	John W. Boyle
FWT	Patrick Lego
FWT	George W. Skinner
Wiper	Carlos Bravo
Wiper	Paul R. Peitzcker
Wiper	Joseph W. Kraber
Chief Steward	Lynn Schniden
Chief Cook	Jose Beltran
Second Cook & Baker	Paul Cecil Petti
Assistant Cook	George M. Babbs
Messman	Frank W. Schwartz
Messman	Stanley Kuk
Messman	Jacob Swinkels
Messman	Michael P. Jones
Messman	Maurice S. Van Meter
Messman	Lawrence P. Reynolds

VOYAGE 30 — AUGUST 1, 1969 TO OCTOBER 19, 1969.

Ports of call:

Bangor, Washington
Subic Bay, Philippine Islands
Danang, South Vietnam
Sasebo, Japan
Long Beach, California

Crew:

Master	E. W. Wentworth
Chief Mate	Morgan W. Vail II
Second Mate	Raymond J. Neibauer
Third Mate	Eli Donabedian
Third Mate	Robinson Brugman
Radio Operator	Price R. Garner
Purser/pharmacist	Leland P. Christensen
Bosun	Douglas P. Kapule
Carpenter	John K. Gaumer
Deck Maintenance	Peter T. La France
Deck Maintenance	Hom Moon You
Deck Maintenance	Howard L. Whitney
AB	George W. Pope, Jr.
AB	Ronald E. Ericksen
AB	Roger R. Music
AB	Erik P. Williamson
AB	Robert Allbritton

AB	James F. Weber
OS	Donald E. Arnold
OS	Melvin L. Ehrhardt
OS	Burton L. Denham
Chief Engineer	James W. Shaffer
First Assistant Engineer	Edwin L. Tillotson
Day Second Assistant Engineer	James Barnette
Third Assistant Engineer	Harry L. Huffman
Chief Electrician	Norman H. Ramsey
Second Electrician	Ernest L. Tucker
Oiler	Peter Kaneps
Oiler	Adrian Bloomquist
Oiler	Gabriel Maes
FWT	Arthur D. Wyatt
FWT	Albino A. Varares
FWT	Richard D. Enck
Wiper	George C. Roberts
Wiper	Leon Marvin Yarborough
Wiper	Albert K. Watson
Chief Steward	Abraham Baizman
Chief Cook	Albert C. Smith
Second Cook & Baker	Lawrence Erickson
Assistant Cook	Morris Grundland
Messman	Conrad Celloway Tejvco
Messman	Michael H. Oil
Messman	Maurice Van Meter
Messman	Robert J. Lewis
Messman	John Sellett Powell
Messman	Lawrence P. Reynolds

VOYAGE 31 — OCTOBER 20, 1969 TO APRIL 22, 1970.

Ports of call: Long Beach, California
Danang, South Vietnam
Newport (Saigon), South Vietnam
Yokosuka, Japan
Subic Bay, Philippine Islands
Danang, South Vietnam
Qui Nhon, South Vietnam
Danang, South Vietnam
Kaoschiung, Taiwan
Vung Tau, South Vietnam
Newport (Saigon), South Vietnam
Sasebo, Japan

Danang, South Vietnam
Newport (Saigon), South Vietnam
Inchon, Korea
Pusan, Korea
Yokohama, Japan
San Francisco, California

Crew:

Master	Edward Wentworth
Chief Mate	Morgan Vail II
Second Mate	Raymond Neibauer
Third Mate	Eli Donabedian
Third Mate	Robinson Bringman
Radio Officer	Robert Steele
Purser/pharmacist	E. W. O'Hara
Bosun	D. D. Kapule
Carpenter	Charles E. Crater
Deck Maintenance	Arthur Fleming
Deck Maintenance	Douglas C. Newell
Deck Maintenance	Frederick A. Brohlin
AB	T. Johnson
AB	G.A. Drum
Ab	R. Hanley
AB	R. Bryan
AB	Frank Filas
AB	Anthony Ferreria
AB	E. J. Shay
AB	Joseph Kearns
OS	O.J.Patrick
OS	W. Hernandez
OS	T.J. Truskoloski
OS	Edward P. Ferreria
Chief Engineer	J. Shaffer
First Assistant Engineer	J. Nevins
Second Assistant Engineer	P. Bilski
Third Assistant Engineer	Martin Rowe
Third Assistant Enginner	R. Morrison
Third Assistnat Engineer	Emil Lauritsen
Chief Electrician	E. Eckert
Second Electrician	H. Farrell
Oiler	G. Maes
Oiler	R. Ward
Oiler	A. Villi
FWT	E. Shephard

FWT	A. Varrares
FWT	A. Wyatt
Wiper	J. Kittleson
Wiper	M. Erhardt
Wiper	A. Watson
Chief Steward	A. Baizman
Chief Cook	A. Smith
Second Cook & Baker	L. Bemis
Assistant Cook	J. Sullivan
Messman	W. Kuling
Messman	J. Iturralde
Messman	E.E. Hale
Messman	O. Barnes
Messman	J. Powell
Messman	L. Reynolds

Appendix C

Patrons and Volunteers

Board of Directors:
George Henning
Clinton L. Johnson
Bob Lace
Bob McMannis
John O. Smith
Allen Thronson
Joe Vernick

Regional Vice Presidents:
James A. Arnold
Art Crowe
A. David Eslick
Edward J. Heins, Jr.
William Kellet
Frank Liberatore
Otto Marchica
Norris Nahman
Luigi Sorace
Robert E. Thornton
Glen E. Trimble

Deck Department:
Charles Acebo
Espe Acebo
Kay F. Applegate
Charles M. Baca
James D. Baker
Jerry Barham
Bill Bennett
John N. Brindle
Chris Brooks
Jack Brooks
Joe Bull
Dan Burns
Leroy Buus
Mark Campanelli
Bill Cantrell
Lee Chamberlain
Larry Clifford
Roy Coats
Donald P. Collins

Malcolm Cross
Vince Davidson
Tony Desota
Adrian Dokken
Irene Draghi
Chuck Ducker
Napolean Duncan
Frank Filas
Edith Fisher
James A. Garwood
Alvin Gettler
William O. Gordon
Tom Gregoire
Cliff Hagenbuch
Herbert Hahn
Ed Harnby
Larry Hennon
Dave Hoffman
Larry Hoffman
George Hughes
Thomas E. Hughes, Sr.
Brad Hult
Hartley C. Hult
Hugh Hunter
Jack Hutchison
Trevor Johnston
Gregory L. Johnson
Pat Johnson
Rorvick Johnson
Trevor Johnston
Claire Julien
William J. Julien
Charles D. Kallaher
Dale D. Kelly
John E. Kelly
William Kennedy
Dean Kruegar
Jack Landburg
Robert D. Lawson
David Lee
Rex Link
Fred Litsch
William G. Loenhorst
William Loenhorst, Sr.
Sharon Lopaka
Bill Luegar

Bill Martin
Joe Matanzo
Rod Mayfield
Harry McCrillis
Jim McIntyre
Jack McKeehan
Bill McWald
Michael F. Meyerhofer
Janice L. Michaelis
Lewis Miller
Brad Milne
George Moreau
Jack Neilson
James S. Nolan
Tom O'Laughlin
Richard Olson
Larry Pepin
Ray Person
Hans Philipsen
Harold Plouffe
Ernest Price
Mary Prizmich
Pete Prizmich
Leon Pugh
Mel Pulhamus
Ede Rinehart
Jim Rodder
Earl Rossney
Harold L. Runnels
Harold Russel
Ralph Shafer
Eric Sherreitt
Bob Simpson
William W. Skinner
Albert Smith
Ed Smith
Thelma Smith
Fred Souther
John H. Stendahl
John Struyk
Bill Taylor
John Terberg
Glenn Thomas
Stanely J. Tokich
Jerry Turner
Nelson VanWormer

Ricardo Veiyra
William H. Vincent
Ruby Vincent
Kellard Walker
Tim Walker
Albert Watkins
Rose Watkins
Larry Welsh
Jerone F. Werner
Dave Wilkinson
Georgette Wilmeth
Don Wilson
Jack Wyman
Shirley Young
Norbet Zackman
Verena Zackman

RADIO SHACK:
John Coleman
Earl Darnell
Andrew J. Draghi
Jay Flynn
Harry Goldstick
Emmett A. Harvey
Bob Lace
Norman Lester
Robert S. Lukenbill
Frank Minton
Saul Yochelson

ENGINE DEPARTMENT:
Irvina Aldrich
Robert Alexander
Dean E. Ayers
Doug Bader
Jerry Barham
Ernie Barker
Bob Belander
Omar Brand
Hughes Brown
Red Bruton
Bill Bennett
Chris Brooks
Red Bruton
Daryl Brye
Fred Cederblom

Larry Clifford
Nicky Clifford
Howard Cox
Rino Danielson
Kenneth E. Dawson
Tony Desoto
Donna Dorn
Thomas Dorn
Claude Gammel
Chuck Gardner
Art Gardner
Art Grissom
Harold Hansen
Clyde W. Harrell
Bernard E. Hein
Douglas Heitkamp
George Henning
Jim Higman
Pete Jacobelly
Stan Jensen
C. John Johnson (deceased)
Darwin "Bud" Jorgenson
James D. Kennedy
Don Knight
Nina Knight
Tony Laich
Paul Landier
Leonard Lane
Ernie Langner
Bill Lingrey
Lou Loring
Phil Martin
Reynaldo Martinez
George Masters
Orvil Miller
Joe Mulkey
Bill Munford
Margaret Munford
David Nadzan
Phil Newman
Lewis Nicodemus
Richard C. Nutting
Fred Oehler
Tom O'Laughlin
Don Parish
Charles Perara

Joe Person
James Peckham
Joe Person
Russell W. Peschke
George Plyley
Bob Powell
Frank Prentiss
Harold Ramsden
Phil Rosenfield
Dave Rosenfield
Tom Ruatta
Harold Russell
Albert Smith
John D. Smith
Leroy J. Smith
Ron Stahl
Pete Sparks
Jack Talbert
Roy Taylor
Chad Topping
Jim Topping
Charles E. Trousdale
George R. Tuttle (deceased)
Gordon Vincent
Jim Vorhis
Eric Walker
Al Watkins
Art Weatherly
Robert Williams
Art Windsor
John Wingerson
Ray Young
Tony Young

STEWARD'S DEPARTMENT:
Scott Anderson (deceased)
Hope Borja
Ken Carpenter
Isaac B. Givens
Cathleen Johnson
Darlene Jones
Max Jones
Caroline Kallahar
Jim Pelot
Midge Porche
Orviv J. Porche

Tom Ruatta
Barney Starr
Dave Vaughn
Rose Watkins
Jeannette Whitten

ARMED GUARD:
Robert Abbot
Charley Baca
Loring L. Bigelow
Charlie Coffee
William Hartzel
Thom Hendrickson
Robert Herrara
Richard Hudnall
Luke Leslie
Mike Leslie
Sid Leslie
Ted Liddle
Gerald May
Joe Piccolini
Bill Privett
Rodney Raymond
Charles Savona

STAFF:
Bob Bodwell
Melina Boswell
Saul Brindle
Jim Davis
Eliose Dawson
Tanja Desmari
Margaret Gordon
Flo Hamel
Lloyd R. Hamel
George Henning
Hartley Hult
Doug Huntzinger
Clint Johnson
Pat Johnson
Claire Julien
William J. Julien
Ken Keith
Bob Lace
Janet Laich
Carmen Lane

Cleo Liddle
Jenny Lukenbill
Donald R. MacLean
John E. Marriner
Shiela McIntyre
Bob McMannis
Jean Meyerhofer
Mary Minshall
Jim Mullins
Bill Munford
Capt. James Nolan
Pete Poulter
Carol Pugh
Al Rasmussen
Louise Raymond
Ken Riley
John Romeo
Frances Smith
John Smith
Mary Stahl
Mary Anne Struyk
Oscar Thompson
Allen Thronson
Bob Tompkins
Chuck Trousdale
Mary Trousdale
Jerry Turner
Joe Vernick
Ruby Vincent
Ruth Werner

GIFT SHOP:
Marie L. Cole
Shirley Filas
Beverly Hult
Fran Smith

OTHER VOLUNTEERS:
Eugene Allen
Paul Artman
Joe Avila
Loring & Louise Bigelow
Ray Brunk
Charles & Kim Carlon
Herb Chatterton

Verne Echelby
James Flynn
Isaac Gwens
William Kellett
Joe Lewis
Jan Mahelis
Arthur Morrison
Clarke Mumford
Dave Ohlson
Walter Reinheimer
Robert Swank
Richard Thomas

CHARTER LIFE MEMBERS:
Charles & Espe Acebo
Jim Ackerman
Wayne M. Adcock
Ara Avak
Dean E. & Edith Fisher Ayers
James D. Baker
George B. Barber
Jerry W. Barham
Ernest E. Barker
William & Evelyn Barnard
Cdr's Edric S. & Marion D. Bates
Warren & Yvette Bauman
Charles & Marian Beal
Tom O. Berry
Phillip Berumen
Brad & Bea Best
Randall Bishop
Edward & Paula Joe Blackburn
Ronald B. & Jeanette Blume
Orin Burhl Bond
John F. Borum
Omar & Doris Brands
Aaron Franklin Braziel
Burton & Doreen Bril
John & Alice Brindle
Kenton & Evelyn Brinkley
Jack B. Brooks
Hughes & Jacqueline Brown
Edwin & Blanche Bruton
James G. Butler
John W. Cairns
Donald C. & Jean Carson

Fred R. Cederblum
Glen G. Chapman
Angela & Edward Charles
John Wook Chong
Joseph & Rosalie Clingerman
I. Roy & Loleita Coats
Harry H. Coleman
Donald & Violet Collins
Edward J. Connell
Dale K. Cooper
Joseph & Dorothy Costello
James C. & MAry Ann Costigan
Doris Ann & Stephanie S. Coulter
Roy J. & Hazel Cox
Malcolm M. Cross
Cyril J. Cudahy
Jerry Cudahy
Richard & Charlotte Dahl
Kenneth & Elois Dawson
William H. Dawson
Leon R. & Pamela Dewick
D. G. Dimit
Victory & Diana Distefano
Edward H. Dobler
Richard & Edna Docherty
Thomas & Donna Dorn
Andrew J. & Irene J. Draghi
Napoleon Duncan
Carl & Laura Ebert
George H. Emerson
Peter & Virginia Ernzer
Vern & Judy Eshelby
B. L. & June R. Evans
Frank & Shirley A. Filas
Marvin John & Mildred Foss
Walter H. Fraser
Capt. Richard P. Frayer
Kristian & Helen Fulsebakke
Capt. Hiram C. Gallop
Claude A. Gammel
Robert C. Gammel
Terry T. & Lilliam Garabedian
James & Kay Garwood
Morton J. Gelb
Homer N. Gibson
Richard & Edith Gillelen

Joe L. Gilmaker
Joe Giocomarra
Isaac B. & Rowena Benitez Givens
Clifton Abbott & Jadwiga Goddard
Harry & Fae Goldstick
Wade & Barbara Goodin
William & Margaret Gordon
Henry C. & Patricia Grieb
Audrey & Monique Griffis
Lloyd A. Gunderson
Herbert Paul Hahn
Sol Hakam
Kenneth & Harriet Hall
Lloyd & Flora Hamel
Harold & Wilma Hansen
Duane G. Hansen
Charles W. Hardin
Charles L. & Maria A. Harkness
Emmett A. Harvey
Floyd (Red) Hayes
Bernard E. & N. Jeane Hein
Edward & Eva Heins, Jr.
Kenneth C. Helgeson
George & Doris Henning
George Robert Hensel
Kenneth Hepler
Fred R. Hicks
James E. Higman
Malcolm & Dorothy Hinchcliffe
Richard E. Holdaway
Royce & Hermelina Holland
William A. Hood
Paul H. & Emiko Hoshi
Orville R. Hubble
Charles & Mary Ann Hudson
Thomas E. Hughes, Sr.
Douglas Huntzinger
Max Hamilton Jacobs
Jack & Margie Jacobsen
William R. & Margaret K. James
Clinton & Pat Johnson
Robert Johnson
Clell & Joan Johnson
Warren Eugene & Betty Johnson
Jay & Patricia Johnson
Gregory & Cathleen Johnson

Max W. & Darlene Jones
Charles & Helen Jones
Charles & Mary Nell Jones
Darwin K. Jorgenson
William J. Julien
Ted Kalivas
Chares & Caroline Kallaher
Edwar & Alexandra Kalpakian
Charles W. & Carol Kanavle
Austin C. & Helen M. Kane
Carl & Dorothy Karfs
Joseph & Ann L. Katusa
Kenneth & Helen Keith
Dale D. Kelly
Clennon & Esther Kemp
James David Kennedy, Jr.
William F. Kerr
Roy L. Kidman
Charles & Norene King
Bill & Esther Klaunig
Nina C. Knight
Donald & Annette Knight
Norman & Agnes Knowlton
Herbert & Dolores Kuhnke
Robert & Rose Kunst
Robert & Edith Lace
Tony & Janet Laich
Jack & Marguerite Landberg
Robert D. Lawson
Spencer Lawson
John L. & Vivan H. Le Flore
C. A. & Patricia Lenzen
Norman & Marylin Lester
Lloyd & Barbara Liddle
Lester G. Lien
Rex B. Link
Victor & Carmen Lluis, Sr.
Peter Loenhorst
William Loenhorst, Sr.
William & Ida Longo
Sharon McClendon Lopaka
Lyle L. Lorenzen
Robert & Genevieve Luckenbill
Arthur MacLaren
Donald & Joyce MacLean
Robert J. Mader

Capt. Peter Mahi
Theodore & Josephine Manning
Phil & Ruthie Martin
Reynaldo S. & Jeannie Martinez
James E. Mason
George & Shirley Masters
Don F. Matics
George & Marcy Mattern
Capt. Charles S. Maxim
Robert Maycock
Harry & Margaret McCrillis
Franklin R. McDonnell
John & Mariell McGonnell
Jim & Shiela McIntyre
James W. McIntyre
Jack & Mary Lou McKeehan
Richard & Louise McLean
Robert L. McMannis
George & Edith McTiernan
Capt. Kurt-Olaf & Hazel Meyer
Capt. Donald F. Miley
Orval & Florence Miller
Lewie Miller
Fred & Flora Minton
Paul & Norma Jean Mitskoff
Maynard & Flora Mobley
Robert L. & Lynn Moor
William & Edith Morris
Donald Murphy
Charles & Delores Nafie
Norris S. Nahman
John J. & Emma W. Nelson
Stanley Neufeld
Millard F. & Ruth Newman
Lewis C. Nicodemus
Jens Nicholaisen
James B. & Laurine B. North, III
Bill & Jeanne O'Shea
Capt. Richard & Jean Olson
John W. Osborn
Jim & Dru Paine
Angie Fay & Jim Peckham
Robert & Lucille G. Perez
John & Kimberly Pettus, Jr.
Claude & Clara Phillips
Donald W. Pike

Deane & Marjorie Plaister
William "Bill" Polero
Orviv J. & Midge Porche
Clifton & Deloris Priest
Henry & Dolores Preimesberger
Pete & Mary Prizmich
Leon W. & Carol Pugh
Richard & Mary Pulliam
Lee & Joy Reasoner
V. Noble & Rose L. Redmon, Jr.
Leonard Regan
Vernon & Sandra Richardson
Myron & Mary Richardson, Jr.
Frank & Barbara Robinson
Walter & Dorothy Rock
Charles O. Rogers
John & Pat Romeo
John L. & Mae Anne Root
Margaret & Earle Rossney
Darrell & Eddene Roush
Attilio T. Ruatta
Robert & Mary Rubenstein
Ben & Louise Ruckle
Harold & Lorraine Runnels
Harold & Joanne Russell
Bruce & Amelia Sathre
Marlin S. Sennett
J. B. Shackelford
Nathan & Ilene Shaphran
Walter H. & Paula Shears
Bob Simpson
John & Frances Smith
Leroy G. & Bernice R. Smith
Fosdick J. & Grace Smith
Albert & Thelma L. Smith
Andrew & Sylvia Smith
Charles C. Smith
Pete & Clytie Sparks
Dan Spears
Jerry W. Spray
Ronald & Mary Stahl
Roger B. & Louise H. Steppe
Fred & Barbara Stevens

Elmer H. & Kathryn M. Stevens
Leon & Donna Stoddard
Lewis W. Striplin
John & Rosilyn Struller
John & Mary Anne Struyk
John O. & Loura Camille Svensson
Kedley R. & Dolores Swaby
Earl "Bill" & Clarabel Terry
Paul Roy Thomas
Glenn E. Thomas
Darrell & Mary Thompson
Edwin & Catherine Thopson
Harold O. Thompson
Allen & Vivian Thronson
Stanley & Ruth Tokich
Robert D. Tompkins
Clifford C. & Barbara Topliff
James A. Topping, Jr.
Goerge D. & Glays L. Trahan
Glen E. & Bonnie Trimble
Charles & Mary Trousdale, Jr.
Jerry & Barbara Turner
Nelson & Itha Van Wormer
Joe Vernick
William & Ruby Vincent
Eric Walker
Albert & Rose Watkins
John & Betty Webster
Jerome F. Werner
Vagn Akton & Martha Westergaard
Leroy R. Westervelt
Louis H. White
Stanley & Carol Willner
Georgetta & George Clyde Wilmeth
Donald & Verna Marie Wilson
Art & Marion Windsor
Raoul R. & Fern L. Wolff
Robert & Eleanor Woodford
Frederick W. Woodworth
Stephen E. Wright
James R. & Shirley M. Young
George & Georgette Zeiger

BIBLIOGRAPHY

Chapelle, Howard I. *The History of American Sailing Ships.* New York: W.W. Norton & Co., 1935.

Cooke, Alla L., *Lane College: Its Heritage and Outreach*, Jackson, Tenn: Lane College, 1987.

Field, James A. Jr., *History of United States Naval Operations*, Washington, D.C.: GPO, 1962.

Ingram, Robert L., *A Builder and His Family*, San Francisco, Ca.: n.p., 1949.

Queenan, Charles F., *The Port of Los Angeles, From Wilderness To World Port*, Los Angeles, Ca.: Los Angeles Harbor Department, 1983.

Ridgway, Mathew B., *The Korean War.* Garden City: Doubleday & Company, Inc., 1967.

Sawyer, L.A. and W.H. Mitchell, *Victory Ships and Tankers.* Devon, England: David & Charles: Newton Abbot, 1974.

Index